Sex Fiends, Perverts, and Pedophiles

Sex Fiends, Perverts, and Pedophiles

*Understanding Sex Crime
Policy in America*

Chrysanthi S. Leon

NEW YORK UNIVERSITY PRESS
New York and London

NEW YORK UNIVERSITY PRESS
New York and London
www.nyupress.org

References to Internet websites (URLs) were accurate at the time of writing.
Neither the author nor New York University Press is responsible for URLs
that may have expired or changed since the manuscript was prepared.

Library of Congress Cataloging-in-Publication Data
Leon, Chrysanthi S.
Sex fiends, perverts, and pedophiles : understanding sex crime policy in America /
Chrysanthi S. Leon.
p. cm.
Includes bibliographical references and index.
ISBN 978-0-8147-5258-6 (cl : alk. paper)
ISBN 978-0-8147-5326-2 (pb : alk. paper)
ISBN 978-0-8147-5313-2 (e-book)
1. Sex crimes—United States. 2. Sex offenders—United States.
3. Child molesters—United States. I. Title.
HV6592.L46   2011
 364.15'30973—dc22   2011007841

New York University Press books are printed on acid-free paper,
and their binding materials are chosen for strength and durability.
We strive to use environmentally responsible suppliers and materials
to the greatest extent possible in publishing our books.

Manufactured in the United States of America

To Rob and Sue Settlage
and to Franklin E. Zimring

Contents

Acknowledgments

Twenty years ago, my religious community struggled to acknowledge the risks and realities of child sexual abuse, including how to teach children to regard authority, and whether we could accommodate people who had been victimized as children as well as former offenders who sought support after they completed their sentences. Those efforts opened up old hurts and new fault lines. The resulting realization that we ought to be able to do better, at the community and social levels, inspired this book. I therefore offer my deep gratitude to all of those who do the difficult work of protecting the vulnerable and healing the harmed.

Thanks to Judy Randle, Dorit Rubinstein, Mark Harris, Jonathan Simon, David Sklansky, Ben Fleury-Steiner, Aaron Kupchik, and especially Frank Zimring. I appreciate the suggestions of the many people in Berkeley and beyond who responded to this material during various conferences, including "Probing the Penal State," organized by Loïc Wacquant and the Institute for Governmental Studies, and the Northeastern Law and Society meetings for its junior scholar sessions. I am grateful for archival assistance from Christine Sun, Lynette Chua, Stefanie MacArthur, and Michelle Pfaulmer and for proofreading by Kerstin Carlson, Jordan Leitner, Kevin Ralston, and Dana Alvare. Staff at the Kinsey Institute for Research in Sex, Gender, and Reproduction and at the Interuniversity Consortium for Political and Social Research provided access to wonderful data. At the University of Delaware (UD), I thank my outstanding graduate and undergraduate students for sharing the journey of intellectual inquiry into these difficult subjects, my department and the university community for collegiality and understanding, and especially for the pretenure sabbatical semester and the Dean of Arts and Sciences' Faculty Research Support grant. Ilene Kalish, Despina Papazoglou Gimbel, Christine Dahlin, and the reviewers for NYU Press offered outstanding revisions at many stages.

The people and policies at progressive institutions like the University of California, Berkeley, and UD make it possible for scholars with young children to write. At Berkeley, I particularly thank Cathy O'Sullivan of the Early Childhood Education Program, whose love and skill in caring for Maggie, my daughter, were crucial. Many people at the UD Early Learning Center, including Rhodah Harrell and Eileen Blouse, allowed me to work because I knew my children enjoyed world-class care. Miles, thanks for keeping it all together.

Finally, I thank Frank, a tolerant and generous mentor, incisive critic, and wonderful example of how to improve the world through rigorous empiricism. I dedicate this to Frank and to my parents: all three are models of how to live and work for truth and justice.

Introduction

> Californians have a tremendous opportunity to make our communities safer by voting Yes on Proposition 83, Jessica's Law. It is a comprehensive initiative that would strengthen California's laws against child molesters and sexual predators.
>
> Both major political parties and every major law enforcement and crime victims group in California support the proposition. As district attorney, I know firsthand the importance of passing Proposition 83. I see how sexual predators exploit the loopholes and weak laws to repeat their crime over and over again.
>
> —Jan Scully, Sacramento County District Attorney, October 6, 2006

American media and politics are saturated with stories about sex crime. As the prosecutor describes above, there is a widely shared conception of what the problem is and how to address it: sexual offending is carried out by predators who repeat their crimes and must be stopped through new, tough laws. As a result, since the 1990s, scores of new laws have increased prison sentences and attached extra penalties and restrictions on released sex offenders.[1] Because these laws are often tied to states' criminal justice funding, they directly influence the functioning of police, court, and correctional personnel, as well as the makeup of prisons and parole systems. The particulars focus on "managing" sex offenders through notification laws and various forms of biological and psychological monitoring. While the public may support the idea of treatment for some offenders, risk assessment and control are far more characteristic of the contemporary approach to sex crime, and prevention is rarely addressed.

Popular tough-on-crime legislation such as Proposition 83, the ballot initiative referenced above, often capitalizes on fears of the violent recidivist who is beyond the reach of any approach except incapacitation (that is, sterilization or castration or even execution). The spirit of California's "three strikes and you're out" approach has informed sentencing reform in states across the country, with most states shifting from indeterminate to determinate sentencing structures in whole or in part.[2] Interestingly, violent crime rates have consistently fallen during the period of panic over recidivists.[3] But the efficacy of "governing through crime" outweighs the facts.[4] Today, policy makers continue to seek ever-better ways of signaling their concern with crime and their solidarity with victims and their families. For example, Proposition 83, known as "Jessica's Law," won approval by a large margin of voters in California's November 2006 election. Jessica's Law tried to solve the crime problem by increasing criminal justice oversight of known offenders. Jessica's Law in its California iteration increased sentences for existing sex crimes, added lifetime GPS monitoring of sex offenders, dramatically expanded eligibility for the state's civil commitment, and restricted where released sex offenders may live.

In the current climate, many people interested in questioning some aspects of our approach to sex offender punishment believe it is too politically dangerous, even when hundreds of millions of dollars are at stake.[5] As Ray McNally, a Republican consultant, said about Jessica's Law, "Pity the poor politician who decides to stand up against this initiative. They'll be roadkill by morning."[6] Unlike other measures on the same ballot, there was very little debate among commentators and no "war of commercials" on radio or television about this proposition (the only commercial that mentioned Jessica's Law condemned a gubernatorial candidate who had expressed limited concerns about an earlier version of the bill). The experts who were featured in the public arena were a strange group. Aside from a convicted sex offender who *supported* most aspects of the law, critics got little airtime. Not even the victims' rights group California Coalition Against Sexual Assault (CalCASA), which circulated press releases about the risks of forcing offenders to move out of well-supervised areas, received attention.[7] Other critics did not even try to reach the public. At a training meeting for a coalition of therapists and correctional officers who work with sex offenders, everyone agreed not to voice practical concerns over the implementation of Jessica's Law—these low-status experts are rarely heard under the best of circumstances, and protests would only waste capital on a losing cause. As I will show, the public support, and even the policies themselves, resemble past efforts dating back to the 1930s. Unique to the present, however, are the dominant orthodoxy and the silencing of critics.

This state of affairs is not good for debate in a healthy civic society, and it is not good for policy making, regardless of the law's content. In order to understand the current dynamics surrounding social and political responses to sex crime, I put contemporary sex offender punishment in historical context. My findings challenge previous attempts to theorize law made in response to sex crime, and I add empirical grounding to contemporary explanations of penal expansion.

Data and Methodology

Increasingly, conclusions drawn from social research are viewed with most confidence if they are the product of triangulation.[8] Borrowed from navigation, "triangulation" in social research means the use of multiple methods in order to guard against the effects of error in one method. This type of multifaceted approach should be familiar to criminologists and to other interdisciplinary scholars, who know better than most that the question or problem, rather than the pet approaches of a particular discipline or profession, should dictate which strategy is used.

My approach is one of multiple methods, including descriptive statistics, archival research, and participant observation. Specifically, I present numerical data that describe criminal justice patterns, combined with a social policy analysis of both the legal changes since 1980 and the institutional changes affecting criminal justice policy in California based on archival and ethnographic research.

Throughout the book, I will track the ways law, media, and psychiatric and criminological scholarship imagined sex offenders in the United States during the twentieth century. In the next paragraphs and in appendix A, I discuss the various measurement techniques I used to achieve something as close to representativeness as I think is possible in examining how discourse, policy, and implementation interact. In short, I tried to identify all the predominant ways of talking about the problem of sexual offending in each realm, and to pay attention to which seemed to recur the most or to hold the most influence, while also pointing out less common perspectives and why they held less weight. Although I am interested in which discursive strains dominated and why, I try to avoid making causal claims about discourse and action. While sensitive to debates about how and whether "culture" can be operationalized, Mary Douglas's definition—"culture, in the sense of the public, standardized values of community, mediates the understanding of individuals. It provides in advance some basic categories"—frames much of my approach.[9] Relationships among punishment policy, public perceptions, and expert opinions vary meaningfully over time. Although the roots of current sex offender policies extend much further,[10] I begin with the sexual psychopath era, from about 1930 to 1950, continue into the era of rehabilitative debate, from about 1950 to 1980, and then go to the containment era, 1980 to the present. I describe the sex offender–related media coverage from two major newspapers; social guidance media; state-of-the-art scholarship in criminology, psychiatry, and psychology; and state legislative activity in California. Together, these measures reveal the discursive field surrounding sex offenders—the toolkit of ideas, beliefs, and strategies available to those who made, supported, and implemented policies. Nicole Hahn Rafter, a criminologist, advocates for this kind of mixed-data approach, which takes seriously popular as well as scientific forms of knowing. In her recent work on sex crimes in film, she explains the connection between the cultural turn in sociology and the need to tell stories in popular media:

> While much of this work is speculative, it seems that the fragments of cultural information in our minds form themselves first into frames and then into schemata or templates—bigger and more solid frames—that we draw on in the form of assumptions, social norms, principles, and so on, using them as handy guides to behavior so we are not obliged to think through every action or reaction from the start. Schemata then aggregate into even larger mental structures—ideologies (including assumptions about the nature of heroes and villains), paradigms, logics, and narratives of the self (perhaps including the self as a victim or perpetrator of a sex crime).[11]

The sex offender discursive field, therefore, provides ways of knowing, which will shape future actions as "guides to behavior" as well as "narratives of the self." To capture this field, I systematically reviewed the sex offender coverage in published articles in flagship American scholarly journals and in two prominent U.S. newspapers since 1930, and by seeking out all archived social guidance media related to sexual deviance.[12] For correctional policy and implementation, I address national trends and provide snapshots from multiple states, as well as an extended case analysis of the state of California across the eras. While California cannot represent patterns in other states or at the national level, it has been at the forefront of innovation in correctional policy. As a populous state, it has driven the national correctional numbers. As a model for other states, California pioneered therapeutic sterilization laws in 1909 and led the push for sexual psychopath laws in the 1930s. It later shone during the golden age of rehabilitation. Today, California suffers from some of the worst symptoms of the actuarial approach to punishment, including prison overcrowding and a shameful record of parolee recidivism.[13]

California has also been a model for sex offender treatment and management: legislators invested in a state-of-the-art research and treatment facility for sex offenders in the early 1950s in response to a series of publicized sex crimes; and in the 1960s and 1970s, California's Mentally Disordered Sex Offender Program was the standard-bearer for sex offender treatment practitioners across the country. More recently, the Sex Offender Treatment and Evaluation Project helped pioneer the relapse prevention approach to sexual offending[14] and the state opened a new facility for sexually violent predators at Coalinga State Hospital that has received sustained national and international attention. Yet despite this commitment to noncarceral treatment and research, California has also increasingly filled its prisons with sex offenders.

Due to its sheer size and scope, California's experiments with sex offender control have provided the grist for much of the existing scholarship in the area. As a result, both the knowledge base and the implementation of sex offender policies often relied on data and interpretation of California samples. For all of these reasons, California is a particularly meaningful site for investigating the genesis and evolution of contemporary modes of sex offender punishment. In some ways it may be more unusual than typical; for example, its correctional and civil commitment populations are larger than those of most other nations. But as California goes, the world often follows. Policies made in California tend to spread, just as sensational stories that originate there tend to dominate the news. As my conclusion will suggest, California may also offer a model for modulating some of the most extravagant policies for sex offender management.

The combined approach to the study of punishment over a more than eighty-year span allows me to discuss broad changes, while grounding my conclusions in a detailed study of local forces. I also use sex offender punishment as a case for studying formal social control as a larger phenomenon. Specifically, my work contributes to the history and sociology of punishment in the United States, the sociology of professions, the study of the gap between law on the books and law in action, and discussions of professional discretion in political and judicial decision making.

David Garland's *Culture of Control* describes the "structured field of crime control and criminal justice" and how it came to be.[15] He admonishes, "Do not mistake short-term movements for structural change. . . . Do not mistake talk for action. . . . Do not assume talk is inconsequential. . . . Do not confuse means with ends. . . . Do not conflate separate issues. . . . Do not lose sight of the long-term."[16] I apply Garland's insights to a particular subset of issues and examine them with a long view: the framing of sexual offending and its responses from 1930 to the present. This provides an empirically grounded historical comparison of one crime control problem, which is often seen as emblematic of the general field.

The Scholarly Context

There is near unanimity among those who study punishment trends that we are now in the midst of a peculiarly punitive era, with approaches to crime and punishment that are unique to late modernity. For example, Garland's work on the contemporary "culture of control" is one of several influential explanations of our penal present that each, in varying ways, offers causal models. Many of these considerations descend from Michel Foucault and his efforts to identify the mentalities and rationalities that underlie governmental institutions and policies.[17]

Almost all of this contemporary theorizing has normative motivations and implications: the penal apparatus is out of control, so to change course we must understand it.[18] Many of these accounts also blame a vengeful public: As Garland explains, "There is now a distinctly populist current in penal politics that denigrates expert and professional elites and claims the authority of 'the people', of common sense, of 'getting back to basics.'"[19]

There is also a distinct Marxist strain in contemporary critiques. For many, the special punishments imposed on sex offenders highlight the uniqueness of the current regime. For example, Loïc Wacquant emphasizes the connections between changes in the organization of labor, social welfare, and punishment, elaborating on Marxian theorists like Rusche and Kirchheimer.[20] As Wacquant writes,

> The logic of punitive panopticism and segregative imprisonment that has informed the management of dispossessed, deviant, and dangerous categories in America following the renunciation of the Keynesian social contract is now applied with all the more force to sex offenders, since their misdeeds are more scandalous and touch more directly the foundations of the familial order at the very moment that the family has to compensate for the disappearance of state protections against the risks of working life.[21]

Wacquant thus joins other scholars in pointing out that sex offender crackdowns coincide with the state's retreat from its past responsibilities to its citizens in the areas of welfare and work, suggesting an attempt to substitute public safety for other kinds of security.[22] But these may be coincidental and not causal.

In recent years, scholars, policy makers, and the public have reconsidered certain aspects of general punishment trends since the 1980s. For example, Krisberg and Marchionna found that "by almost an 8 to 1 margin (87% to 11%), the U.S. voting public is in favor of rehabilitative services for prisoners as opposed to a punishment-only system. Of those polled, 70% favored services both during incarceration and after release from prison."[23] Nonetheless, new and improved sex offender punishments are constantly suggested and often enacted. Thus it is unclear whether sex offender punishment reflects the intensification of general penal trends or whether it has a unique trajectory. While I avoid strong causal claims, I have marshaled a wide variety of data to question available theorizing and suggest new, contextualized explanations of sex offender punishment.

Social Construction and Social History

The influence of social theorist Emile Durkheim is nearly universally evident among writers who address the relationships among society, crime, and punishment. Durkheim's insight that the act of punishing strengthens social bonds remains integral to understanding who and how societies punish. His related description of crime as a social fact is similarly fundamental.[24] Rather than existing as a natural or God-given truth, the definition of crime is produced by people and will vary across time and place. For example, the offense of adultery is no longer part of the criminal codes in most U.S. states, but had once resulted in numerous executions in the early American colonies. Adultery has been transformed from a capital crime to a private misdeed.

Social constructionists and social historians have long understood that the framing of threats to children requires deep contextual analysis. In particular, Philip Jenkins's seminal work on changing conceptions of the child molester and Katherine Beckett's account of changes in the media's framing of child sexual abuse provide the groundwork for the present research.[25]

Scholars have also studied the tendency to view the sex offender as a monster and as a scapegoat at the intersection of public fears and reactionary policy. Focused on exaggerated responses and hyperbolic claims, scholars, including Richard Ofshe on the satanic abuse panic, Jonathan Simon on Megan's law, Franklin Zimring on adolescent sexual offenders, and Eric Janus on preventive detention, have all described the often unfounded assumptions and generalizations that have led to ill-advised public policy.[26] Much of this policy making appears to be Durkheimian in nature—a way of drawing boundaries that demonstrate social values and create solidarity.

A great deal of the scholarship that delves into social beliefs and reactions to sex crime builds on Stanley Cohen's concept of "moral panic":

> A condition, episode, person or group emerges to become defined as a threat to societal values and interests; its nature is presented in a stylized and stereotypical fashion by the mass media; the moral barricades are manned by editors, bishops, politicians and other right thinking people; socially accredited experts pronounce their diagnosis and solutions; ways of coping are evolved or (more often) resorted to; the condition then disappears, submerges or deteriorates and becomes visible.[27]

Moral panic scholarship on this topic has focused on the social construction of the "monster" and has shown how the reaction to what is often an overblown threat takes on a life of its own.

The historians Philip Jenkins and Estelle Freedman, in particular, draw our attention to important complexities in the framing of sex crime as a problem. Jenkins and Freedman explain shifts in public interest in sexual offending using many of the same kinds of archival sources I reference. Jenkins's book, *Moral Panic: Changing Concepts of the Child Molester in Modern America*, provides a rich account of three eras, which formed the basis of my own periodization.[28] One of his early chapters focuses on "the age of the sexual psychopath"—this period also forms the basis for Freedman's work, which highlights the ways in which discourse about sexual abnormality allowed the re-drawing of moral boundaries put into crisis by the world wars and postwar social changes.[29] Both scholars contributed not only wonderful leads for archival material but also provocative interpretations of the causes and meanings of preoccupations with sex offenders.

Freedman identifies two eras of "sex crime panic," from 1937 to 1940 and from 1949 to 1955, which she sees as illustrative of a new public discourse on nonmarital, nonprocreative sexuality. Freedman identifies in these sex panics a newly focused punitive attention to homosexual deviants (the inadequately masculine) and violent sex criminals (the hypermasculine) as well as the stigmatization of victims of sexual assault. Freedman explains the sex panics by focusing on shifts in professional and social arrangements, which she describes as

> three convergent trends. First, as courts and prisons became important arenas into which American psychiatry expanded beyond its earlier base in state mental hospitals, the recently established specialization of foren-

sic psychiatry sought new explanations for criminal behavior. Second, the social stresses of the depression drew attention to the problems of male deviance. Third, the social scientific study of sexuality became respectable, and the influence of psychoanalytic theories on American psychiatry during the 1930s provided an intellectual base for a sexual theory of crime.[30]

Jenkins similarly views interest in sex crime as a window into other social phenomena. He focuses on child molesters and covers a longer historical period, extending the critique of the sexual psychopath era to the early end of the contemporary focus on sexual predators.

Freedman's article came out in 1989, while Jenkins's book was published in 1998. Given the exponential increase in sex offender policies since their works and those of other scholars, including Lynch and Beckett who also have examined these trends, not only is there more to analyze but my longer historical view allows for the realization of different patterns. In particular, where each of these works emphasize distinct periods,[31] I see a long progression from multiple ways of talking about sex offenders to a simplified, totalizing narrative. Most important, I also offer a different interpretation of what Jenkins calls "the liberal era" and what all view as a lull in the governance of sex crime.[32] The longer historical view combined with a focus on how different components of the discursive field present conflicting narratives allows me to see the same period of time as signifying not a break from the periods before and after, but as a test of rehabilitative rhetoric that laid the groundwork for contemporary policies.

From Construction to Practice

In addition, while owing much to the historical and sociological perspective that Freedman and others have brought to public debates about sexual offending, I focus on the relationship between criminology and forensic psychology and the importance of sex offenders as subjects for both disciplines. Other scholars of this topic have ignored variations among discourse, legal changes, and changes in formal social control, instead assuming that talk equals action, and that action leads to expected changes in practice.

While it is clear that public attitudes and changes in the construction of threats play a role in policy change, their causal role is not so clear. Major shifts have taken place since 1930 at the policy level and as further measured by criminal justice trends. These shifts are related in part to changes in the politics and structures of criminal justice, and especially to the kinds of expertise considered relevant to crime control. In the following chapters I will examine these shifts as they apply to sex offender and general punishment trends in the United States. The correctional numbers show a phenomenal increase in sex offender incarceration over time.

The best information available for showing longitudinal punishment patterns for particular offenses is from yearly reports of prison admissions to state institutions (long-term historical data cannot be reliably compiled into national figures, but the California numbers shown in figure 1.1 generally track national trends in sex offender punishment since the 1960s). Figure 1.1 shows sex offender admissions, as rates per 100,000 Californians in order to correct for population growth.

The timing reflected in this figure is surprising, given the insistence by both moral panic scholars and those who examine larger punishment trends that the present is peculiar. Prison admissions for felony sex offenses remained flat until the 1960s despite extensive media attention to sensational sex cases, punitive public attitudes, and frequent passage of new laws aimed at sex crime, each of which I describe in the next chapter. These contradict what we might have expected from accounts about "panics" surrounding sex fiends and psychopaths in the postwar period. It also contradicts penal theorists who consider sex offender punishment as exemplary as well: from 1940 to 1971, there was a 48% decrease in sex offender prison admissions, while the big period of expansion occurred from 1971 to 1984, when there was a 486% increase. After 1984, there were some fluctuations, but nothing comparable to the pre-1984 increase.

If we could create a line graph that would track public concern about sex offenders, it would bear a very different shape, with some peaks and valleys, but with neither the flat period from the 1930s to the 1970s nor the dips in the 1990s—of course, such a graph is impossible because "public concern" is not something we can easily measure over time. However, proxies for public concern include media coverage (however imprecise, given the major structural changes in news reporting over the twentieth century) and the more easily quantified passage of state and federal laws. Sex offender–related law making over this period showed spurts of activity that broadly correspond to the periods of moral panic that Estelle Freedman and other historians of twentieth-century sex law have identified,[33] but with massive growth in the 1990s, more than ten years after sex offender prison admissions began to grow exponentially. I dissect the particulars of these trends in later chapters; for now this proves that public anxiety alone cannot drive sex offender punishment or the larger imprisonment boom. If public anxiety could do

FIGURE I.1. *Admissions to California Prisons for All Felony Sex Offenses,*
1932–2007, per 100,000 Residents

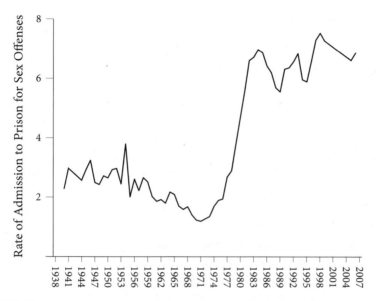

All California incarceration data in this and subsequent figures (admissions, institutional population, and time served) are from the California Prisoners series published in various forms by the California Department of Corrections, first through the Bureau of Criminal Statistics, and later by the Offender Information Services Branch Data Analysis Unit. Rates are calculated using the annual state population as published in California Legislature 2004, Table B-1.

this, the law-making boom of the 1990s would have come *before* the prison expansion, not *after.*

Notwithstanding the unexpected relationship between public concern and punishment numbers over the long term, we might argue that the policy-making trend since the 1980s shows a long-overdue recognition of the seriousness of sexual offending and that criminal justice reflects our toughened attitude. Public opinion and policy changes nationwide have shifted to take sexual offending in general more seriously. While media and politics have paid attention to sex crime as a problem since at least the early twentieth century, there has been a marked shift in the severity of responses that are called for, and there have been some changes in how sex crimes are actually handled. For example, a 2008 report on sexual offenders in Delaware specifically claimed, "Criminal sexual behavior that in the past might have been handled as a misdemeanor, addressed privately, or even considered a mental health issue, is now more likely to be prosecuted as a felony."[34] Available criminal penalties for a variety of sex offenses have certainly increased since the early 1990s.[35] In addition, over the past few decades, the Bureau of Justice Statistics reports that the rate of prisoners sentenced for violent sexual assault has increased at a higher rate than the general prisoner population.[36] But these policy changes, and rate increases, belie the stagnation that has generally occurred for the prosecution and sentencing of rape. As will be discussed in later chapters and is well known to sexual violence scholars, neither clearance rates nor median time served for forcible rape have changed much in the last forty years—despite changes not only in public attitudes but in law enforcement training and techniques (e.g., sensitivity training as well as the use of DNA collection and analysis).[37] Victimization rates also do not uniformly reflect the expected decline as a result of all the new laws aimed at preventing recidivism.

Thus there are two "problems" in the current scholarship: the seemingly overblown response to a particular category of monstrous sex offenders that moral panic scholars emphasize, and the contrasting lack of measurable successes in using the law to address real patterns of sexual violence. I believe this stems from a refusal to acknowledge the multiple and contradictory goals that currently motivate various punishment policies. In subsequent chapters I will lay out the various policies and the stakeholders who are involved in their promotion and application to sex offenders. I have linked stories about sex crime with the way the punishment laws work and have used this linkage to show that the United States has gone off track in several pursuits of justice and social change.

Plan of the Book

In general, I move from discourse analysis to implementation analysis, although some of each can be found in each chapter. Chapter 1 briefly introduces the discursive categories that appear throughout: the images of the offender and the common fallacies that underlie many strategies for responding to sex crime.

The next several chapters describe three eras in the history of sex offender punishment, combining accounts of public anxiety about sex crime with the strategies promoted by experts in psychology and psychiatry and in government (construed broadly to include elected officials as well as criminal justice and correctional authorities). Chapter 2 describes the sexual psychopath era, roughly 1930–1955, in which the media construct and the law refers to a monstrous sex fiend who is plagued by uncontrollable desires and must be captured. In the era of rehabilitative debate, 1950–1980, described in chapters 3 and 4, public interest in new concepts from the psychiatric fields provided a limited testing ground of rehabilitative techniques. But their apparent failure helped pave the way for the current dichotomous approach to sexual offending—punish the offenders and treat the victim. In the containment era, 1980 through the present, described in chapter 5, a peculiar mix of ideologies and strategies are applied to convicted sexual offenders—treatment, incapacitation, and retribution are all featured in a wide range of approaches, although incapacitation dominates.

Chapters 6 and 7 focus on the major discursive shift that has taken place since the 1950s: the displacement of alternative explanations for sexual offending by that of the bogeyman. The ascendance of the undifferentiated image of the monster sex offender appears to have usurped the alternative versions in the policy field. Thus policies typically require the justice systems to react to all sexual offending with the same penal severity. These chapters explain the major shifts and missteps by psych experts that led to their sidelining except as correctional workhorses. Chapter 7 examines the increasing synchronicity of prosecutorial statements about sex offenders and those of hard-line victim advocates and the explicit alliances between police, prosecutors, and victim advocates that characterize the containment era. Chapter 8 moves solidly into implementation analysis by interpreting trends in sex offender criminal justice data across the eras. These data suggest that the most important influence on sex offender punishment may have little to do with ideas or practices unique to sex offenders.

In chapter 9, the conclusion, I explain the implications of each strand developed in the book. The historical perspective suggests that future penological theory and scholarship must examine multiple dimensions in order to draw strong conclusions. Focusing on ruptures and shifts in one dimension has led to overstating the significance of penal change and moral panic. Finally, I consider the possibilities for policy reform, noting several recent state-level successes. Given the sheer numbers of sex offenders currently under correctional control and the staggering costs associated with the numerous special conditions imposed upon them, sex offender policies will have to change.

Punishment Stories

A . . . man accused of raping as many as 20 women, and convicted in June of nine counts of first-degree rape, was sentenced
to life in prison plus 136 years Friday. . . . According to prosecutors and police, Sahin picked up a series of women, primarily
prostitutes, between February and October 2007. And in almost
all the cases the pattern was identical—Sahin would pick up a
prostitute, drive her to a dark, isolated dirt road along the Ches-
apeake & Delaware Canal, display a knife and often hold it to
her throat, and force sexual relations. At least one woman, who
admitted she planned to have sex for money with Sahin, said he
forced sex at the outset when she asked for payment up front.
Sahin allegedly told police that sometimes he just "needed" sex,
but didn't have the money to pay for it. . . . [Judge] Jurden . . .
highlighted one victim's testimony who said she pleaded with
Sahin to think about if he had a daughter facing such a situation. Sahin responded that if he had a daughter "who did what
you do for a living, she'd deserve it."

—Sean O'Sullivan, "Knife-Wielding Rapist Gets Life
Sentence," *Delaware News Journal*, August 15, 2009

The stories we tell through our media and in other public ven-
ues are important. In *Governing through Crime*, the sociologist Jonathan
Simon tells the story of how the problem of crime became an influential
template for reshaping governmental authority in America since the 1960s
and describes the consequences for the way American institutions operate in the early years of the twenty-first century. As part of this argument,
Simon describes the cultural work that is inspired by crime in predeter-
mining certain roles and scripts: "Crime is a genre, in the dramaturgical
sense. It comes with certain kinds of roles: vulnerable victims, willing
offenders, vigilant prosecutors, and harsh but fair judges (and all the deviant variations those set up). When we govern through crime we pass out

these scripts to hundreds if not thousands of real people with little in the way of an audition and no accountability for the consequences."[1]

The story above of the knife-wielding rapist sent to prison for life is not a typical story for many reasons. Stories about violence against women, aside from the occasional heinous murder, are not nearly as common as stories that offer more sensational appeal. More often than not, over the long term, typical stories are about child victims, not about rape and other assaults on adults.

In addition, we expect punishment to achieve multiple and often contradictory goals. I highlight the story of Sahin's punishment in order to attune readers to the tensions among symbolic approaches to punishment that use a single case to achieve a social goal and those that individualize punishment to the individual offender and crime. In fact, as I sat in the courtroom to hear Sahin's sentence, I noted reactions in myself that exemplified at least two goals of punishment: my gut reaction was to celebrate the messages sent to Sahin, a Turkish transplant to the East Coast of the United States, about the value of women. That life sentence told Sahin's victims that they mattered and that their bravery in testifying against him was worthwhile. But after my internal "hurrah" at the judge's words, I began to wonder whether anyone else received that message. The court translator had to give Sahin and his family the judge's message secondhand, and the translator likely focused on the details of the sentence rather than on the judge's framing. Being sentenced to life in prison will not in itself change Sahin's view of women, and it probably will not change anyone else's either. His family and community will more likely focus on his lengthy punishment as being unjust rather than as a social message they could internalize, especially since some have wondered if Sahin's Muslim affiliation played a role in the severity of the charges brought against him. I became further concerned about locating the tangible effects of this message when I realized that there was no major news coverage of the sentencing, despite the fact that the crimes had been featured daily in the local print and television news while they remained unsolved. Neither Sahin and his family nor the local community likely heard the punishment message, although his victims probably did.

The lack of interest in Sahin's sentence by the media reflects the reality that crime fears are more newsworthy than the denouement of the plot that comes at sentencing. In the following text, I examine the expectation that sex crime policies will send symbolic messages, and I contrast symbolic displays through public statements and public policies with the measurable changes in criminal justice responses to sexual violence that can be identified through institutional changes and through exploring the way institutional decision makers put these symbolic policies into practice. Many criminologists would argue that the public and policy response has become disproportionately focused on sex offenders, perhaps out of fears about homosexual pedophiles and other pariahs.[2] Both perspectives—one that sees a successful crackdown or a symbolic victory such as Sahin's sentencing, and one that sees a fruitless panic—make assumptions about the nature of criminal sexual offending, about cultural and scientific beliefs over time, and about the character and quantity of punishment. Too often, scholars, advocates, and even community members focus on one punishment goal and ignore the others. Those who try to pass reforms that consider just one of these perspectives tend to misunderstand the motivations of those who oppose the reforms. Instead, we must look carefully at how we have responded to specific categories of sexual offending over time in order to understand the implications of our current approach and to correct them where necessary.

Sex crime stories have had a vast appeal for many decades. As Philip Jenkins documents in his book on the changing conceptions of the child molester, advocacy claims makers have made child molestation a staple of news media.[3] Organizational constraints and the pressures to sell papers have also helped keep certain kinds of sex crime stories in the public view.

As the criminologist Christopher Greer argues based on his study of more recent print media in Northern Ireland, "the press representation of sex crime, particularly in the tabloids, is becoming a source of (a certain kind of) entertainment . . . a cultural form designed to shock rather than educate, reinforcing existing stereotypes. . . . At best, representations give an inaccurate and misleading impression of the nature and extent of sex crime in society."[4] Greer sees this entertainment value as a relatively recent phenomenon that can be explained by the combination of changing commercial pressures on media, increased social awareness, and populist punitiveness.[5] But the longer historical view suggests that this entertainment value is not new.

Even more important, sensational coverage skews public beliefs. As the historian Paula Fass writes about the Leopold and Loeb case in 1924, "When it finally left the front pages months later, the newspapers, which had started by sensationalizing an unusual kidnapping, had succeeded in normalizing a truly sensational case."[6] Fass demonstrates through this case the way that repeated exposure to sensational tales ends up obscuring statistical "normality" in favor of the story most often repeated.

As someone who is both a researcher and advocate, as well as someone who can bridge the divide between "offenders" and "victims," I am therefore concerned with the impacts of the stories we tell about sex crimes as well as the punishment of sex crimes—both in discourse and practice. Salient characteristics of such stories have changed dramatically over time, and these changes can be connected to legislative and policy implementation changes.

Images of the Sex Offender

Today, public perceptions of sexual offending reveal a paradoxical combination of a moral, will-based model of criminality with a biological, disease-based model; this combination in effect covers all bases, inviting any therapeutic or punishment technique and simultaneously denying that anything could ever possibly work. Throughout the twentieth century, the monolithic notion of the sexual bogeyman, whether it is called a "sex fiend," "sexual psychopath," or a "sexually violent predator," has justified control strategies that have assumed individuals who are quite distinct from that monstrous image to be from the same mold. By the containment era, which spans from 1980 through the present, the psych experts who offered more nuanced accounts, differentiating among types of sex offenders, are largely unheard by those who determine most penal outcomes, as demonstrated in the discussion of Jessica's Law. Rather than calling for a complex response that draws upon multiple fields and strategies, today the most prominent experts are advocates who call for "closing the loopholes" to enable indeterminate punishment, as in the quote from Jan Scully, at the beginning of this book's introduction. In subsequent chapters, I will more deeply investigate the trajectories of what I identify as the three most salient images of sex offenders, which appear across time: the monster, the patient, and the nuisance. I introduce them briefly here, followed by a set of related fallacies that together set the stage for my study.

The Monster

In a 2002 casenote, psychiatrists report on a subject they called "Mr. A," described as a fifty-six-year-old married man, who was referred for treatment of pedophilia. "He reported that his fantasies were repetitive, and while he experienced a sense of shame, he felt unable to control his fantasies: 'I've become a monster.' Despite his impulsive behaviors, he had never been arrested, and he reported no other paraphilic behaviors, such as exhibitionism."[7]

In popular culture, the idea that "sex fiends" lurk in the shadows has featured prominently in popular discourse about sexual violence since at least the 1930s, as I will describe further in the next chapter. This representation reflects many of the associations with sexual offending that continue to dominate: Deviant desires are so beyond control and so terrible that merely thinking about them must be a precursor to action. Even a contemporary man suffering from compulsive sexual fantasies about children puts his problem in these terms, despite the fact that he had not taken any steps toward achieving those fantasies.

The monster appears in slightly different forms, whether as a true stranger, an outsider known to the community but identified as deviant because of his class, lifestyle, or appearance, or as a familiar person who turns out to be a "monster among us." Often, when the monster appellation is applied to a real person in the media, it is to a murderer—and this murderer's sexual homicides implicate other sexual offending by association. The monstrous sex offender is either a confirmed murderer or a potential murderer, and any other kind of sexual offending is frightening in part because it may escalate into acts of murder. Although often cast as a stranger, the monster sex offender may also be an ordinary man who turns out to be an evildoer in our midst. This is one way in which the horror of child murder is hyped in the media as especially fearsome: It cannot be predicted or prevented. Despite some variation, monsters have the following in common: sexual deviance, uncontrollable impulses, and the near certainty that they will cause harm and injury. As a result, the monster is not typically a candidate for therapeutic rehabilitation. Instead, the monster must simply be stopped.

Whether a sex offender is truly unknown or whether it is only his potential for violence that is unknown, the monster image represents a crucial way of thinking about the people who commit sex crimes, which has come to dominate not only popular fears but public policies as well. I investigate the origins of this notion and find that prior to the containment era, at least two other ways of thinking about perpetrators of sex crime have competed with the monster image: One (the patient) is located more in the psychiatric field and the other (the nuisance) is more often used in criminal justice.

The Patient

It may be difficult for some people to see why we adopt a whole hearted psychotherapeutic approach to the child molesters and exhibitionists who make up the majority of our patients. Some may feel that in so doing we are condoning their offenses. . . . But when we see a surgeon carefully repair a bank robber's wounds, we do not conclude that he condones robbery.[8]

Those who treat sex offenders are tasked with carrying out one of punishment's goals, yet they are often viewed as undermining the symbolic role of the law: By treating sex offenders, therapists may appear to be discounting the seriousness of the offending. As the psychologist quoted above notes, this seems to be a problem peculiar to the therapeutic treatment of criminal offenders, and it is especially troublesome for sex offenders. This creates an almost untenable position for such practitioners. In addition, the psychological disciplines cannot credibly claim to cure monsters; therefore, its experts (hereinafter psych experts, including professionals trained in counseling as well as doctors of psychiatry and psychology) must define a specific type of sex offender as their proper subject: The sex offender becomes the patient. The patient image suggests a person who has a pathology that is amenable to treatment and whose troublesome behavior is not a sign of terminal and permanent difference. While psych experts have always been invested in this construction, at times others have promoted it as well, including the popular media, criminal justice experts, and offenders themselves.

But inherent in the representation of the "patient" is defensiveness about whether citing therapeutic approaches to sexual offending is also a means of denying or evading criminal responsibility or just deserts under the law. This will be a recurring theme in this book, as public experts have missed several opportunities to handle this problem more effectively. The missteps (documented in chapters 3 and 4) are combined with the secondary stigmatization of those who work with sex offenders (chapter 7) to undermine the plausibility of the sex offender as a treatable subject.

The Nuisance

Interviews with judges, attorneys, psychiatrists, probation officials, and a study of the leading authorities lead to the conclusion that the adult consensual homosexual offender is not a menace to society and does not exhibit a proclivity toward children. When he engages in homosexual conduct in public he is simply a nuisance. Sentences imposed by the court indicate judicial recognition of this fact.[9]

Getting law enforcement officials to take sex crimes seriously is one of the great feminist victories of the twentieth century: Conduct that had been dismissed as being nuisances became criminality worthy of punishment. As referenced above, debate during the mid-twentieth century raged over whether homosexual conduct should be considered criminal; in some places criminal justice agents effectively decriminalized it in practice (see chapter 5 for an extended analysis). While the legal classification of consensual homosexual conduct was eventually resolved, questions evident in the early twentieth century about sexual assault that did not cause physical injury or involve force persist today. Thus, nuisances were once considered to be a larger group of offenders that included consenting homosexuals in addition to child abusers who coerced participation or who otherwise committed their crimes without overt force.

The difficulty in enumerating the harms of sexual violence and the dangers of sex offenders will be another theme throughout this book, as this reflects another area of unresolved debate that merits more explicit attention in order to move social policy forward. As will be shown, the nuisance category has shrunk dramatically both in popular conceptions and in legal classifications: More sexual offending is now viewed as intolerable. But the shadow of past tendencies to dismiss sexual predation as a mere "nuisance" continues to shape contemporary policies and practices, especially the efforts of advocates who seek signs that society takes sex crimes seriously.

Understanding this image as it applies to sex offender benefits from viewing other work on the social construction of danger. The anthropologist Mary Douglas contrasts the categories of purity and danger, and she describes the relational interpretations that cause objects to be placed in "pure" or "contaminated" categories. For example, a shoe on someone's foot is neutral, but a shoe placed on a dining table is dirty and contaminating.[10] The sociologist Ruth Simpson contrasts notions of danger and safety by describing three frameworks for viewing the world: the confident framework assumes safety and makes note of the dangerous; the cautious framework assumes danger and makes notes of the safe; and the neutral framework makes independent judgments of danger item by item.[11] Simpson also describes the contextual nature of the identification of danger, but focuses on the tension created by violations of assumptions about danger: "In defining our expectations, they create opportunities for surprise, uncertainty, and deviance. Violations and contradictions of frameworks generate the surprise that leads to humor and horror. Uncertainty about which framework to use in a specific situation produces excitement and panic."[12]

Although most of her article uses examples from popular culture or truisms relating to mundane objects, Simpson briefly connects her theorizing to assumptions about sexual violence: "Incest horrifies in part because it violates the safety zone of the family."[13] I develop this insight by looking at historical trends in which kinds of conduct moved someone into the category of "danger" (the monster) as well as by examining the way conduct from persons otherwise unmarked as dangerous could be explained away through models of sickness that failed to contaminate the identity of the perpetrator.

Nuisances are not typically considered to be dangerous. While nuisances could be consensual homosexual offenders, as in the quote above, conduct we take "seriously" today was viewed quite differently in the recent past. As the historian Stephen Robertson explains in his overview of legal practices in New York City before 1950,

> The relatively small number of prosecutions for carnal abuse in New York City reveal that working-class parents continued to treat only [physically injurious acts] as sexual crimes that warranted legal action. Juries, made up of middle-class as well as working-class New Yorkers, tended to agree. Only rarely were they prepared to even indict men that prosecutors established had "fondled" or manipulated a child's genitals; instead, they usually transferred the case to the Magistrates Court to be dealt with as a misdemeanor.[14]

Similarly, a case excoriated in the *Los Angeles Times* in the 1950s shows the persistent "nuisance" labeling of child molestation. The case also served as a vehicle for decrying official inaction—another recurring theme in public discourse and another way of using punishment to send social messages. The *Times* described the offender in this case, Bernard Stringfellow, as a mild-mannered interior decorator who rubbed up against little girls in movie theaters.[15] Stringfellow was eventually civilly committed to a state hospital under the sexual psychopath laws, but not until he had acquired a very long criminal record. At his commitment hearing, he was depicted as "a little, high-domed man . . . who admits molesting more than 100 little girls."[16] Today Stringfellow would be called a serial molester or sexually violent predator, but in 1950 he was treated as a nuisance who pushed the system's tolerance too far, moving him into the category of someone who should be treated psychiatrically.

In fact, the nuisance was not really thought of as a "sex offender" but was typically someone in the community or family who committed acts such as fondling a child (e.g., by offering candy in exchange for a sex act), peeping, flashing, or otherwise engaging in public sex. The nuisance usually had no serious criminal history. Repetitive or public nuisance offenses might signal a pathology and the potential for escalation, but such an offender was not thought of as causing injurious harm. Most important, the deviance he displayed was not so severe that he was a "fiend"; instead he was viewed as controllable, or at least tolerable. He was largely seen as a noncriminal or very minor problem in the first era I discuss in this book (1930–1955), but he is increasingly likely to be charged as a misdemeanant in the second era (1950–1980). By the containment era, the kind of offending previously dismissed as a nuisance or diverted from confinement is now enough to qualify him as a true bad guy at the policy level, but he still presents difficulties for decision makers who do not see him that way. Figure 1.1 illustrates this historical shift, which I will describe in greater detail in subsequent chapters.

These three ideal types—the monster, the patient, and the nuisance—are ways of thinking about sex offenders that coexist with a series of false assumptions that are deeply entrenched in popular discourse as well as in public policy. Subsequent chapters demonstrate these fallacies in wide circulation.

Many ideas about sex offenders circulated before 1980, within and across the various sources available to the public such as within the news, within films, and via public comments from criminal justice officials, government officials, and academics—these multiple ideas are reflected in the first set of circles in figure 1.1.[17] Words and traits used to describe sex offenders included compulsive, evil or willful, sick or treatable, dangerous or harmful, as well as normal and abnormal (biologically or psychologically). These seem logically inconsistent with each other, yet contradictory beliefs were often expressed simultaneously. Throughout the 1970s, the representations begin to consolidate, with certain fields presenting more consistent views of sex offenders that contrasted with those documented by others (e.g., the psychiatric perspective became more cohesive and contrasted with views expressed by those within social movements). By the containment era, there was a largely monolithic portrayal.

Fallacies Surrounding Sex Crimes

The following fallacies are deeply held beliefs. They are influential in the framing of new laws and in the dispositions of individual offenders. By highlighting the differences between popular and professional knowledges and alternative ways of knowing and acting on sex offenders that held sway in previous eras, I ultimately offer strategies for dislodging these fallacies from their prominent places in our media and policy.

FIGURE 1.1. *Images of Offenders*

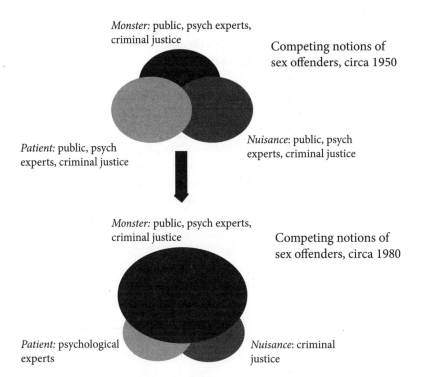

Monster: public, psych experts, criminal justice

Competing notions of sex offenders, circa 1950

Patient: public, psych experts, criminal justice

Nuisance: public, psych experts, criminal justice

Monster: public, psych experts, criminal justice

Competing notions of sex offenders, circa 1980

Patient: psychological experts

Nuisance: criminal justice

The stranger fallacy: The biggest threat is posed not by people known to us but by random sex attacks by monsters. This fallacy is often accompanied by hyperbolic statements about the increasing incidence and prevalence of this kind of crime.

The bogeyman fallacy: The people who commit sex crimes have a unique, essential identity. They are of a different kind—distinct from the general population in terms of their deviant and compulsive sexual interests, criminal offense patterns, and likelihood of reoffending. Once identified, they can only be incapacitated.

The singular sex offender fallacy: All sex offenders are equally deviant, dangerous, harmful, and incurable. There is no reason to differentiate among them—all require the harshest response.

The continuum fallacy: There is a continuum of deviance on which every sex crime exists, and offenders will inevitably escalate from noncontact offenses to murder.

The victim-or-offender fallacy: To promote therapeutic rehabilitation for offenders is to deny the harm caused by the offense or to favor offenders over victims. This is supported by the notion that sex offenders neither deserve nor respond to treatment.

The knowledge-is-power fallacy: By keeping convicted sex offenders under public scrutiny, the community can participate in policing known offenders and can prevent recidivism.

The new law fallacy: The prosecutor's call for Jessica's Law at the outset of this book is one of numerous calls to action that assume new laws will prevent future victimization. But the new laws are almost always narrowly conceived penal strategies that focus on previous fallacies, rather than on broad, social-change agendas.

A final leitmotif of the following chapters needs a brief introduction here: There is tension between a way of thinking about sexual offending that I describe as "normalizing" and a way of thinking by those who take a "bogeyman" approach. Many other scholars of contemporary society emphasize the dialectics of normal and abnormal and insider and outsider, often building on Durkheimian and Marxist theory. For example, the sociologist Jock Young argues that the displacements and alienations of late modernity lead people to cling to essential identities and to insist on oppositions such as the criminal other.[18] I will return to this scholarly conversation in chapter 9. As I describe historical moments that illustrate this tendency as it relates to sex crime, I define normalizing discourse as that which emphasizes two characteristics. First, normalizing discourse assumes a universal potential for sexual aggression: anyone could commit sex offenses, but social controls typically keep deviant urges in check. Second, given this etiological view that does not see sexual offending as the product of a wholly alien type, but rather of an uncontrolled but common urge, normalizing discourse declares that offenders can stop offending through treatment or other controls. In contrast, the bogeyman is a monstrous, irredeemable deviant, an entirely separate type of person who can be stopped but never cured.

The Sexual Psychopath Era

1930–1955

On February 2, 1928, the nude and headless body of a young boy
of about eighteen years of age, apparently of Mexican extrac-
tion, was found in a ditch by the side of Hudson road, near
Puente. The body was covered with a sack which had formerly
contained chicken feed. An autopsy was performed, which dis-
closed that death had been caused by gunshot wounds, and that
decapitation had apparently taken place immediately subsequent to death and probably not more than twenty-four hours
prior to the discovery of the body. The appellant, in the presence
of his nephew, the prosecution's chief witness, stated to his parents that he had killed a Mexican boy and left his body beside a
road near Puente. . . . Upon his return the following morning,
he removed the head of a male person, resembling a Mexican,
from the back of his automobile, and stated to his nephew that
he had to kill the Mexican because he "knew too much."
                                    —*People v. Northcott* 1930, 642

In 1930, the Supreme Court of California rejected Gordon Stewart
Northcott's appeal in the infamous "Wineville murder farm" case. Northcott had been tried and convicted of murdering several boys and disposing
of their bodies on his chicken farm. After declaring the facts too gruesome
to recount, the court recounted the facts as excerpted above. The court also
described the motivation for two other alleged murders:

It was the theory of the prosecution that the appellant had kidnapped or
abducted these boys, who were brothers, and brought them to his chicken
ranch in order that he might practice a most unnatural and disgusting act
upon them. The evidence very definitely establishes that the appellant is
a moral pervert and degenerate of the very lowest type. When upon the

stand in his own defense he readily admitted that for a number of years he had been addicted to the practice of the unnatural crime against nature.[1]

Intense public attention surrounded the story as soon as the investigation was made public. A mob attempted to remove Northcott from the local jail in order to force him to reveal the location of other children's bodies. At Northcott's hanging at San Quentin, a *Los Angeles Times* reporter, one of 140 witnesses, described the way the twenty-two-year-old "had to be carried to the scaffold. His eyes were bandaged at his own request."[2] The *Los Angeles Times* and *New York Times* covered Northcott's mother's appeals of her life sentence for her role in the crimes, keeping the case in the public eye throughout the 1930s. Northcott's story has had incredibly long-lasting appeal. In 2008, Clint Eastwood retold the tale from the perspective of one of the victim's mothers, in his film *Changeling*. Almost a century later, the gruesome details and ultimate resolution—through the extermination of the bad guy—continue to be a prototype for media portrayal of sexual offending and its appropriate "solution."

In this chapter I will survey the prominent discourse, law, and policy regarding sex crimes from 1930 to 1955. I set the stage for later chapters that focus on particular sites of knowledge and action: popular media, law makers, criminal justice actors, advocates, and public experts. Northcott is emblematic of particular fears, sensationalized not only by the tabloid media, but also by courts and even some criminal justice actors. He was a predatory, calculating child molester, with multiple victims whose bodies he tried to hide. But in addition to being portrayed as a rational actor, he was also compulsively "addicted" and "degenerate." He was not only homosexual in his interests, but he was also a transgressor of racial boundaries. Northcott was the iteration of the bogeyman as depicted in the 1930s and 1940s: the sexual psychopath.

Before the Psychopath Era

Before describing the key features of the sexual psychopath era (from 1930 to 1955), it is necessary to recount some of the public campaigns surrounding sexuality as well as instances of criminological thinking about sex crime in the period just prior to the 1930s. The American Social Hygiene Association, formed in 1913, became a major force in public education during World War I.[3] Its campaigns included posters distributed widely in schools and community settings like the YMCA. Because their goal was decreasing stigma and shame in order to encourage healthy sexual habits, the association's discourse surrounding sexual activity had normalizing rather than demonizing strains. The idea the association promoted was that natural inclinations must be controlled. Without explicitly naming sex crime or offending as part of its concern, the association's poster series (created in 1918 for boys and in 1922 for girls) cautioned against excessive sexual fantasy or activity. For example, in the boys' series of posters about "keeping fit" the emphasis was on diet and exercise; a poster titled "how the mind affects the body" cautioned that "continued thinking on sex matters causes harm."[4] Another pictured a young man in a factory setting with the caption, "The man or boy absorbed in constructive or interesting work and thoughts has no time to bother with smutty stories."[5] In addition to avoiding compulsive fantasy and pornography, the posters urged boys to channel their "sex impulses" to "act, dare, possess, strive" for the social good.[6] The messages encouraged willpower: "The youth who achieves self-control can go joyfully and clean into marriage."[7] There were also posters that valorized pure femininity, which primarily aimed to prevent venereal disease, but used more general language: "The chivalrous youth protects the honor of all women and girls" and "Treat every girl as you would like to have another man or boy treat your sister, girlfriend or sweetheart."[8] While encouraging abstinence and prophylactics, people within the social hygiene movement created a space for viewing problematic sexual urges as something all young people must control, not just as a problem attached to a small group of dangerous strangers. However, they also contributed to the stigmatization of sexually active women, for example, by stating, "A girl who would yield to one man has probably had relations with another. Very likely, she is diseased."[9] This kind of stigma is one feature of the victim blaming that often chills sex offense reporting.

In contrast to this normalizing discourse, the emerging discipline of criminology, as understood by the American audience at the turn of the twentieth century, tended to view offenders as categorically different. Cesare Lombroso, an Italian anthropological criminologist, is today widely associated with biological fatalism and bad research methodology, because of his infamous identification of "atavistic" subtypes in a noncontrolled criminal sample. But he is also a criminological founding father. Lombroso's attention to sex crimes was largely excised from English translations, but newly available editions allow us to re-examine his contributions. Lombroso's focus on sex crimes is relatively minor compared to his other interests, but what he proposes contradicts expectations. His chapter "Sexual Sensitivity (Lesbianism and Sexual Psychopathy)" in his treatise on female criminality as well as a selection on sex crime from the fifth edition of his treatise on male criminality[10] both focus more on situational crime than on atavism or other biological explanations. After describing these, I compare these texts to the notions of criminality that dominated the sexual psychopath era.

When Lombroso discusses sex-related crime in *Criminal Man*, he writes quite a bit about female criminality, emphasizing that sex crimes by both men and women are often opportunistic, rather than the result of an inborn drive or "special type" of offender. Instead, sex crimes result more often from the "natural" result of a lack of noncriminal sexual outlets and moral restraint. For example, in *Criminal Man*, he wrote, "When equilibrium between the call of nature and moral duty is established, we will see a rapid reduction in sex crimes, which derive as much from a lack of love as an excess of passion."[11] Further, these "occasional crimes" are social in nature, rather than biological; that is, they are "encouraged by the primitive level of rural society, lack of prostitutes as sexual outlets, or barriers to marriage."[12] Lombroso also condemns the effects of "religious institutions like the Catholic Church" because "where priests are condemned to celibacy, the confessional offers an occasion and instrument of crime. . . . Statistics show relatively high rates of sex crimes, particularly pederasty." Other opportunities for sex crimes against minors include "the proliferation of schools, particularly boarding schools. Schools provide opportunities for contact between teachers (who are often poor and therefore single) and pupils." Rather than being the behavior of monstrous individuals, sexual offending in this view could be understood by its social context.

This social explanation of sex crimes as natural urges gone wrong is the predominant theme in *Criminal Man*, though Lombroso does mention in passing that "some sex crimes are caused by congenital tendencies in born rapists with a cretinal diathesis that either stimulates the genitals or provokes insanity."[13] It is this biological explanation, which we most often associate with Lombrosian explanations of crime, that captures the fascination of one strain of sex offender science, as exemplified by Dr. J. Paul De River, an expert who dominated the sexual psychopath era.

A Period of Panic?

This period from about 1930 to about 1955 functions as a baseline for the purposes of my historical comparison—I describe the sex offender discursive field at this time in order to understand what changed over time and to draw some tentative conclusions about policies and implementations that were facilitated or obstructed by the dominant paradigms. In contrast to subsequent eras, which can be best defined by the prevailing penal strategy (treatment and then containment), the 1930s, 1940s and early 1950s were characterized by a diverse and inclusive mix of ideas and strategies that cohered around fears of "the sexual psychopath" or "sex fiend"—such as Northcott.[14] Fear of the sexual psychopath emerged from dominant criminological theories of degeneracy and feeblemindedness at the beginning of the twentieth century, which were popularized by newspapers seeking readers.[15] Sexual psychopaths were perceived as deviants with a compulsive sex disorder who were running rampant among us and therefore must be identified, classified, and captured.

The various strategies suggested and promoted by various public sources for eliminating the threat of sexual psychopaths included incapacitation, biological research, public education or awareness, and rehabilitation. During this era, the legal system and the government maintained some distance from the most vitriolic of public concerns, ignoring calls for castration and instead funding research and institutions for treatment as well as passing new laws to increase punishment. Undeniably, public pressure did determine some policy, as scholars writing during and after the sexual psychopath era have noted.[16] But numerous and competing strategies were available to policy makers, and they generally enacted the less punitive ones. Figure 2.1 provides California prison admission data for just this era. Admissions for forcible rape are represented by squares, while "other" sex offense admissions are represented by triangles. The two horizontal lines are the averages for each offense for the period (0.81 for rape and 1.79 for "other" sex offenses). Despite slight variation, these lines show overall flatness in the rate of imprisonment for sex offenses during this era—moral panic does not seem to have translated into punishment change as measured by incarceration during this period.

Even though prison admissions did not change much over time, two broad and related discursive changes took place during the sexual psychopath era. First, sexual criminals (and offenders in general) were no longer seen as suffering from a biological defect (an *identity*) but instead were thought to be suffering from mental illness or *behavior* that could be modified, in some cases allowing the individual to rejoin the "normal" world. This reconsideration is not unique to sexual offending but reflects the influence of the larger mental hygiene and humanist psychology movements as well as the general medicalization of criminality.[17] However, expert discourse about sex offenders in particular underwent a split: While academic psychiatry and criminology relinquished the biological paradigm, influen-

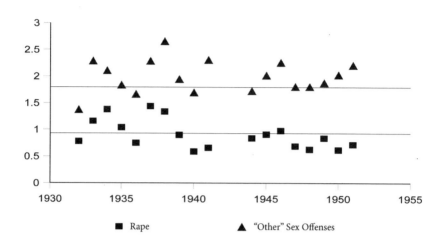

FIGURE 2.1. *Admissions to California Prisons, 1932–1951, per 100,000 Residents*

■ Rape   ▲ "Other" Sex Offenses

tial figures associated with policing and the practice of criminology continued to seek out signs of crime written on distinctly deviant bodies. A second change occurred within legislative activity, from rooting strategies exclusively in incapacitation to emphasizing research and treatment. Cultural expressions about sex crime and punishment reflected some of these ideas, often retaining ideologies and strategies long after the mainstream experts abandoned them. The sexual psychopath era, therefore, resists classification solely in terms of moral panic: To say that public anxiety led to policy change elides the particular changes, as well as the ways in which policies were implemented.

Talking about Sex Crimes and Sex Criminals

The discourse surrounding sexual offending from 1930 to 1955 was varied and often contradictory, as the articles about Northcott reflect. Coverage of other sensational cases in the *Los Angeles Times* and the *New York Times* during this era expands the picture of public perceptions as well as the context in which various experts and government authorities were making sex crime policy.

One of the most common kinds of stories about particular cases can be characterized as "sex fiend sought" stories, which were really about the crime victim rather than the offender. These generally gave some details about a murdered victim, including age and gender as well as her occupation, such as dancer, nurse, student, or wife. These stories hinted at sexual assault either in the details of how the body was found—"nude" or "choked with panties"— or by using a phrasing of the time, "criminally assaulted." Often, however, the only indication that the case was considered a sex crime was that the authorities sought a sex fiend or sexual psychopath. The story rarely identified the race of the victim, except for in cases where "Negro" boys had been found murdered.[18] The assumption seemed to be that certain kinds of victims could only have been killed for sexual reasons; thus, reflecting circular reasoning, the suspects were sexual criminals.

During this era, newspaper readers were exposed to these and other brief mentions of sexual psychopaths or potential psychopaths,[19] but, more important, they could read extensive coverage of a handful of sex murders. The public was offered detailed, sensational accounts of the minutiae of trial proceedings, as in the Northcott case. The sustained and alarmist descriptions of these cases reified the monstrous image of the sex offender. The tendency to infer sexual connotations to murders had been a key feature of the press coverage and public discourse surrounding the murder by Leopold and Loeb of young Bobby Franks in 1924, a case that received international attention and shaped beliefs about sex crime through the subsequent decades. As the historian Paula Fass explains,

> The sensationalism occurred, in part, because Leopold and Loeb were unlikely killers but also because rumors about the mutilation of the body and the body as the site of perverse practices started almost immediately after the discovery of the unclothed child, well before Leopold and Loeb were suspects. As early as May 24, Chief of Detectives Michael Hughes tried to squelch these rumors by noting that "after a hard day's work on the Franks mystery, I am convinced . . . that it was a plain case of kidnapping for ransom—not a case of a victim of perverts." The coroner's report found no evidence of sexual abuse, but these allegations lingered throughout the life of the case, and the judge had to continually remind the prosecutor that the rumors had been disproved. The rumors were subsequently inflamed by psychiatric reports and wide-ranging interviews that suggested boyish compacts and alluded to perversions (a code word for homosexuality) between Leopold and Loeb.[20]

These sexual psychopath cases cast long shadows, remaining salient even when the trial was over or the defendant executed. For example, the North-cott case directly informed later cases. In a 1939 trial a prosecutor was reprimanded for mentioning Northcott and another infamous child slayer, Albert Dyer. After the jury was told to disregard the references, the prosecutor insisted that he mentioned the infamous names not to "inflame [the jurists'] passions" against Adams, a defendant charged with child molestation but not murder, but to combat the belief "that these things don't occur in this metropolitan area of ours, in this modern life we are living, because they do occur—they occur time and again without number."[21] But the Supreme Court of California didn't accept the excuse and agreed with the defense that the prosecutor had acted prejudicially:

> In connection with the Northcott and the Dyer cases, to which the deputy district attorney had referred, it need only be said that they were not only the most outrageous in character, but also were the most notorious that have occurred within the state of California in recent years. Each of them received so much newspaper publicity and were so much the subject of general conversation that it would have been unbelievable that any person who had read the newspapers at all, or who had indulged in ordinary conversation with his neighbors or friends, was not made familiar with the details of the atrocities perpetrated in each of those cases. . . . the purpose of the deputy district attorney in making reference to those cases was not confined to that of assuring and reminding the jurors that occurrences of the nature of that involved in the instant case were not uncommon,—but that, by recalling the Northcott and the Dyer cases to the minds of the jurors, they might entertain a feeling of hostility toward [the] defendant and . . . would "render a verdict such as you will be proud of and can adhere to in the days to come."[22]

Nationally, these sex murders were well known. Within California, merely naming the defendants was shorthand for signally sexual danger. The facts of these cases built on and further constituted commonly held beliefs about sexual offending. This view of the Adams trial also shows that an individual incident of nonfatal child molestation provided an opportunity for conjuring the horror of child murder. Jurors could "do something" to protect their communities and to demonstrate their values by punishing one sexual deviant, who served as a metonymy for the larger threat.

While crimes against adult women were also depicted in the media, as shown in the "sex fiend sought" articles and social guidance media described in more detail later in this chapter, the most sensationalized cases, and those that ended with executions, involved child victims. Albert Dyer, the name of one of the murderers invoked in Adams's child molestation trial, was described in newspapers as a "dull, stupid man," harkening back to the "feeble-minded offender" of earlier decades.[23] Dyer worked as a neighborhood crossing guard and was familiar to local children. When three elementary school girls went missing, Dyer tried to help find them.

Characterizations of Dyer referred to his mental defects, but focused on his sexual degeneracy. Dr. J. Paul De River, the nation's most famous and controversial expert on "sexual psychopathy" at the time, provided the sexual angle for the case, testifying that "as [Dyer] perpetrated each murder by strangling them to death he became more sexually excited and when he had completed his third and last murder before he began his infamous assaults on the victim's bodies, everything turned black to him he was so emotionally overcome."[24] This could be a voice-over in a cautionary tale or a line from detective fiction. But it is instead De River's expert testimony.[25]

Another account of Dyer's trial depicted a deputy brought to tears as he testified about the gruesome crime scene; another cited attempts to break into the jail to lynch Dyer and his wife, who was also held in custody.[26] The *Los Angeles Times* included a photo of a mob of housewives who lined up to get a seat in the courtroom, illustrating the opposition between the normative order embodied by the feminine ideal and the disorder threatened by sex fiends in our midst.[27] This also reflects the fact that the pages of the newspapers inspired people to action.[28] While nationally known and effective in shaping cultural beliefs, at the local level these sex homicides galvanized social protest as well.[29]

Subsequent cases superseded even the Northcott and Dyer cases in their impact. In 1949, coverage of six-year-old Linda Joyce Glucoft's disappearance included the parents' impassioned pleas for her return, numerous photos of the chubby girl with Shirley Temple curls and dimples, and then relentless coverage of the murder scene after her body was found "strangled, stabbed by an ice pick and slashed with an ax."[30] The coverage of Glucoft's murder and in particular the image of her grieving parents, was so much a part of the public consciousness that *The Dangerous Stranger*, a film described later in this chapter, featured a staged reproduction of the parents and cautioned children not to cause their own families such sorrow by being "boobs" and taking candy from strangers. The investigation quickly identified "grandfatherly" Fred Stroble, a neighbor of the Glucofts, as the perpetrator. Within a matter of days, Stroble fled to Mexico, prompting a manhunt, complete with posses on horseback. Stroble was executed on July 25, 1952.

Burton Abbott was the final sexual psychopath to receive sustained attention in this time period. Abbott was a husband, father, and an accounting student at the University of California, Berkeley. He was convicted of kidnapping and murdering Stephanie Bryan, a fourteen-year-old schoolgirl who disappeared on April 28, 1955, in Berkeley. His execution was carried out in 1957, missing by moments a call from the governor offering a stay.[31] Abbott's mother spent the next fifty years trying to prove his innocence;[32] in 2002 his case was added to the material describing the proud history of the Alameda County District Attorney's office on their public Web site.

While the news coverage of sex crimes offered a certain amount of pleasure and titillation to consumers, other forms of media focused on solutions to sex crimes. Stroble's story also inspired the feature film *The Sniper*, released in 1952, which billed itself as both entertainment and as a warning for women about how to avoid victimization.[33] But there is also a purely educational category of media that has had important influences on the *doxa*, or taken-for-granted ideas, surrounding sexual offending. (For an explanation of "doxa," please see appendix A.)

The most influential of these media was *The Dangerous Stranger*, a "social guidance" film intended to warn children about the dangers of trusting people they didn't know. Sid Davis, a stuntman, had read about Glucoft's disappearance and tried to warn his daughter about the risk of kidnapping but felt his daughter was not getting the message. So he borrowed money from John Wayne, for whom he had acted as a double, and produced the first of what would turn out to be hundreds of educational short films. Created with the "counsel and assistance" of the Los Angeles Police Department (LAPD), the film offers several vignettes about children lured by strangers. The narrator is a friendly neighborhood police officer who tells viewers, "Remember the kids who get in trouble with strangers are the ones who forget what they've been told." The film was distributed nationally to schools and police departments by the company that produced the Encyclopedia Britannica; it was even revised and redistributed in the 1970s. It arguably informed multiple generations of schoolchildren regarding the perils of sex crime. But one of the troubles with this film and the others like it was the lack of specific advice for avoiding victimization. The most concrete recommendations that the narrator made was the now proverbial "don't take candy from strangers."

Beyond this, other films in the series suggested that children should "always get the license number, and description of any stranger who takes a young person off alone, no matter what they tell you."

Although light on constructive advice, social guidance media shaped and reinforced particular ways of thinking about sexual offending. Popular writings about crime and criminals also offered a particular interpretation of sexual criminality. As the historian Paula Fass writes, detective fiction often invited readers to the "boundary of human consciousness where analytic intentionality blended with irrational passion."[34] This conception of sexual criminality as both irresistibly compulsive and ominously calculating did not automatically correspond with calls for punitive solutions, however. For example, the best-selling book *Terror in the Streets* was written by the journalist Howard Whitman to stir public fears about "hoodlum crime," which he characterized as a problem borne of a "new" criminal type who lacked any empathy for people. He told a litany of terrible tales like the following, of little Shirley Jean, who had asked her father if she could stop and buy a pack of gum: "She didn't get home. But she got the gum alright. A piece of it was frozen in her mouth when she was found in the frost-silvered weeds the next morning, dead, ravished, her little body pitifully torn."[35] Interestingly, Whitman did not use Shirley Jean's story to call for increased prison sentences, executions, or castration.[36] Although he used the same kinds of descriptive techniques used by newspaper reporters and screenwriters, and Dr. De River, after capitalizing on fears, Whitman called for police patrols to prevent criminal opportunities and he insisted that criminals needed to be caught early and rehabilitated:

> I should like to see the theory of responsibility substituted for the theory of punishment. . . . When society gouged out the eyes of rapists, it didn't stop rape. . . . The entire dismal picture of our prisons two-thirds full of repeated offenders testifies to the general failure of punishment. . . . Joe the Knifer . . . must be re-educated toward the mature pattern, "I am a part of society. I am, as an individual, individually responsible."[37]

Whitman's peculiar mix of sensationalism and rehabilitative rhetoric shows that the sexual psychopath era was really a bridge into the normalizing perspective that came to dominate in subsequent decades, not a period of unremitting "crackdown."

More often than not, the threat of the unknown sexual psychopath or sex fiend is transformed in both print and cinematic media from the familiar represented by Dyer, Stroble, and Abbott into a complete unknown who enters a community in order to commit a terrible crime and then flees. These kinds of unknown threats are depicted in articles describing unsolved crimes as well as in the admonitions of J. Edgar Hoover, who ran a series of national articles aimed at stirring up concern about sex criminals.[38] But few people recognized or attempted to resolve the inconsistency between the threats the public was exhorted to protect itself from and the threat that presented itself when child murders are solved or when other sex crimes are investigated. Sexual psychopath murderers, for example, were typically offenders who knew their victims, thereby confounding much of the "monster" stereotype.

But some did note the inconsistency between image and reality. A quote from a Los Angeles police officer illustrates the problems created by the lack of differentiation in the public's view of the sexual offender: "The same people who are so incensed today and who are urging drastic measures like castration for sex criminals, are the same ones who in a couple of years will be importuning us to quash a case against some pillar of the community—some churchman or kindly old grandfather."[39] This conflict between the punitive response to monsters and the desire to protect respectable citizens defines this era—and, as available data show, this conflict most often was resolved through nonprosecution or the use of minor charges. This inconsistency appears to have chilled law enforcement efforts at the local level, even as Hoover and others made national exhortations.

While the most pervasive representation of the dangerous sex offender may have been the stranger, there was some acknowledgment that acquaintances could commit sex crimes—this was unavoidable, for example, in the case of Fred Stroble, described as a favorite of the neighborhood children.[40] The short film *Boys Beware!* is emblematic of the way this familiar danger was often framed as a monster in our midst that we needed to unmask.[41] That film, which provides a series of vignettes showing boys seduced by adult men, cautions against "dangers involved that never meet the eye." Specifically, it warns boys not to let their guard down: "He may appear normal, and it may be too late when you discover he is mentally ill."

These kinds of public education tools portrayed homosexuality as a mental illness, as in this description of an adult who befriends a teen: "Ralph was sick, a sickness that was not physical like smallpox, but no less dangerous and contagious, a sickness of the mind. You see, Ralph was a homosexual, a person who demands an intimate relationship with members of their own sex." Although Ralph turns out to be a "passive homosexual" who is sent to jail, in another vignette a teen who accepts a ride from a recent acquaintance finds himself "riding in the shadow of death . . . sometime that evening,

Mike Merrit traded his life for a newspaper headline." Even in these films, which portray the dangers associated with acquaintances, the bad guys are called "strangers" in order to facilitate an easy solution through the concluding public education message. Thus, even when the circumstances involved a guy who appeared to be normal, the problem was re-framed as that of a dangerous stranger when it came to the closing advice. As Mary Douglas, an anthropologist, explains, "It is part of our human condition to long for hard lines and clear concepts. When we have them, we have either to face the fact that some realities elude them, or else blind ourselves to the inadequacy of the concepts."[42] This research shows the tendency to maintain the monstrous essential identity and simultaneously apply that label to everyday dangers.

This critique is not just the product of hindsight but was made contemporaneous to the release of these films. A family studies professor at Oregon State University published a review of *The Dangerous Stranger*, which made just these points:

> The film has received severe criticism on several counts. First, it attempts to attain its objective through building the concept that any stranger is dangerous and children should steer very clear of any person with whom they are not acquainted. The child is not taught to judge situations in any way, nor to believe that most people are good—only to fear strangers. There is a serious fallacy at this point in that probably more children experience sexual advances from persons with whom they are acquainted than from strangers. A study in Detroit showed that 72% of all child molestations were committed by someone the child knew. Such evidence suggests a need for helping children to judge specific situations. The error becomes even more serious when the film implies all sexual molesters are men and casts these more or less in the stereotyped villain's pattern. This builds a mistaken idea that sex deviates can readily be spotted by their physical appearance.[43]

But this professor was a marginalized expert, and his critique did not penetrate the gestalt in 1952 any more effectively than similar comments have since.[44]

In addition to the contradictions between sex offenders being portrayed as either strangers or familiars, other discourse included contradictory ideas about why sex offenders committed their crimes and how we should handle them. These discussions of etiology, level of risk posed, and how distant sex offenders were from the rest of us were heavily shaped by police, lawyers, judges, and mental health practitioners.

Experts and the Marketplace of Ideas
Dr. J. Paul De River and the LAPD Sex Crimes Bureau

The Stroble case and the interest surrounding it compelled Earl Warren, the governor of California at that time, to call a special session of the legislature, during which he invited experts to offer their opinions.

> California has two basic needs for solution of its sex crime problems, according to 10 psychiatrists who testified in the State Building here yesterday. One is immediate. The other is long-range in purpose but was recommended to start at once.
>
> The first would require that every convicted sex offender be examined by a psychiatrist, psychologist or criminologist so that he may be classified for correction and treatment.
>
> The other is a program of research work and training of needed personnel—psychologists, criminologists and social workers. The psychiatrists suggested $500,000 as a starter for the program. (*Los Angeles Times*, December 8, 1949)

This session resulted in legislative funding for a variety of new responses to sexual offending. There were to be two new sources of institutional knowledge of sexual offending: one based in policing and the other in the civil commitment program created by the sexual psychopath laws. Both of these illuminate a fragile coalition between criminal justice interests, including those of police, prosecutors, judges, and probation and parole officers, and the interests of therapeutic professionals, including counselors and evaluators.

J. Paul De River rose to prominence for his role in the nation's first Sex Crimes Bureau, created as part of the package of measures enacted in the wake of Warren's special conference on sex crime. At the height of his career, De River was a national figure whom Estelle Freedman has called a "crude popularizer" of the concept of sexual psychopathy. His involvement in high-profile investigations, including the Black Dahlia murder, made him famous and was further supported by two "casebooks" based on his experience with the police in Los Angeles (*The Sexual Criminal* and *Crime and the Sexual Psychopath*).[45] Published by a specialty press that offered other volumes dedicated to police science, De River's books received significant national attention, including mentions in the *New York Times* book section under "Science," a review in the *Journal of Criminal Law and Criminology*, and a *Newsweek* review.[46] De River was also featured in *12 Against Crime*, which was a police reporter's attempt to "publicize the work of 12 non-police specialists, little known technical experts whose modern detection methods aid the law enforcement agencies of the country."[47] Thus, De River was known popularly and within the criminological community, although there is nothing to suggest that he was a major player in academic psychiatry, due to his lack of published scholarship.

De River first came to public attention in California in the early 1920s as a cosmetic surgeon. He stated in the *Los Angeles Times* that "it is every person's social and constitutional right to have his nose altered."[48] De River believed that one's appearance was very important to one's psyche. This reflects De River's preoccupation with reading the body and interpreting it through a Freudian lens and emphasizes that his entrée into psychiatry was not through the academy but through his application of popularized notions to his clinical experience.

De River's casebooks featured incredibly graphic photos. Although the books were produced for police training purposes, the publisher marketed them broadly. Thus, the casebooks contributed to the sensationalized view of sexual offending: they provided uncensored images of ex-sanguinated and mutilated bodies, crimes attributed to "lust murderers." These images of raped and tortured women and children are shocking today and must have been so in the 1940s and 1950s. De River also showed pictures of the offenders he interviewed (not identified as suspects, but nonetheless described in captions as the killers). For example, his chapter on juvenile sadism shows the bloodied body of a twelve-year-old girl and also shows the line-up picture of "Case of X: Juvenile Sadist. He is cold, egotistical, and defiant."[49] In many ways, the text that accompanied the pictures was of much less importance—the pictures themselves reinforced the message that sexual criminality was incredibly harmful and dangerous. Even though De River's explanations of criminal conduct and beliefs of etiology were more nuanced, the pictures blazoned a simple, sensational message.

Along with the pictures, De River's casebooks included transcripts from his interrogations of suspects as well as his elaboration of different subtypes. De River's work follows Cesare Lombroso's flawed methodological tradition, relying on a correctional convenience sample to generalize about sexual criminality. It shows the influence of Lombroso's biological and situational explanations of sex crime, with an additional emphasis on moral failing described in Freudian terms. De River also provided biographies for the offenders, which reveal the implicit role of social class and ethnicity in his construction of sexual deviance. Like Lombroso had, De River saw sexual perversion as the result of sexual development gone wrong—from this perspective, an offender was not a monstrous type but was someone who developed incorrectly, often because of poor upbringing related to his or her racial and class position. But anything in this explanation that could be viewed as potentially normalizing is completely overshadowed by the other elements of the casebook, which construct sexual criminals as horribly violent and deviant others.[50]

De River fell out of favor with the LAPD and the city council in 1950. His daughter, who developed a Web site to correct false information about her father in a recent book about the Black Dahlia murders,[51] believes that he was the victim of political maneuvering. Regardless, De River made a lasting contribution to the "bogeyman" view of sexual offending, and he also helped secure the place of psychiatric expertise in public and policy debates about sex offenders. As the self-described founder and director of the LAPD Sex Crimes Bureau,[52] he also played a role in implementing sex offender law. The particular strategies he promoted are discussed below.

If De River enjoyed a period of national prominence as a psychiatric expert who reinforced popular interest in sex murderers, J. Edgar Hoover, the director of the FBI, maintained a position as the single most influential person in promoting attention to sex crimes. Hoover decried the vaguely defined problem of increasing sex crime in syndicated articles such as those which appeared in 1937 and 1947.[53] In addition to his direct engagement in public discourse, Hoover provided a model for local police departments and their public relations efforts. A number of criminal justice agencies took their cues from Hoover and produced materials that either focused exclusively on educating the public about the dangers of sex crime or that featured their work on sex cases as part of their larger service to the community. For example, a stop-action film produced by the police department in St. Paul, Minnesota, highlighted its work in helping "girls or women who have been molested by sex perverts."[54] Like the social guidance films, the police film advised the public to aid police by reporting crimes: "Don't hesitate to call the police; when mashers force their attention, prompt action may prevent tragic consequences." The image that accompanies the narration is a pristine red rose, from which dirty male hands begin to remove the petals. By the time "tragic consequences" is uttered, the rose is entirely destroyed. Law enforcement officers promoted themselves as defenders of feminine virtue, with the "masher" or "sex pervert" as the demon to be slayed.

Hoover's influence on police officers is also evident in how departments prioritized training. For example, Val B. Satterfield, an assistant professor of clinical psychiatry, was invited by the St. Louis police department to train the officers on "sex molestation."

St. Louis has never had an acute sexual molestation problem, and no pressures of any type encouraged this selection. . . . The program was started in the Summer of 1949 and was very timely in that the project was well along when national interest became focused upon a nation-wide flurry of cases of sexual molestation. Again, this increased activity did not hit St. Louis with any force, but the newspapers and general public were reassured by the well organized plan of the St. Louis Department. As a result of this interest a new state law covering the management and institution of sexual psychopaths was passed by the legislature, and considerable favorable publicity came to the City of St. Louis.[55]

St. Louis caught the wave of "national interest" in sex crime, and officials used the training program to enhance the city's professional status: "It has given the community a sense of security and has acquainted the department with the material required for a closer application of prevention and enforcement to the real needs of the community."[56] Contemporary scholars of punishment, including Jonathan Simon and others, have identified this kind of governmental response to crime as illustrative of the peculiar present. This research into the sexual psychopath era reveals the early importance of sex crime narratives and, in particular, the important role of the heroic police officer, as seen in the above-described social guidance films.

Commentators like De River and Hoover provided a way of thinking about criminals that focused on the sexual aspect of criminals' drive—a largely undifferentiated account of a monstrous offender. De River's particular brand of criminology is striking not only for its policy influences but also because it foreshadows a trend that continues throughout the twentieth century—a break between the academic mainstream and the commentators who captured public attention and as a result shaped punishment. While De River was a media and criminal justice darling, he by no means represented the leading minds of the field.

That role belonged to Dr. Karl Bowman, who embodies the transition from explanations of crime that were more biologically based to the approach of "mental hygiene" in the forensic field. Mental hygiene focused on the mind and on emotions, rather than on anatomy or biology.[57] Bowman is most famous for his evaluations of Nathan Leopold Jr. and Richard Loeb during their trial for the abduction and murder of Bobby Franks. That case marks the rise of psychiatric expertise as a plausible tool for grappling with social issues such as sexuality and crime during childhood. More specifically, the historian Paula Fass credits the evaluations Bowman and his coevaluator Dr. Harold Hulbert provided as offering a new way to make sense of criminal deviance: "First the newspapers, through which the case initially exploded into the public arena, and then other cultural agencies participated in a public discourse that offered Americans the new terms normality and abnormality to understand transgressive behavior. Indeed, the judicial hearing that determined Leopold and Loeb's fate was guided, not by legal questions of responsibility, but by a psychiatrically driven defense that popularized those terms."[58]

After a rise to international fame following the Leopold and Loeb trial, Bowman continued to also study the potential connections between endocrine function and mental illness. He moved from Boston to San Francisco, where he conducted research at the Langley Porter Neuropathic Institute (later the Langley Porter Clinic). While there, he won competitive grants for his research on sexual deviance. Bowman, a medical doctor not originally trained in psychiatry, joined many others who studied sexual offending in describing "sexual psychopathy" as an inappropriate diagnosis: "The range of psychiatric opinion as to the definition and possible applications of the term is so broad and the relevant scientific data and formulations so tentative, that the term is nearly meaningless."[59]

Another prominent national expert, David Abrahamsen of Columbia University, also disputed the popular perception that sexual psychopaths were a distinct type: "There is no such entity as 'sexual psychopath' and this is a term that should be abolished."[60] Abrahamsen reported on a study of 1,800 inmates at Sing Sing, which showed that 30% had committed sex crimes at one time or another. Academically affiliated psychiatric researchers on sex offenders labored against popular assumptions about sexual offending as unique behavior committed by a particular kind of monstrous offender. But their normalizing discourse never prevailed.[61]

Doctors like Bowman and Abrahamsen had to tread carefully: They wanted criminal justice and corrections to institutionalize mental health evaluations, but they did not want laws to entrench specific terms or diagnoses that were popular but not empirically supported. They wanted authority and jurisdiction, but not the conflation of legal and psychiatric notions. In 1965, the psychiatrist and historian Seymour Halleck wrote in hindsight that psychiatric criminology had peaked in the 1920s. By the 1930s, the prestige of working in the court and prison system paled in comparison with private practice and its opportunities for practicing psychoanalysis. Psychiatric criminologists felt constrained to "housekeeping" duties, rather than having the freedom to explore the cutting edge of their field: "After World War II psychiatrists began to value most highly the gratifications that came with treating motivated individuals. . . . To a large extent the decline of psychiatric interest in criminology may have reflected this inability of both physicians and correctional administrators to reconcile the values of individual psychotherapy with those of social rehabilitation."[62]

By the 1940s, the remaining interest in psychiatric criminology focused on special offenders, following public and legislative interest in the sexual psychopath.[63] While Halleck does not emphasize this point, it remains a crucial reversal. Psychiatric expertise stopped driving crime and punishment policy, abandoning it to the remaining psychiatrists willing to work within the dominant framework.

But at the end of the sexual psychopath era, even if academic psychiatrists were moving on, psychiatric knowledge was privileged in criminal justice and punishment processes, in public discourse, and in policy. For example, in an article that proclaimed a rising number of "sex perverts" in the Los Angeles area, its subheading read "Use of Psychiatric Clinics Urged as New Way to Fight Crime."[64] During the special session called by Governor Warren in response to the Glucoft abduction, psychiatric experts offered a range of solutions, each of which involved some level of assessment by their colleagues:

[Psychiatrist Charles] Tranter said the task is to catch sex perverts before they commit a crime. He said many could be intercepted in city jails. People who are brought in for some other crime are more likely to be prospective sex offenders than average citizens, he declared. Put these perverts under treatment by a State agency, offered Dr. Tranter, on a sort of indefinite probation status. . . .

Dr. Bromberg, one-time psychiatric service head at New York's Bellevue Hospital, recommended scuttling the words "sexual psychopaths." Those words, he said, leave the impression that nothing can be cured. The contrary is true, he said. . . .

[Dr. Frank Tallman, the Mental Hygiene Department director, advised] child guidance programs in schools to correct early-life maladjustments, [as well as broadening the sexual psychopath law, to allow] an individual to turn himself in to officials for treatment of abnormalities.[65]

Each of these strategies is based on the potential for therapeutic intervention to control or perhaps cure the causes of sex crime, echoing the general optimism at the time that most offenders could be rehabilitated.

While psychiatric expertise received a wide audience, other academics also weighed in. The sociologist Edwin Sutherland's explanation of the diffusion of sexual psychopath laws and his critique of the laws were published during the height of public interest in the sexual psychopath.[66] Morris Ploscowe, a prominent judge from New York, also published a contemporaneous critique of the way psychopath laws targeted low level offenders and warehoused them rather than treating them: "They confuse sin and crime; they fail to distinguish nuisance and danger; they confound offensive sex habits with serious mental abnormality."[67] These critiques may not have had the mass appeal of other discourses, but they were part of the discussion and resurfaced a few decades later when concern about civil commitment reached wider audiences, including the courts.

The public received contradictory messages about sex crime and punishment rates and was generally not exposed to comparative or longitudinal data. Government officials exercised discretion behind the scenes while making public statements that acknowledged fear. In 1949, Governor Warren declared, "The public is aroused and it has a right to expect action."[68] The suggestions presented at the special session of the legislature came from a range of sources of expertise and provided for several uses of incapacitation, rehabilitation, and experimentation; these suggestions culminated in the creation of the Sexual Deviation Research Act.

Expanding the Toolkit: What to Do with Sex Offenders

Sex crime was usually framed as a problem of increasing incidence and prevalence, which lent urgency to proposed policies. Some local- and state-level law enforcement officials as well as some psychiatrists echoed the popular discourse and emphasized the looming threat (by citing measures of increase, which were produced as a result of the police department's own escalated activities). For example, Captain William Barron, the head of the Los Angeles sheriff's juvenile division, told the delegates to Warren's special session that his department had accumulated a file of more than 3,000 sex offenders during the preceding three years.[69] Prosecutors frequently cited increasing incidents of sex murder as something they had to combat.[70] Similarly, in an article titled "Sex Perverts Pour in Here, Inquiry Told," De River emphasized that 1,690 sex crimes were reported in 1947 and that 1,175 arrests were made in the first half of 1947.[71] A 1956 article referred to a California Department of Mental Hygiene report that showed that hospital admissions of sexual psychopaths increased from 400 to 512 in the twelve-month period beginning March 31, 1954.[72] Correctional and other professional associations also noted that increasing sex crime rates were part of their calls for new legislation to address the problem of sexual psychopaths. For example, in 1947, the New York State Magistrates Association declared "a national and statewide increase in sex crimes."[73] The *New York Times* reported that the Prison Association of New York made similar calls for new legislation, including civil commitment, each year from 1944 to 1948.

As far as we can tell by cross-checking these reports with other sources, the numbers cited by alarmists appear to be exaggerations. Despite the popular belief in increasing sex crime rates that were supported with anecdotal or single-year data, the *Los Angeles Times* reported in 1948 that the State Department of Corrections saw a downward trend in sex crime, as measured by convictions and fingerprint files. Richard A. McGee, the director of corrections, told the *Times* that admissions of child molesters to state prisons remained about the same from 1943 to 1948.[74] Similarly, while in California there was an uptick in civil commitments to hospitals for sexual psychopaths during this period; official reports show only about 300 such commitments in 1954.[75]

How can we account for the gap between perceptions by the public (and the public statements of some officials) and the practices of punishment? The most likely explanation is the gap between the specter of the violent, threatening psychopathic fiend and the nonthreatening, "regular guy" who appears in court. At a time in which the criminal justice system gave relatively unregulated discretion to police, prosecutors, and judges,[76] rarely, if ever, did an actual defendant match that sensationalized figure.

The individual offenders who were depicted in the media as "sexual psychopaths" were tried for murder and sentenced to death, not considered for civil commitment. But Northcott, Dyer, Stroble, and the others represented bogeymen to the public. Likewise, experts who fomented fears of increasing sex crime and who referred to the threat of mysterious fiends added weight to that image.

Quantitative data were rarely part of the popular discourse surrounding sex crimes, but some experts did dispute the perception of an increasing threat, evident at the 1937 symposium on the Challenge of Sexual Offending, held by the National Committee for Mental Hygiene, where speakers explicitly denied that sex crime had increased. Instead they declared that the public outcry reflected the culture's general repressive attitudes toward sex. This was repeated a decade later during Earl Warren's special session on sex offenders, when the chief of criminal identification for the State

Department of Corrections cautioned that there had not been "as great an increase in sex crimes as . . . the public believes, due to the concentrated interest that has developed."[77]

Data are fragmentary, but it seems that public officials, at least in Los Angeles, may have opined about "monsters" but they most often charged sex offenders who appeared in court with misdemeanors. A *New York Times* article covering the Warren special session had quoted the following rather optimistic statistics: out of 10,665,000 Californians, 1,078 were imprisoned during "the period" constituting 8.8% of prison admissions; and 3,000 men were arrested for child molestation with a 93% conviction rate, most often for a misdemeanor charge and resulting in a six-month sentence.[78] These data do not match the figures available from the official publication of the Department of Corrections, *California Prisoners*, which shows about 600 felony admissions to prison for sex charges during 1949. Most of the arrests reported in the *Times* must have been for misdemeanors (or were exaggeration).

Various discursive strains lent support to at least three strategies for the sex crime problem, as exemplified by three major pieces of legislation in California (variations of which were passed across the country). The first type of law authorized civil commitment as a mechanism for intervening with and incapacitating sexual deviants. California's state legislature passed the first iteration of its sexual psychopath law in 1939. Then, in 1947, California passed the nation's first sex offender registration law in order to give police departments a way to keep track of known offenders by creating a list of suspects for use when new crimes occurred. Finally, marking the beginning of the end of the sexual psychopath era, the hybrid Sexual Deviation Research Act of 1950 funded a variety of state responses to sex crime. This shift from incapacitation to more inclusive policies was accompanied by various levels of support and debate among scholars and researchers in media, law, and psychology.

The Death Penalty, Sterilization, and Castration

Nearly every commentator called for more and better incapacitation as a first response to a perceived sex crime wave: Members of the legislature and the executive branches, community representatives, and newspaper editorial board members, to name a few, all called for improving California's power to identify and detain sex offenders. Courts were viewed as constrained in their ability to adequately punish sex criminals, so public and professional organizations pushed for penalty enhancements and laws specifically directed at sexual psychopaths. After Albert Dyer was sentenced, the editorial board of the *Los Angeles Times* emphasized that death was a crucial part of the solution for the sex crime problem in California, calling it "the only outcome of the case the public could afford to sanction": "Even if Dyer is mentally defective, there is no reason for his continued existence. He could never be safe to have at large. . . . Eradication of such types is necessary for public safety. . . . In any scale, the safety of children must weigh more heavily than his forfeited right to live."[79]

Similarly, fourteen years later, with the Stroble execution still framing public debate, a prosecutor also called for the ultimate incapacitation: "Amendment of California's 'Little Lindbergh Law' to provide the death penalty for kidnaping [*sic*] for the purpose of forcible criminal attack and other morals offenses, was urged."[80]

Many bills were proposed during the next fifteen years that tied a sensational crime to the need to expand the death penalty for perverts. While most of these bills did not pass, the death penalty for sex homicides was part of the criminal justice system response to "sex fiends" (sex homicides were rare events, but a disproportionate number of executions were for sex homicides as opposed to other kinds of murder). This passage also shows that, even in 1951, a district attorney was likely to use a media sensation—in this case through a law named after a child crime victim—to call for more death-eligible offenses.

Nationwide, incapacitation through the death penalty was publicly supported, enacted into law, and actually used with relative frequency for sex offenders. Historical data contain information on 506 U.S. executions involving a sex crime from 1930 to 1950 (a total of 3,058 executions took place during this period).[81] These data suggest that just under 1 in 5 executions in the United States during this period were sex-related. Depending on how well publicized each execution was (locally and nationally), it could have had a significant impact on how people viewed both the dangerousness of sex offenders and their appropriate punishment. As with all patterns in execution, the use for sex crime varied regionally. In California, at least 13 of the state's 197 executions during this time were sex-related (only about 6%).[82] While I do not argue that these executions for sex crime defined public opinion, their relative regularity and speedy implementation provided a sense that the criminal justice system could be counted on to handle the worst of the worst when necessary. For those who opposed execution, it may also have fostered a sense of "over-reaction" to sex criminals.

Certain members of the public responded to sex homicides like the Northcott case with calls for castration or the death penalty, both of which were framed as "cures" but without any real therapeutic interest:

> When I read accounts of a sex crime I am again amazed at the stupidity of the public in general and the lawmakers in particular. Surely everyone knows that there is a cure for the sex maniac . . . any surgeon can do it in a few minutes.[83]

> Why does this country permit, and take no steps to wipe out, this ever increasing crime, what is wrong with America, a nation that once was considered, in the eyes of other nations, a land that protected its woman-hood? . . . .
>
> The writer knows of only one remedy, a sure cure against these fiendish attacks, and that is the death penalty.[84]

Few psychiatrists supported this view, however, as demonstrated in the following testimony to the state assembly on this subject:

> All agreed that surgery is not the cure. "It may end the sex drive," speaking of castration, said Dr. Crahan, but he declared it probably would result in psychological troubles just as serious. He said that where such surgery has been performed, the resultant "cure" is usually temporary insofar as eliminating the man as a potential criminal.
>
> "The 'cure,' " he said, "can be attributed to shock. You probably would get about the same result if you cut off the man's leg."
>
> Dr. Hacker on the same subject said that surgery creates a profound change. "You could," he said, "by brain surgery reduce a mental case to the level of a vegetable," but added that would not be a cure of a mental illness.[85]

Incapacitation through castration was among the publicly supported strategies, but it was not entrenched in the law or supported by most experts. After Governor Warren vetoed a bill requiring surgical castration, the editorial board of the *Los Angeles Times* wrote, "Surgery is a beautifully simple solution for such a revolting crime—if it would work. But it is wrong to write surgery into a law which would give the public a false sense of security."[86]

But some experts did join public calls for incapacitation through sterilization and castration. These themes appear in a 1937 op-ed piece titled "Social

Eugenics," which described a speech given to a Los Angeles ladies' club by a doctor affiliated with the Federal Health Service. Dr. J. G. Robinson advocated sterilization as a response both to medical threats like venereal disease and to "the great black plague that continues to take its toll of morons, imbeciles, defectives of every kind, including what J. Edgar Hoover calls the most loathsome of all criminals, the sex fiend."[87] Since "like begets like," Dr. Robinson and the op-ed author agree that the crime problem must be addressed by limiting the reproduction of the "lower breeds."[88] The language of disease, contamination, and infection elevated public worries about sexual psychopaths to that of an epidemic or crisis.

Robinson was not an isolated crank; rather he exemplified an older model of criminology that maintained a foothold even as behavioral explanations took precedence. While the role of social eugenics in preventing the reproduction of "defectives" of various kinds is well known, the role of *therapeutic* sterilization for sex offenders has not been explored. In fact, California's sterilization law, passed in 1909, was originally intended for therapeutic purposes (it was revised in 1913 and 1917 to reflect reproductive goals).[89] In 1923, as sterilization came into wider use in California and elsewhere, the state legislature created California Penal Code Section 645: "Whenever any person shall be adjudged guilty of carnal abuse of a female person under the age of 10 years, the court may, in addition to such other punishment or confinement as may be imposed, direct an operation to be performed upon such person, for the prevention of procreation." This is telling: Sterilization is included "in addition to such other punishment" for child molesters with young girl victims. This law remained on the books and was in use until the 1970s; it was renewed in 1996 with a chemical castration provision.

This blending of punishment, treatment, and reproductive control is rooted in the popularized interpretation of Cesare Lombroso's "born criminal." This simplified explanation of criminality as a biological problem, and therefore requiring biological intervention, is a discursive strand that persists today.

Civil Commitment: Therapeutic Interventions

Alongside the castration and sterilization interests in the 1930s, rehabilitation became a prominent strategy, most notably through the "sexual psychopath" laws. Under these laws, individuals could be committed to state hospitals either in place of criminal sentencing or as based on recommendations independent of criminal charges. California passed its law in 1939 directly following the Albert Dyer "child slayer" case. It was one of five states that led the initial period of sexual psychopath laws from 1935 to 1939.[90]

Nationally, these laws enjoyed support from multiple sources. Law enforcement officials and psych experts consistently called for new, specialized institutions to treat sex criminals. A *New York Times* article reported that "a survey of twenty-five up-state police chiefs revealed that a majority believed sex offenders should be examined and treated by psychiatrists and confined in prisons or hospitals until cured."[91] While we would expect psych experts to support a technique that relied on their own expertise, the support from police chiefs seems remarkable from today's vantage point, demonstrating the authority of the therapeutic ideal by this time.

Research, Experimentation, and Supervision

While California and many other states responded to pressure to pass sexual psychopath civil commitment laws, New York reacted somewhat differently. In 1943, Mayor Fiorello La Guardia's Committee on Sex Offenses recommended enactment of civil commitment laws for sex offenders. Then, every year from 1944 to 1948, the *New York Times* reported on the Prison Association of New York's call for sexual psychopath laws to provide for civil commitment and funding for research. Each year before 1948, the call was a minor part of the coverage; legislators proposed such laws, but they either faltered in committee or were vetoed by Governor Thomas Dewey. In 1948, the headlines and articles focused on the sexual psychopath recommendation, including a special research project at Sing Sing, which was eventually passed into law and received funding. Thus, while California regularly passed new laws to enhance law enforcement response to sex crime throughout the 1930s and 1940s, New York focused almost exclusively on funding research.[92] The civil commitment component of these laws may have taken longer to pass in New York because of the proximity and influence of critics such as Columbia's Abrahamsen, Judge Morris Ploscowe, and Paul Tappan, who authored a government-sponsored critique of New Jersey's sexual psychopath laws. In contrast, De River's advocacy on behalf of the concept of the "sexual psychopath" may have facilitated California's speedier passage of civil commitment laws.

Supporters touted specialized institutions for sex fiends both for their potential for treating known sex criminals and for serving as research sites. In practice, it appears that this research did not provide a knowledge base that would help identify and treat sexual offending, but rather focused on biological markers of homosexuality and on law enforcement techniques. For example, police officers used polygraph testing during investigations to extract information about sex crimes, while the minds and bodies of hospitalized and incarcerated sex offenders provided another source of knowledge. An unpublished government document suggests that research on sex offenders at Sing Sing may have been part of the Central Intelligence Agency's investigation into the use of truth serum and LSD as tools for coercing confessions.[93] Psychedelic research was also conducted in the late 1950s by two doctors associated with the Langley Porter Clinic—the facility where California's sexual deviation research took place—although we do not know if sex offenders were the objects of study.[94]

The saliency of this research and experimentation is the focus on investigation and identification rather than treatment. This interest in experimenting with bodily interventions also shows a historical connection from the sexual psychopath era to the present. Since at least the 1930s, sex crime has been perceived as so urgent a problem, and its perpetrators as potentially so different from the rest of society, that there has been little to restrain experimentations with techniques that could later migrate to other populations. The Sexual Deviation Research Act continued this tradition. Although supported as a way to advance therapeutic interventions, the research it funded was not treatment. Instead, researchers at the Langley Porter Clinic used the money to identify chemical markers in the blood of known homosexuals and to test Bowman's theories regarding the interactions of endocrine secretions and sexual deviation.[95]

Community Responsibility and Public Education

Less bodily forms of surveillance and supervision were also a component of sex offender policies during this era. In 1947, California passed the nation's first registration law, requiring sex offenders to register themselves with local law enforcement. With a list of usual suspects in the form of registered, previously convicted offenders, the police could close new cases more quickly.

One way to prevent monsters from acting out was to intervene with minor offenders who displayed monstrous potential. A letter to the editor responding to one of Hoover's syndicated columns on this subject agreed: "We fail in our duties to report the minor offenses so that they can be nipped in the bud. We fail in our personal desire not to become involved or embarrassed."[96] In addition to decrying the criminal justice system's indifference to the handling of sex offenders, Hoover also blamed public apathy toward "'harmless' perverts." His list of responses to the problem of sex crime is long, but among these are calls for community awareness, for law enforcement to empower the public to make complaints, and for people to apply informal social control on those who harbor perverts.[97]

Conclusion

As Jonathan Simon argues, responding to crime is a crucial way for government actors to signal that they are fulfilling their public duties: "Across all kinds of institutional settings, people are seen as acting legitimately when they act to prevent crimes."[98] This research into the sexual psychopath era illustrates responsiveness to public excitement about sensational sex crimes as a crucial pathway to governing, but not as a crucial influence on punishment practices. Legislators, police, prosecutors, judges, and high-ranking leaders such as governors were able to use the threat of the sexual psychopath to appear responsive, while simultaneously calling for more self-government and continuing to exercise discretion. New laws were promoted and passed without increasing formal social control.

Policy makers and front-line responders were sufficiently insulated from the public and sufficiently confident in the legal system's ability to deliver justice that they could acquiesce in public but resist in practice most calls for harsh sanctions against sex offenders. The gap between the image of the dangerous sexual psychopath and the way the criminal justice system actually responded to this image is significant for a variety of reasons. First, other historical accounts of a series of moral panics during this era looked only at discourse, largely ignoring practice and thus missing a central mystery. We do not have access to sex offense arrest rates either statewide or in cities for this period. It is difficult to analyze imprisonment sentences, and we know little about how misdemeanor charges were handled, which we have reason to believe are important. But what we do have are prison admission statistics, which show the flatness indicated in figure 2.1 near the beginning of this chapter. This flatness is important because public concerns loom as largely in this era they do today: Therefore, public attitude fails as an independent variable for explaining change in penal policy.[99] In addition, this flatness is in spite of the new laws passed throughout the era, revealing that there was no change created by policy itself as measured by admissions.

This gap between what was said about sexual psychopaths and how individual offenders were handled shows the importance of the insulation of decision makers and experts from public pressure—officials could respond to public fears without changing the way the system addressed the individuals who were the real-life sexual offenders. Recognition of this discretion, and the biased ways in which it benefited some offenders over others, as well as generally devaluing the victimization of women and children, came to a head in subsequent decades.

An anxious, vengeful public, incited by sympathy for child victims and a reactive government, is not enough to explain increased imprisonment rates. But although the discourse may not matter in the ways other scholars and commentators have assumed, the gap between image and practice in the sexual psychopath era contained some of the roots of our contemporary cultural understanding of sex offenders: a combination of a disease model of sex crime with a moral choice model.

The Era of Rehabilitative Debate

1950–1980

> The popular conception of the sexual offender as a horrendous
> person, devoid of the normal human attributes, is simply not
> correct. I have been working closely with sexual deviates for fif-
> teen years and have yet to be slobbered on or to discover any
> horns and claws. . . . Most of them have easily identifiable prob-
> lems and most of these problems have come about in not too
> dissimilar ways.
>
> —Slater and Bishop 1964, 13–14

Based on his more than fifteen years of experience as a clinical psychologist who treated sex offenders in state and federal corrections and in
private practice, "Manning R. Slater" (a pseudonym) published a book in
1964 that provided "the most startling, the most revealing confessions of
sexual perversions ever put in print."[1] After several decades of exposure to
principles of psychotherapy and the emergence of humanist psychology and
self-help, when Slater's book was released there was room for public debates
about the nature of sexual offending and the potential for therapeutic cure.

Ostensibly intended to lessen the stigma, the book was aimed at a popular,
not scholarly, audience. A reviewer for the *Journal of Criminology, Criminal
Law and Police Science* noted, "Judging from the increasing amount of literature on sexual deviations and sexual offenses, it appears that both public and
the busy practitioner of the behavioral sciences (criminology included) have
become more and more aware of the importance of what some call a 'symptom' and others call an 'illness' of our society."[2] The reviewer, Hans Illing, was
a well-regarded correctional therapist, with many years of experience in group
therapy. He was deeply critical of Slater's contribution: "I fail to see the value of
the book, either in presenting 'sensational' material or in suggesting that something was accomplished."[3] But Illing does not say anything else about the book

and gives no hints as to his opinion of its content. Given the book's largely humanistic approach and its promotion of therapy, the public's appetite for insight into how sex offenders could be treated must have diverged from what more mainstream correctional psych experts like Illing wanted to broadcast.

In this chapter I will examine rehabilitative discourse, which focused on sexual offending from about 1950 to 1980. In the 1930s and 1940s, governmental and public energy surrounding the problem of sexual deviance was funneled primarily into the passage and refinement of laws to civilly commit certain offenders, often with rehabilitation underneath more incapacitative intentions. A decade later, rehabilitation was a dominant correctional ideology, for sexual criminality as well as all other offending. This was the era of the medical model of deviant conduct. By the 1950s California's flagship sex offender treatment program was fully functional and the general problem of crime seemed to call for therapeutic interventions.

Talk about the Problem of Sex Crime and Sex Criminals
Rehabilitative Frames and Claims

The social history surrounding social control of sex offenders during this era of uncertainty about rehabilitation is too vast to fully describe here. But one flash point for debates that must be acknowledged was *Sexual Behavior in the Human Male*, by Alfred Kinsey, which was published in 1948. The book and its author received international attention, and the book remains a touchstone for the study of sex. The historian Miriam Reumann argues that the Kinsey report forced America to reassess sexuality, in the process making it fundamental to national identity and national character.[4] For example, critics viewed Kinsey's statistics as documenting the failings of American society rather than just individual problems with sexual desire. From the extreme of the abnormal sexual psychopath to the worrisome possibility that sexual deviance was actually normal, sex was a major center of debate during this period. As the timeline included in the appendices demonstrates, debates also included homosexuality, pornography, and changes in the framing of mental illness and abnormality.

By far the most important ideological question in corrections between 1950 and 1980 involved the potential for and proper role of the rehabilitation of criminals.[5] The public and officials in many sectors were willing to allow psychiatrists the opportunity to "engage in a valiant struggle—the rehabilitation of patients accused by law of psychopathic criminality."[6] Many scholars have written about the importance of the medicalization of social control in the mid- to late twentieth century, and in particular the importance of psychiatry and its related treatments in shaping the normal and the abnormal.[7] But no one has fully described how pivotal the subject of sex offenders turned out to be for psych experts at a time when the status and credibility of psychiatry were hotly debated.

In 1959 the *Los Angeles Times* published a six-part series that highlighted the rehabilitative efforts of the California Department of Corrections: "California's Penal System Designed to Cure Criminals: Praise and Criticism Heaped on Procedures."[8] Echoing media accounts from earlier decades, the article describes both an increasing sex crime problem and the central role of psychiatric expertise:

> Sex crimes increased 14% here last year. Arrests for indecent exposure alone were up 35%. There were 2,668 incidents of child molesting, exhibitionism, forcible attack and attempted attack. The FBI has estimated that a woman or a child is attacked every 6 seconds in the United States, around the clock, 365 days a year! Aware of this worsening situation, California has met it with two unique legal instruments—the Sexual Psychopath Act . . . and the indeterminate sentence law.[9]

After setting up the problem, the *Times* article describes the most important feature of the state's response—the ability to individualize punishments and keep offenders confined until they are rehabilitated. Both civil commitment and the criminal justice system's indeterminate sentencing facilitated "psychiatry's endeavors to change the spots on the leopard."[10]

Despite more sustained media interest in child murders during the sexual psychopath era, there is continuity in the media's portrayal of the problem of sex crime through this era of rehabilitative debate. A rough comparison of coverage in the *New York Times* and *Los Angeles Times* between the two eras indicates more media reporting on nonhomicidal sex crime, and more coverage of adult victims as well as children. However, when adult women are the reported victims, there is a continued tendency to imply blameworthiness (as with, for example, depictions of victims as provocative, "party girls").[11] Otherwise, the content is largely similar: The "increasing" incidence and prevalence of sex crime was a common theme in news articles as was the portrayal of sex offenders as "sick." The experts best suited to comment on sex crime continued to run the gamut from psychiatrists like Karl Bowman, who led the sexual deviation research funded by the 1950 act, to local police, superior court judges, and community leaders.

Echoing the criticisms of the previous era, which placed some of the responsibility for the sex crime problem on society, one commentator blamed parental inattention: "Too many parents don't know where their kids are. . . . How often did you hear about this sort of thing in years past when parents met their kids at school or switched them if they didn't get home on time?"[12] Other authorities called upon communities to participate in crime prevention and detection, repeating the mantra of the social guidance films:

> "Get the license number of a sex offender's car." That's the request of Sgt. Ted Jonoski, West Los Angeles juvenile officer, in the event that a child or adult is involved in a sex molestation incident. . . . "There has been no sharp increase in sex crimes in the West Side," he declared. "Neither are we engaged in a sudden drive against the sex criminal. "It's a constant war that we wage," he said. "We're after the sex offender every day. Parents can assist by telling their children what to do if approached by a molester. Positive identification will help us find the suspect."[13]

Another commentator reported that the public made sex crime control difficult: "The efforts to halt sex crimes were being hampered by the reluctance of most women to report such incidents to the police. [Commissioner Arm] urged women who had been molested to call the Bureau of Policewomen."[14]

In addition to fears of increasing sex crime, official confirmations and assurances negating this fear, and indictments of public failures to report crime, new complaints about sex offender policy also arose during this era. Popular films debated the responsibility of government actors and of society to allow sex offenders to make good after paying their debts. In many ways, these films captured the zeitgeist of this era. Films that featured the molester as scapegoat included *The Mark* (1961), *Straw Dogs* (1971), *The Offense* (1973), and *The Naked Civil Servant* (1975).[15] Overall, these films challenged the idea that all sex offenders are monsters deserving punishment and exclusion, and they also suggested that policies that were too broad would undermine rehabilitation.

The Mark

In 1958, Charles Israel, a screenwriter from Los Angeles, penned a novel about a sex offender who had been imprisoned for a molesting crime involving a young girl and who was released from prison and tried to succeed on the outside. Later turned into a major motion picture released in 1961, *The Mark* shows a sex offender who was not a monster but rather was grappling with many of the same issues as the rest of us. The film, featuring Rod Steiger, "tells a basically poignant tale of a young man living with the fear that his previous involvement in a sex crime will be discovered and ruin his now exemplary life."[16] *The Mark* confirms that there was an audience for material that presented sexual offending without the popular fallacies that were also in circulation at the time. That is, alongside the entrenched misconceptions, insights about "normal" sex offenders also appealed to the public, especially when such insights were framed as psychological dramas that portrayed the possibilities and limitations of psychotherapy as rehabilitation.

The story of *The Mark* follows Jim Fuller, the protagonist, as he negotiates life outside of prison. It is a Hollywood version of what an ex-con faces, and it is also a product of the 1950s, rather than the contemporary, harder-line viewpoint most often expressed toward former prisoners. Jim is an empathetic character from the outset. We see his struggles and his stumbles, and we root for him.

The novel, written with many appealing elements, is similar to the two other kinds of popular portrayals of sex offenders discussed in previous chapters. Like the mental hygiene films and sensational newspaper stories of child murders, learning about sex offenders promises to equip us for protecting ourselves. Like the first-person accounts of sex offenders in therapy, *The Mark* lets us in on something illicit, ostensibly because it will be good for us. We get special insight into something titillating. *The Mark* joins in that tradition but also challenges the judgmental impulse because we are encouraged to humanize the main character.

After Jim's essential goodness is established, and he is beginning to build trust within his new community, everything begins to unravel. His love interest, Ruth, turns out to have a young daughter, but when he tries to tell Ruth about his offense, she will not listen. When a sex crime occurs in his area, the police find him through the sex offender registry and call him in for extended interrogation. As each stress takes its toll on Jim, we begin to see flashbacks to his offense. Gradually, we learn more about the pressures that led him to seek attention from a young girl. Typical Freudian explanations of unresolved conflict with his domineering mother and sisters explain why he sought the "easier" company of a child.

The film climaxes when a newspaper reporter writes about him and includes a photo of Jim with his girlfriend's child. In the denouement, we wonder whether, faced with public condemnation, Jim can possibly survive. He loses his job and his rented room, and his relationship appears to be over as well. The message is clearly that the odds are stacked against people like

Jim. Even having done everything he was supposed to in coming to terms with his own problems and reintegrating in society, his status as a child molester prevents a new beginning.

During this period, talk about sex crime and sex criminals broadened from hyperbolic depictions of child murders to debates about how much harm sex crime caused, whether sex offenders were treatable, and how to determine and handle the dangerousness of sex offenders. Unlike the previous and subsequent periods, experts differentiated among types of sex offenders, even while predominant assumptions about who sex criminals were and what should be done with them continued to reflect more simplified conceptions.

Experts and offenders continued to try bridging the distance between the heinous monster reified in the sexual psychopath era and the actual offender. This bridging occurred in at least two ways. The first way was through the analogy to addiction, which was frequently discussed as a persistent but treatable condition and which had its own set of civil commitment laws for narcotics users.[17] Sex offenders themselves, and those who worked in correctional and therapeutic settings with them, tried to capitalize on the public's increasing acceptance of drug addiction, alcoholism, and mental illness by analogizing sexual offending to these compulsive disorders. This was by no means an easy sell and there is not much evidence that it succeeded. Second, and even less successfully, some, like Slater, tried to overcome the perceived distance between sex offenders and everyone else by comparing their conduct to other kinds of criminal "acting out." The former was far more common than the latter, but both indicate a desire to "normalize" sexual offending. I will explain the roads not taken in the contemporary era and also place the current schism between experts and advocates in historical context.

Recasting the "Problem"

The promotion of sexual criminality as a "situational lapse" analogous to narcotics use is evident in the materials documenting the heyday of California's Atascadero State Hospital. In 1955, hospitalized sex offenders created a pamphlet, "The New Approach: Sex Offender to Good Citizen," distributed by the state to promote civil commitment; this was followed by a staff-produced report on Atascadero's "Therapeutic Community," which highlighted the innovative use of group therapy to correct sexual deviance.[18] In 1955, therapists in correctional psychiatry could proclaim that they had the new approach to creating good citizens out of sex fiends.

Building on endocrinal theories of criminality that had been part of the criminological discourse earlier in the century, and focusing on the importance of the sex glands in shaping personality and emotion, Atascadero's Emotional Security Program focused on normalization: "Sex offenders are of no particular type and are not restricted to a specific occupation, or to a set economic or social level. The majority were respected members of their communities, rearing their families, engaging in gainful occupations, living the average life, apparently as happy, useful citizens. These differences have led to the adoption of the term 'emotionally ill' when referring to the sex offender."[19] This quotation highlights the patients' attempt to define themselves as "average"—not deviant or monstrous—and as merely suffering from an emotional illness, implying their amenability to treatment. The experts offered similar accounts of sex crime's etiology as social and emotional maladjustment. Dr. James Judge, Atascadero's chief psychologist, explained sexual offending as neurosis: "Meaningful and comfortable communication with others is impaired. As emotional isolation intensifies, important reality checks are lost and the person falls back on his frequently very inadequate personal resources. No man, even the strongest, can live solely by himself. This, the neurotic tries often to do. The usual result is dismal failure in a conflict of instinctual drives."[20]

A contemporary account of the origins of sexual offending similarly describes deviant arousal as a coping mechanism for dealing with sexual abuse—sex offenders masturbated as children to deal with the stress of their own victimization, and this led them to become offenders themselves.[21] Thus, some sex offenders are normal men who have socially inappropriate instincts, which they lack the emotional resources to control. This fits the model of what Nicolas Rose and others have written about the goals of the psychiatric profession during this era in terms of claiming the normal subject.[22]

The patients' pamphlet from the early Atascadero program explains that treatment is necessary because "the person committing the sex crime did so compulsively, and at the same time he was aware of a sense of guilt and 'didn't want to do it.' "[23] A later account of the program's goals echoes this sense of illness but also of will: staff from the Department of Mental Health described revisions they proposed to the commitment law as attempts to "give offenders a strong motivation to remain in society without violating society's rules of sexual conduct."[24] In addition to portraying sex offenders as deterrable, this also portrays them as rule breakers, not heinous monsters. The "patient" image therefore portrays sex offenders as both rational actors and mentally abnormal; able to respond to legal threats and subject to compulsive desires. But because these impulses can be controlled if not cured, choice can counter compulsion.

The image of the rehabilitated subject as projected by the offenders and the correctional therapists was a respected member of the community, gainfully employed, and usually white. This image of the reformable sex offender reveals a crucial aspect of rehabilitative logic—rather than trying to remake subjects who are further from the ideal, sex offenders most "amenable to treatment" were those not incapacitated by sexual disorders or those acting out of violence, but only those who were slightly mixed up. These offenders, though temporarily inpatients in the civil commitment facility, were really thought of as "outpatients" who could quickly return to society. The patient image signals a pathology that is amenable to treatment, not an identity. This is a theme that Alfred Kinsey and his researchers focused on during interviews they conducted at Atascadero. The Kinsey researchers visited Atascadero in 1956 and collected a variety of unpublished internal memos, correspondence between California Department of Mental Health and Atascadero staff, and interview notes with staff ranging from directors to nurses. For example, Dr. Abe, an Atascadero psychologist, told Kinsey researchers that "about 50% of the civil committees at Atascadero really did not need to be hospitalized, and another 25% could be handled outside the institution in patient therapy"[25]—thus according to the staff themselves, the sex offenders selected for civil commitment were not especially disordered.

This message was also offered to mass audiences. In 1964, a confessional, intimate view of sex offenders (an excerpt from it opened this chapter) was published as *Sex Offenders in Group Therapy* by a pseudonymous psychologist. The book offered a privileged sneak peek into the minds of sex deviates. While "Slater" and his ghostwriter, George Bishop, were capitalizing on their reading audience's prurient interests, they claimed that their purpose was really to humanize, as the quote that opens this chapter explains. Within the slim 160-page volume, there are more than a dozen explicit statements about how similar sex offenders are to "normal" people, and there are also numerous attempts to paint sexual offending as comparable to any other criminal conduct, such as robbery, check forgery, or pickpocketing,

> Public acceptance is very important in the successful rehabilitation of an emotionally unstable person. For example, little or no stigma is attached to a reformed alcoholic who manages, with the help of Alcoholics Anonymous or some other agency, to overcome his problems and returns to his

place in society. . . . But what of another type of emotionally disturbed human being, the child molester? He, no less than the alcoholic, is fighting a titanic inner struggle against inhibitions rooted in his early childhood, inhibitions that have driven him to "act out" his problem in a specific manner in times of great stress. Yet he, and the unfortunate individuals who manifest other forms of sexual deviation as a result of these inhibitions, are social outcasts occupying somewhat the same position as did victims of tuberculosis before the current age of enlightenment.[26]

In total, the book was an extended argument for the use of therapy to treat sex criminals rather than sending them to prison.

Slater's book was by no means isolated. Howard Whitman's *Terror in the Streets* included a section devoted to first-person accounts called "Meet the Criminals," which included a "verbatim" transcription of a prosecutor's interview with the famed sexual psychopath Fred Stroble. The interview demonized and pathologized the "wretched little man."[27] Books devoted to sex offender confessions continued to be published throughout the next twenty years, including *Hidden World of Sex Offenders* (1969), which, like Slater's, also repeated the stories of a small group of sex offenders based on therapy session transcripts. In addition, other popularized clinical studies included *The Sex Offender* (1978), *The Sex Offender and the Criminal Justice System: Why They Did It* (1986), and *Sex Offenders* (1988). Unlike the more scholarly studies published by well-known figures including Guttmacher (1951), Karpman (1954), and Kinsey's associates (Gebhard et al., 1965), the popular books meant to humanize sex offenders also clearly capitalized on public appetites for scandalous material, similar to the De River casebooks of the previous era.

Altogether, these texts show the public's willingness to listen to claims about sex offenders that address something other than monstrosity, and they perhaps explain why therapeutic rehabilitation continued to be a publicly supported strategy for sex offenders up until the late 1970s.

Beliefs Regarding Harm and Dangerousness

The assumption that sexual deviance would progress from noncontact to contact offenses, and from offenses that caused minor to major harm, was a significant theme in the evolution of knowledge about sex offending.[28] This attention to harm was in part because of the feminists and child advocates who campaigned to acknowledge sex crime, but it also relates to previously existing ideas within psychiatry and criminal justice. In 1948, Dr. J. M. Nielsen, a neurologist and psychiatrist representing the Los Angeles County Medical Association, explained that "any molester of a child is guilty of potential murder even if the murder is never committed. No matter what happens, the child has suffered a tremendous harm which can never be erased. The molester should be put behind bars for life."[29]

But in contrast with contemporary near unanimity about the harm of sexual offending, experts and the public evidenced uncertainty regarding the impact of various kinds of sexual victimization before 1980. For example, while many examiners assumed a child molester was dangerous, others based the assessment on whether the child experienced any harm or on whether the offender might use force in the future.[30] Writing in the *American Journal of Psychiatry* in 1951, Dr. Bowman cited a series of studies of the victims of child molestation that suggested that "the harmful effects of such sexual relations to the child victim have been at times exaggerated" and cautioned that in many cases we should "question whether the crime is 100% the fault of the offender or whether in a considerable number of cases the child may have contributed more or less to the situation and have some degree of responsibility for what occurs."[31] Bowman claims that harm is not universal or necessarily devastating.

By the end of this era, most research published in the *American Journal of Psychiatry* about sexual offending disproved this by showing the traumatic effects of sexual victimization on children and on adults victimized as children. Today, anything that would be called child molestation is assumed by the public and policy makers to cause harm—this signals an important shift from the thinking of doctors like Bowman and from the dismissal of some sexual offending as mere nuisance that remained part of the cultural toolkit until the containment era.[32]

Crucially, attempts at normalizing offenders coincided with this de-emphasis of harm. Occurring at the same time as feminist and child protection movements were bringing public attention to the prevalence of sexual violence, this made such experts appear to be aligned with offenders and against advocates. In some cases, the experts truly were insensitive to victims, but in many cases, they were reflecting and reproducing the dominant cultural views of women, children, and sexuality. Rather than setting out to be "apologists" for offenders and therefore antagonists to victims, experts found themselves unable to talk about the ways in which sex offenders were just like everybody else without also devaluing—or at least seeming to devalue—the harms offenders caused.

In response to the minimizing of harm, others during the later portion of this era tried to bring the discussion back to just deserts. For example, Susan Brownmiller expressed distaste for debates about rehabilitation that threatened to undermine the law's punishment message:

> I am one of those people who view a prison sentence as a just and lawful societal solution to the problem of criminal activity, the best solution we have at this time, as civilized retribution and as a deterrent against the commission of future crimes. Whether or not a term in jail is truly "rehabilitative" matters less, I think, than whether or not a guilty offender is given the penalty his crime deserves. It is important to be concerned with the treatment offenders receive in prison, but a greater priority, it would seem, is to ensure that offenders actually go to prison.[33]

This is a prime example of contradictory goals for the punishment of sex offenders, and now it is explicit: Punish the guilty as they deserve, and make treatment secondary. In the marketplace of ideas, opposing sides began to emerge during this period, which eventually undermined the credibility of normalizing experts.

Experts and Practitioners

Psychiatrists have long struggled with general issues of how to negotiate the murky area in which legal and psychiatric categories overlap, for example in the well-known debates over legal and medical insanity.[34] This uncertainty has proven an especially difficult problem for sexual offending. As debates about the clinical merit of "sexual psychopathy" showed, describing sexual offending as a mental disorder was a tricky issue. Even when therapists and assessors claimed sexual offending to be a mental disorder, there remained the problem of how to categorize, include, and exclude offenders. Further uncertainties surrounded whether psychiatry could actually deliver, given the public and political support for attempting therapeutic rehabilitation. Finally, the perils of practicing within correctional environments, and with taking clients through correctional contracts added another ethical dimension—is the therapist's responsibility to the offender/patient or to the community/victim? These questions remain relevant and unresolved today, even if not as publicly debated as they were at the height of interest in therapeutic rehabilitation.

Consider the following exchange printed in the letters section of the *American Journal of Psychiatry* in 1974:

> For a number of years I have been a court examiner for Los Angeles County and have been frequently called upon to render opinions as to the "dangerousness" of sex offenders. . . .
>
> The court faced with a defendant who has committed multiple heterosexual crimes against children does not need a psychiatrist to declare that the man is dangerous. Any reasonably competent probation officer's report would have come up with the appropriate inescapable conclusion.
>
> . . .
>
> ERIC H. MARCUS, M.D.
>
> Dr. Sidley replies
>
> If it is impossible to predict reliably, we psychiatrists shouldn't try. If we do, we end up being overconservative and locking up too many people. We then harm justice rather than serving her.
>
> NATHAN T. SIDLEY, M.D.[35]

The exchange between the psychiatrists above highlights their uncertainty about what signals danger. The court evaluator is in the business of making these determinations because the law requires a psychiatric expert to do it, while the reformer suggests psychiatry should stay out of such determinations. But even if sexual offending is really caused by a mental disorder, if the offender is dangerous enough, then psychiatry as represented by the evaluator does not want him—he should be "dealt with through correctional channels." Why take responsibility for a problem that may not be solved by therapy? The academic psychiatrist may be willing to experiment, but the evaluator is the one who will be held accountable.

This exchange reveals the psychiatrists' disenchantment with the kinds of forensic assessments they were increasingly asked to perform by the state, already apparent in 1974. By providing "criminal prediction," they undermined the value of their expertise by the use of their discretion, which was essentially subjective, to sort out the dangerous offenders. In the 1970s, these doctors sought to distinguish their more nuanced work from the kind of determination "any reasonably competent probation officer" could provide.

Decades earlier, by the late 1950s, the great minds and esteemed figures of psychiatry had already abandoned the criminal as their ideal subject, either out of choice as some suggested,[36] or because the courts were disappointed in their work and shut them out of all but the cases except "when sexual or irrational motivation is obvious." However, those who continued to treat and evaluate criminals continued to normalize—sex offenders were often portrayed by psychiatrists during this time as being temporarily different from the rest of us as they grappled with emotional disease but were capable of returning to normalcy through treatment. For example, Dr. Charles Graves, the director of the Iowa state mental hospitals that housed sexual psychopaths, reassured the community where the psychopath ward would be located that the offenders were "nice guys: They're just sick. They're in a jam because they have a peculiar make-up."[37] In 1963, staff from the California Department of Mental Hygiene proclaimed to the *Los Angeles Times* that its sexual offender program boasted a 26% recidivism rate for released civil committees.[38] The article, "Better Cure Rate for Sex Offenders Sought," offered a snapshot of the "typical repeater" who was "white, married, a father, about 35 years of age, born of American parents, a blue collar worker, Protestant and a veteran. He has some high school education, but is not a graduate."[39] This portrait, laboring against popular opinion, is that of the repetitive sex offender as being more like us than being different—the offender was not an atavistic or feebleminded offender or an irredeemable deviant without any ties to upstanding society, but was someone with a problem that could be fixed.

Refining the Toolkit: What to Do with Sex Offenders

The push to provide treatment in order to rehabilitate sex criminals was nationwide. See, for example, a New Jersey grand jury's statement on the issue:

> "There is a desperate need for more intensive and, if necessary, prolonged treatment of sex deviates." In a presentment handed up to Superior Court Judge J. Wallace Leyden, the January term jury, which was discharged today, said its attention had been drawn to the preponderance of sex crimes. It said it did not find that thirty-day suspended sentences or $100 fines were sufficient deterrents to the second commission of a sex crime. "It is distressing that the public does not realize the importance of increasing the capacities of our state and county institutions for treatment of those unfortunates who suffer sex disorders," the panel said. "The promise of a sex offender to seek his own psychiatric treatment is not enough; he should be placed in an institution where he will receive treatment until his malady is removed."[40]

While civil commitment remained the most-promoted strategy for responding to sex crimes during this era, there continued to be debate surrounding other kinds of responses, including the restriction of obscene materials based on the assertion that viewing pornography incited sexual violence, the requirement that certain sex offenders register with local police, the use of castration, and the death penalty.

Media coverage of sex crimes often included concern about obscenity and pornography. This reflects a theme feminists picked up later, but it also demonstrates the effects of Hoover's ongoing "anti-smut campaigns" and local law enforcement efforts going back to the Comstock laws, which were themselves a product of women's advocacy and law and order interests.[41] Hoover, elaborating on his "war against the sex fiend" mantra begun in the 1930s, continued decades later with a variation on this theme:

> "The time for half-hearted, oblique action against depravity is past. Although this despicable trade reaps $500,000,000 a year, this diabolical business is costing the nation much more than money, it is robbing our country and particularly our younger generation of decency—it is a seed-bed for delinquency among juveniles and depravity among all ages." Noting that a forcible rape occurred every thirty-six minutes in this country in 1958, Mr. Hoover said: "This truly shocking and shameful state of affairs is made even more deplorable by the knowledge that sex crimes and obscene and vulgar literature often go hand in hand."[42]

This diatribe, containing all the features of the syndicated pieces from the 1930s and 1940s, was originally published in the *Federal Law Enforcement Bulletin*, and it was reproduced in the *New York Times*, *Wall Street Journal*, and in other newspapers throughout the country in 1960. Most opinion from all sources, both expert and popular, emphasized this nexus connecting pornography and violence as being common sense.

But some experts and commentators protested. Karl Bowman repeatedly tried to debunk these assumptions about sex offenders, calling for more research on the connection between pornography and crime.[43] Media commentators also pointed out the hysteria in much of the anti-smut campaigning, such as one columnist who wrote, in response to a state legislator's book ban, that "Assemblyman Barnes, it seems, believes that teenagers, being a susceptible lot, will read one of those words, grab a switchblade and rush out to commit a sex crime. I wonder if it would surprise him to know that the book [*Dictionary of American Slang*] is an essential component of the libraries at UCLA and Loyola Universities, two institutions not particularly noted for matriculating a high percentage of sex fiends."[44] The commentator doubts that a teenager or college student would read suggestive material and respond with sexual violence. Nonetheless, this view was implicit in many accounts and was explicit in writings by Hoover and others.

By the end of the 1970s, Hoover's influence on public opinion about pornography joined the concerted efforts of one segment of the women's movement. While this concern about obscenity may have shaped ideas about dangerousness, it did not directly impact the penal system (there was a small increase in obscenity arrests in the mid-1970s, but there does not appear to have been much impact on the back end of the system).

Sex Offender Registration

Although often considered part of the "third wave" of sex offender law that characterized the 1990s, sex offender registration began in the 1940s in California. Certain sex offenses required offenders to register with their local police agencies.[45] This registration played two major functions. First, it offered the police a ready-made list of suspects for unsolved crimes. Second, it provided an additional layer of police and prosecutorial discretion, which added an incentive for defendants to bargain for reduced charges.

Twelve years after the sex offender registration law's enactment in California—a length of time that should have given ample opportunity to establish its effects—the local media reported that police disagreed about the efficacy of registration: "Some endorse it, because it gives a charge on which to hold a suspect under investigation. Others doubt it affords much actual protection to the public."[46] The authors of an extensive study of sex prosecutions in Los Angeles County found that by the mid-1960s, the number of registrants was already so large that it was "impractical to check each one."[47] In some ways the registration law functioned like vagrancy laws, giving police the ability to charge defendants with the failure to register as a stand-in for other crimes or simply to remove them from the streets. But during this period, an informal policy excused mistakes of law: a three-county study found that prosecutors felt the courts had a duty to notify defendants of their registration obligations in order to hold them responsible for failure to register.[48]

The authors of the Los Angeles study also reported judicial reluctance to impose registration: "A number of judges felt that although the avowed purpose of the registration statute is to facilitate the process of law enforcement by providing a list of suspects with propensities toward the commission of certain crimes, the information obtained under section 290 is subject to some abuse—either through police harassment or by indiscriminate revelation to unauthorized persons. Furthermore, some of these judges believe that registration serves no practical function."[49] Although this kind of debate was not a major aspect of public discourse—the studies were widely read by academics and advocates but were not mentioned in mainstream media—it does reflect the same concern for the harshness of sex offender laws as demonstrated in films such as *The Mark*. Thus, critique was not wholly relegated to internal debates among experts and criminal justice professionals, as it tends to be today.

Castration

While retributive calls for castration continued in the rehabilitative era, others promoted the humanitarianism of allowing castration to provide an alternative to imprisonment. In 1975 courts in San Diego brought attention to a long-standing experimental program in which certain sex offenders could volunteer for castration in exchange for probation—at least four hundred sex offenders were surgically castrated over a twenty-year period.[50] Just as there are those today who debate the ethics of administering lethal injections, members of the medical community in San Diego censured urologists who performed the surgery. Eventually, the defendants could no longer find willing physicians, because of malpractice concerns and the government's threat of criminal prosecution for assault and battery. Declaring that he personally regretted it but had no choice, Judge Douglas Woodworth gave several castration volunteers indefinite prison sentences, which he expected to be lifelong, and lambasted the medical community for neglecting to help one of the defendants he sentenced: "A whole branch of the medical profession has been unwilling to extend a humanitarian service to this man, who faces the prospect of being locked in a cage for the rest of his years."[51] An attorney in Colorado who had represented a volunteer for castration also stated his support for using castration as a benevolent cure for a compulsive disorder: "The Freudians can shout all they want to about being opposed to castration, but this castration took away this guy's problem. His emotional state is real good. He doesn't cry any now."[52] But many other lawyers, not just from the California and Colorado chapters of the ACLU who filed suits, were concerned about whether offenders could freely choose between castration and prison. Further controversy erupted when a prisoner in Germany who had volunteered for castration died during the surgery.[53] This phase of the castration experiment disappeared from public view from the mid-1970s until the mid-1990s, but it remained quietly used throughout the interim and continues today as part of the penal and therapeutic apparatus for sex offenders.[54] But, like the preoccupation with obscenity, castration has never been a numerically significant feature of sex offender punishment.

Execution

When castration was unavailable and other penalties were inadequate, the death penalty remained available as the ultimate incapacitation. During this era, calls for the execution of sex criminals still appeared in public debates, especially around particular cases. Capital punishment for nonhomicidal crimes is a largely unrecognized context of the debate surrounding sex crime in this period. When these cases came up, critics identified civil and human rights issues focused on the death penalty, not on the justice system's handling of presumed sex crimes.

While media reporting of sex crimes tended to focus on white, homicidal killers, the public also continued to fear the black rapist as bogeyman. The racialized nature of sex crime fears was nearly absent from my sample of documentary sources that describe public debates from the 1930s to the 1950s, but other scholarship attests to its importance, especially in the postbellum period and in the early twentieth century.[55] But by the rehabilitative era, media and politics engaged the issue head-on. In courtrooms across the South, black men continued to receive disparate handling when the rape of white women was at issue and this was noted in public debates.[56] In 1959 many commentators lauded a Florida decision as an important symbolic victory in changing this practice. An example of this support was a letter written by Alan Chalmers, the NAACP Legal Defense Fund president. Chalmers wrote that he was pleased that white men could be given life sentences for raping white women but noted that "no white man has been executed for the rape of a Negro woman."[57] This emphasizes the importance of rape in the death penalty debates, but it also reminds us of the continuing importance of the death penalty as a symbolic strategy for responding to sex crimes, in the most Durkheimian sense. Though the number of executions was not high enough during this era to justify viewing the death penalty as a numerically significant tool for combating sex crime, executions clearly continued to play an expressive role.

Cinematic media responded to this in the John Ford film *Sergeant Rutledge*, released in 1960. *Rutledge*, set in the Western frontier after the Civil War, tells the story of a falsely accused black soldier. The film alternates between showing his trial for rape and murder and giving an account of his heroic efforts to save a white woman. The film's heavy-handed message is unavoidable: despite our culture's predilection for stories about the rape of white women by black men, there are other stories to tell. The historian Philip Jenkins sees this as an important shift in media coverage, which shows a "dramatic reduction of concern about sexual threats to women and children" in favor of "allegations of racism in the prosecution of sex crime."[58] This complements the cinematic portrayal of the wrongly hounded child molester as seen in *The Mark*, a character Jenkins also highlights.

Contemporary academics have tended to write about the execution of black men, either through state-sanctioned killings or through lynchings (often informally sanctioned by local officials), as being important to debates about the death penalty or about the constructions of race and gender.[59] But little attention has been paid to the implications of these racialized responses to sex crimes for constructions of criminal offenders and for policy responses to sex crime in general. Writing in 1959 about the lynching of Mack Parker, a man awaiting trial for raping a white woman, a special reporter to the *New York Times* noted that in the South "the crime [lynching] is covertly, if not openly, approved. This is particularly true where a Negro male is accused of a sex crime against a white woman, as was the case in Poplarville . . . few persons volunteered any expression of sympathy for the Negro."[60] The complicated tangle of social control of men and women in racialized and gendered ways is another feature of discourse and practice surrounding sexual violence during this era, even though it was no one's officially touted strategy for responding to the sex crime problem.

The Law: From Sexual Psychopaths to Mentally Disordered Offenders

The most prominently discussed strategy for treating sex offenders continued to be civil commitment. States nationwide considered civil commitment laws, and many passed them, only to rescind them after a short time. In contrast, California's 1939 sexual psychopath law, passed somewhat later than many, remained on the books and was actively used for decades. Initially, this law was promoted as a strategy for indefinitely committing anyone who displayed the tendency toward sexual deviance, reflecting the hope that it could be used for preventive detention and treatment of noncriminal as well as criminal sex offenders. But it was rarely used that way and was also the subject of frequent tinkering, just as it has been typical since the 1990s for state and federal legislators to respond to sensational sex crimes with revisions of the registration and notification laws and of civil commitment schemes. In 1949, after a series of sensationalized child murders and the special session of the California legislature conducted by Warren, the law was further amended to focus on child molesters, requiring sexual psychopath evaluation for certain crimes with victims under the age of fourteen but continuing to allow other offenders to be referred for evaluation.[61] However, unlike contemporary tinkering, from the 1950s to the 1980s most revisions to the California laws effectively *narrowed* the scope of the civil commitment law.

In 1963 California renamed its sexual psychopath law to reflect psychiatric terminology. The Mentally Disordered Sex Offender (MDSO) law amended the civil commitment program to encourage courts to restrict referrals to defendants who showed signs of mental defect, rather than to those who could be described with the ambiguous designation of "sexual psychopath."[62]

The 1972 version of the civil commitment law reflects the criteria for commitment, which remained largely unchanged throughout the period despite attempts to change how the criteria were used in practice. A person could be referred and then committed as a sexual psychopath or MDSO if "by reason of mental defect, disease or disorder, [he] is predisposed to the commission of a sexual offense to such a degree that he is dangerous to the health and safety of others."[63] This meant that courts should refer only people likely to be found by evaluators to have a mental defect predisposing them to sex crimes (though not necessarily a "sexual deviation" according to the *Diagnostic and Statistical Manual of Mental Disorders* [*DSM*]) and who also showed signs of being dangerous (or a "menace," as earlier versions stated). Typically, probable cause hearings were ordered to determine whether the defendant should be committed to the sexual psychopath program for evaluation after a guilty plea, but these hearings could also be held after conviction at trial. Thus, civil commitment was in effect the postponement of sentencing while the Department of Mental Hygiene determined whether the offender met the statutory criteria as a sexual psychopath or MDSO and was also amenable to treatment. If, after a ninety-day evaluation, the department recommended indefinite commitment, the judge generally agreed and would either suspend or postpone sentencing.[64]

Debates about Sex Crime Causes

Almost everyone Kinsey interviewed at Atascadero reiterated the heterogeneity of sex offenders; no single etiological explanation could address each of them. The 1959 *Los Angeles Times* series on correctional rehabilitation portrayed child molesters as "typical" sex offenders but also included a revealing quote from an inmate who participated in gang rape: "You look around and you see guys with good houses and good jobs and women and good clothes and cars and like that. Man, you look at yourself and you know you ain't makin' it. You're a nothin', What you gonna do? Nobody wants to be a nothin."[65] This media account reflects the dialogue among criminology, correctional therapy, and the public at the height of the rehabilitative era. It reflects attempts to recognize social causes of crime, and it reveals underlying assumptions about power and about the intersections of race, class, and gender that informed debates about sex crimes. For example, the offender in this quote is portrayed as a normal man reacting to frustration, reflecting the influence of criminologists like Robert Merton, Richard Cloward, and Lloyd Ohlin whose theories of crime causation focused on social and structural causes and were part of cultural debates at the time.[66] Judging by the idiom attributed to the gang rapist, there may also be an underlying assumption about this rapist as being "normal" for his race and class—the "Negro rapist," acting out against white society, may have seemed like he deserved prison rather than the clinic. This recalls Angela Davis's depiction of the myth perpetuated by rape reformers as well as the white patriarchy. As she points out, even those who are sincerely trying to address sexual violence tend to reify racialized beliefs about black men acting their frustrations out on women's bodies.[67] This racialization of aggressions continues with Phillip Rushton's construction of the "Negroid" offender who is more aggressive and therefore more criminal because of having higher levels of testosterone.[68]

Apart from race, some media and institutional accounts showed a belief that perhaps rapists were not deviants fit for hospitalization because they were acting out power issues, not expressing deviant sexual proclivities that could be treated. The same article that quoted the gang rapist also described an "attacker who achieves 'masculine superiority' by forcibly taking a woman."[69] Similarly, a report by a doctor who treated sexual psychopaths kept in prison rather than sent to the treatment facility at Atascadero described one of his rape patients, whose "resentment exploded, first in petty and meaningless theft and later in a series of raping episodes in protest against the Puritanical environment surrounding his pure wife."[70] This incarcerated rapist was not a psychiatric case; he was a man acting out sexual urges that could not be expressed at home.

Other materials from the Kinsey interviews display the view that rape did not indicate a treatable disorder. Dr. Bessant, in a document prepared for the Norwalk Society for Mental Hygiene, explains that the hospital program he oversaw accepted rapists as sexual psychopaths only in the rare instance in which they displayed a "rather bizarro element" that made them interesting.[71] The sex offenders typically selected for treatment were therefore those who were most like the patients that psychiatrists might see in private practice. It makes sense that such practitioners would select subjects most like those they were already comfortable with. This also indicates the unexamined role of racialized constructions of dangerousness. Although there is no explicit statement from the psych experts at Atascadero or elsewhere that they preferred white subjects, this choice was largely made for them at the front end of the criminal justice system by judges. Thus, the psych experts did not create a racialized system of preferential treatment for white subjects, but they very likely perpetuated it.

While psychiatrists might tell the public and policy makers that therapeutic interventions could be justified for the undifferentiated mass of sex offenders, in practice the offenders selected for treatment were from a much smaller pool of those who fit the treatment being offered, a practice further described in the next chapter. Similarly, while the Atascadero staff in the 1960s and 1970s diagnosed a broad range of conduct as indicative of a Mentally Disordered Sex Offender, when it came to admissions for treatment, those staff accepted only a select group of those MDSOs, sending the others to the prison psychiatric ward.

Even though the scope of subjects for normalization narrowed during this era, the diagnostic categories and treatment modes remained largely constant. The nomenclature changed superficially, from "psychopathy" to "personality disorder" and "mental defect." But these changes were driven more by changes in the field of psychiatry than by real differences in the ways patients were diagnosed or in ideas about how these offenders were abnormal. As depicted in the timeline in appendix B, the *DSM* fine-tuned its diagnoses for sexual offending behaviors from sexual deviation to paraphilia over time, but these diagnoses were always within the general category of personality disorder. Pedophilia, voyeurism, sexual sadism, transvestism, and homosexuality could all be understood as behaviors that resulted from inappropriate objects of sexual fantasy and gratification; people suffering from these disorders belonged in a psychiatrist's office because the behaviors and compulsions were abnormal and caused them distress.

Two significant changes did take place in the *DSM*'s treatment of sexual deviation, one better known than the other. The debate over where and whether homosexuality belonged in the *DSM* is well known.[72] A lesser-known exclusion from the *DSM*'s spectrum of sexual disorders involves rape, and it is therefore another indication of the reluctance of psych experts to treat sexual offending against adult women, which in turn seems to have shaped sex offender law and its practice. The very bare *DSM* edition of 1952 does not explicitly include rape as a sexual deviation, unless rape was "coitus performed under bizarre circumstances as in . . . sadism."[73] But *DSM-II*, published in 1968, clarifies that "rape, sexual assault and mutilation" are part of sexual sadism.[74] Then there appears to be some backtracking, rumored among those who worked on the next revision to be the result of a political compromise pushed by those who worried that rapists would be unfairly able to circumvent the criminal justice system if they had diagnostic criteria available to explain their behavior.[75] *DSM-III*, published in 1980, only described serial rape and that it was "repetitive sexual activity with non-consenting partners."[76] Nonserial rape does not itself indicate a paraphilia:

> Rape or other sexual assault may be committed by individuals with this disorder. In such instances the suffering inflicted on the victim increases the sexual excitement of the assailant. However, it should not be assumed that all or even many rapists are motivated by Sexual Sadism. Often a rapist is not motivated by the prospect of inflicting suffering, and may even lose sexual desire as a consequence. These represent two ends of a spectrum, and for cases falling in the middle, it may be very difficult for the clinician to decide if the diagnosis of Sexual Sadism is warranted.[77]

Whether the political compromise account is true or not, the uncertainty about whether to include forcible rape is characteristic of a two-track approach for addressing sex crime. Viewed in light of the academic and public debates about how to determine what rape was and why men committed it, this backpedaling is not surprising at all. Jenkins claims that feminist activists in the 1970s were responsible for framing rape as normal as opposed to pathological.[78] While feminists certainly did advocate for this in order to address the broader problems with patriarchal society, the construction also fit within the dichotomous approach to sex crime that appeared far earlier, which we see well entrenched in civil commitment practice in the 1950s.[79]

Kinsey's investigation into the treatment of sex offenders also reveals that the psych experts were not interested in treatment that aimed to cure *sexual* disorders of sexual psychopaths. For example, Dr. Bessant explained that "sex deviation" is a symptom of a personality problem. This echoes the *DSM's* inclusion of paraphilia as a subclass of personality disorder rather than a disorder distinct because of its sexual nature. An Atascadero psychologist, Dr. Abe, explains the preference for offenders whose charges were for lewd and lascivious conduct because they "have a better prognosis than others because many were situational."[80] Dr. Abe further clarifies that the ideal treatment subject is the heterosexual offender, because the *homosexual* lewd and lascivious offenders have poor prognoses. Accordingly, therapy for heterosexual offenders in the nation's flagship institution consisted of "analytic group psychotherapy" that focused on alleviating "anxiety producing feelings."

Conclusion

From 1950 to 1980, popular discourse about sexual offending and its solutions continued to focus on "stranger danger." But experts in criminology and the treatment professions also contributed to public debates about sex crimes, and they provided a basis for public and political support for a broader set of tools. These experts viewed sex offenders as human but sick and amenable to treatment. This perspective existed in addition to the continuing view of the sex offender as a heinous monster. Experts believed they understood the Freudian and addictive aspects that drove criminality, including sexual offending, and were granted the ability to experiment without the expectation that they would have all the answers. Thus, popular and expert discourse included some differentiation among sex offenders, even if how to differentiate by determining exactly who was dangerous and what caused harm remained unclear.

But while there is no way to measure a "win" for the normalizing rhetoric, there are several ways that indicate that it mattered (some of which will be discussed further in the next chapter, in which I will move away from discourse and look closer at implementation). First, decision makers, including prosecutors, judges, and probation officers, continued to recommend sex offenders for probation and treatment rather than to sentence them to prison time. Second, civil commitment as an alternative to criminal prosecution remained a well-used track for certain sex offenders throughout much of this period, especially during the 1960s. Third, though few people other than sex offenders or their therapists would claim to believe that sex offenders are "just like us," there was a place for this claim in the marketplace of ideas.

Sex Offender Rehabilitation in California and How It Worked

1950–1980

Throughout its penal system, California today is committed to the philosophy that a leopard CAN change his spots.

It is a philosophy which holds that, through a brainwashing process of firmness, understanding, faith and psychoanalysis, nearly all criminals, no matter how bad, can be returned to the community as useful citizens. . . .

On the theory that all criminal behavior is rooted in emotional disorder, California prisons today are functioning more and more like mental hospitals.

In practice it is often difficult to discern where one leaves off and the other begins, as witness the comparative cases of two inmates.

Both men are in their 20s, both have histories of delinquency and both committed the same crime, abducting and molesting 3-year-old girls.

But one was adjudged to be a sexual psychopath; the other was not. One is in the Atascadero asylum, which resembles a prison only in that it has a fence around it. The other is in the penitentiary.

Within their respective confinements, both men are undergoing psychiatric treatment aimed at their rehabilitation. The only difference is that one has more freedom than the other.

—Hubbart 1959

Notwithstanding the broad rehabilitative project described above in the *Times*, in this chapter I contrast that rosy view with data that describe how the California penal system worked. From the vantage point of mass imprisonment, it is tempting to look back wistfully at periods in which there was broad public and political support for rehabilitative efforts. Examining the era of rehabilitative debate to see how it worked can provide insight into the limits and possibilities of rehabilitative logic. California's efforts to reform sex offenders through civil commitment for psychiatric treatment are in many ways emblematic of the aspirations and travails of the larger rehabilitative movement in corrections. Therefore, these cases in California provide useful information about rehabilitation writ large, as well as about the way rehabilitation justified the differentiation of sex offenders based on factors of race, class, and type of offense. It turns out that rather than experimenting with the rehabilitation of "nearly all criminals, no matter how bad," those offenders who seemed most like "useful citizens" were diverted from prison, while those who had less in common with the decision makers and whose offenses seemed more "harmful" were sent to prison—and little therapy took place in either location. This history is crucial for understanding rehabilitation, as well as the bald deceit that provides constitutional justification for sex offender civil commitment laws in the contemporary era.

The fascination with sexual criminality and the use of so-called sexual psychopath laws have been criticized as a way to crack down on certain categories of deviants such as homosexuals and as a way to expand social control in a potentially dangerous fashion. Using the civil commitment of sex offenders as a proxy for rehabilitation, I investigate here the constraints under which rehabilitation functioned and how the state of California used rehabilitation to track sex offenders into different confinement programs based on factors independent of mental health considerations.

Neither the most deviant nor the most violent of offenders were chosen for civil commitment, at any point between 1950 and 1980.[1] Throughout this era of rehabilitative debate, the Department of Mental Hygiene (DMH) shaped the civil commitment population not only by spearheading statutory change, but also by determining who should be indefinitely committed after the initial observation period.[2] A 1957 review in the *American Journal of Psychiatry* found that "one of every 2 cases sent in by the courts with the preliminary diagnosis of 'sexual psychopath' was, as a result of the observation period, not recommended for recommitment."[3] The 1972 DMH report on a sample of referrals from 1966 to 1970 found that of 2,869 offenders referred for 90-day observation, 907 were determined not to be eligible—that is, 32% were screened out, most as not amenable to treatment, though a significant number were also found not to be mentally disordered sexual offenders (MDSOs) at all.[4] Thus, across time, psychiatrists and other mental health workers in California influenced how thousands of sex offenders would serve their time—in a hospital setting or in prison.

How were assessments of amenability to treatment and dangerousness determined? Despite long-standing fascination with empirically grounded risk assessment and the creation, refinement, and validation of predictive tools for determining sexual dangerousness, assessment of sex offenders has always relied most heavily on decisions made by clinicians who largely base those decisions on record reviews, not clinical observation.

The determination of MDSO status as described in a 1976 article in *Criminology* also portrays this reliance on records. MDSO examiners relied heavily (and often exclusively) on the social histories recorded by probation officers, echoing the debate between two psychiatrists discussed earlier about whether psychiatry really played an expert role in their assessments. The article finds that when clinical symptoms were reported, they included "lack of guilt . . . no indication of remorse or emotional distress" and "failure . . . to assume responsibility."[5] This depiction of MDSO assessment could apply as well to contemporary assessment of sexually violent predators (SVPs): "In general, persons examined evidenced very few of the traditional clinical symptoms associated with serious mental illness. Consequently, the examiner's conclusions were often based primarily upon the defendant's prior behavior."[6]

But a "psychological abnormality" was necessary to justify civil commitment and examiners usually found a *DSM* category that would fit. Some believed that any "abnormal" finding about the subject's behavior or development, including intoxication at the time of the offense, was adequate. While it may be interesting to measure changes in psychiatry's view of sexual deviation by analyzing the *DSM*, it turns out that there is a remarkable lack of reference or citation to the *DSM* in either the clinical literature or in program evaluations. Individuals found to be sexual psychopaths (or MDSOs) were usually given non-sex-related diagnoses. What made these offenders unique and in need of treatment was not their particularly *sexual* mental illness. Instead, their mental illness happened to produce sexually criminal behavior (e.g., like the arsonist who set fires to relieve stress or the gang rapist who could as easily have committed robbery). The psych experts involved in civil commitment reflected psychiatry's general uncertainty about how to diagnose sex offenders.

The *DSM* has been contested and controversial, and it is perhaps better suited to bureaucratic purposes like insurance billing than to rehabilitation.[7] But the disconnect between the *DSM*'s formal categories and the diagnoses by practitioners may be even more pronounced in the area of sexual offending, in part because sex offender law is written to flexibly accommodate a wide variety of problematic individuals as being mentally disordered. This continues to be the case in the containment era, when most SVPs are diagnosed with antisocial disorder, not paraphilia.

If sex offenders selected for civil commitment did not tend to receive diagnoses of sexual disorders, what made them candidates for what was supposed to be treatment targeting their sexual disorders? It turns out that a vague determination about "treatment amenability" was used to justify who should be committed. But the standard for amenability was unclear and its interpretation in practice has been more aligned with institutional capabilities and the preferences of the penal operatives than with the individuals' needs.

The uncertainty surrounding how to determine treatment amenability is described in both published sources and in the notes made by Alfred Kinsey and his colleagues during their visit to Atascadero. For example, a 1952 snapshot found that those whose sexual psychopathy was due to neurosis or personality disorder were better candidates for treatment than others, and findings in 1963 focus on the type of offense and on the offender's perspective toward the victim.[8] Most striking, however, are the findings revealed in the Feagley case (discussed in the following quotation)—offenders who were convicted of nonviolent misdemeanors received diagnoses of being MDSOs amenable to treatment *but not to the treatment available at Atascadero*. Hundreds of these offenders were superficially under the jurisdiction of the DMH, but in practice were sent from Atascadero to prison psychiatric wards, where their experiences were indistinguishable from other offenders and involved no treatment of any kind. The justification of a mental disorder was used on some misdemeanants who no one had any intention of treating: they were deemed "treatable" in order to keep them indefinitely in prison, with perhaps the hope that one day someone would know how to treat them. An example is provided in this description of the Feagley case, which also demonstrates the blurred boundary between nuisance and danger:

On the afternoon of October 25, 1969, Julie and Dena, two eight-year-old girls, were riding their bicycles in front of Julie's house in Menlo Park. Defendant Feagley, who worked as a maintenance man in the area, stopped to talk with them. He asked Julie if she was going to let her hair grow long, and she replied that she was. He then briefly stroked both girls' hair and the back of their necks. After watching Dena show him how fast she could ride her bicycle, he left. That is all that happened.

Nevertheless, when the girls told their parents of the incident the latter called the police, and Feagley was arrested and charged with "molesting" each girl in violation of Penal Code section 647a. These charges were dismissed, however, when he entered a plea of guilty to one count of simple battery,[9] a misdemeanor stipulated to be a lesser included offense. The punishment prescribed for that offense is a fine not exceeding $1,000 and/ or a term of six months' imprisonment in county jail. But a far worse fate awaited Feagley.[10]

Feagley exercised extremely bad judgment when he touched the young girl's hair. More ominously, his interaction with the girls could be what we now recognize as "grooming": interacting with children in order to build trust so that sexual acts can later be demanded in the context of a social relationship. Typically, the law does not criminalize future conduct or bad intentions, although it does provide ways in which police and prosecutors can use their discretion to detain people whose actual conduct merits intervention before it escalates. Which took place in the Feagley case? Was there criminalization of future conduct, of the sort that contemporary scholars criticize as being part of a new "sexual predator template" that departs from constitutional and commonsense principles?[11] Or was law enforcement intervening too early, in part to correct its past habit of neglecting "nuisance" conduct? The story of Feagley's "fate" and its broader meaning frame the interpretation of institutional trends in the following pages.

After looking at large trends in sex offender confinement in California during the rehabilitative era, I will analyze the trends to understand how rehabilitative policies were implemented, focusing on the types of people, types of offenses, and the available treatments.

Two Tracks: Civil Commitment and Incarceration

Civil commitment, in addition to its portrayal in the popular press as the primary tool for addressing sex crimes, was in practice the dominant feature of social control through confinement. Despite the public's continued worries about sex crimes from 1950 to 1980, California prison admissions for sex offenses remained low until about 1970 (when they began a dramatic increase driven by nonrape sex offenses). However, civil commitments rose from an average of about 40 per year in the 1940s to almost 450 in 1955, and they were almost 600 per year at the height of the program in the early 1960s. At this level, support for rehabilitation translated into increased civil commitment.

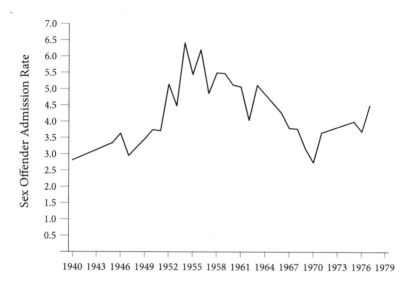

FIGURE 4.1. *Sex Offender Admission Rates in California—Prison and Civil Commitment, Combined, 1940 to 1980*

As shown in figure 4.1, which starts in the 1940s, dramatic changes in the era began in the 1950s. The overall trend in sex offender admissions to confinement over the rehabilitative era shows steep increases peaking in the late 1950s, then an up-and-down movement, and then a steep decline until 1970 when rates modestly increased. Thus, the rehabilitative impulse supported by the public, experts, and officials had some tangible effects on formal social control beyond the other measures described so far.

In table 4.1 I have examined these effects by comparing civil commitment and incarceration for each of the three decades during this era. By the late 1950s, when the civil commitment program was housed at Atascadero State Hospital, it typically admitted one hundred more sex offenders per year than the state prison system. But overall for the 1950s, prison and civil commitment admissions show similar rates. In 1964, almost twice as many offenders went to Atascadero as to prison, although the average for the decade shows less difference between the two. This dominance of hospitalization over incarceration for sex offenders in California continued until 1976, when prison admissions rose while civil commitments slowed and dropped off. Overall, the 1970s show a modest decrease in admissions, while the confined populations show more dramatic decreases.

TABLE 4.1. *California's Confinement of Sex Offenders*

	1950s: Creating Good Citizens	1960s: Selecting the Curable	1970s: Questioning Treatment	
	Admission Rates Per 100,000			
	1955	1963	1970	1973
Civil commitment	3.43 (446)	3.31 (580)	1.51 (302)	2.27 (273)
Prison	2.01 (261)	1.80 (315)	1.23 (247)	1.35 (281)
Total	5.44 (707)	5.11 (895)	2.74 (549)	3.61 (754)
	Median Months Served			
	1955	1963		1973
Civil commitment	18	18		15
Prison	Rape: 42	Rape: 42		Rape: 40
	Lewd/other: 55	Lewd/other: 37		Lewd/other: 52.5

Selected years reflect the best available data for civil commitment.

Total admissions rates are highest in the 1950s, but then decrease in the 1970s to levels that characterized the levels before 1950. Total population rates (in parentheses, not just the newly admitted offenders) are highest in the 1960s. Across categories and decades, civil commitment accounts for much of the trend change, although sex offender prison population rates are larger across time as well. Therefore, this view does not suggest that as sex offender confinement in hospitals declined, those offenders were taken up by the prison system. In fact, despite a brief increase in the 1960s, figure 4.2 demonstrates that social control per capita declines overall.

The shape of the total control and civil commitment lines are nearly identical, emphasizing the large share of total confinement provided by civil commitment. There is no inverse relationship between civil commitment and prison rates. During the middle portion of the era, civil commitment overtakes imprisonment rates for rape and "other" sex offenses, but there is

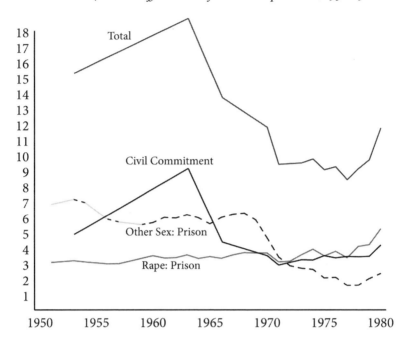

FIGURE 4.2. *Sex Offender Confinement Populations, 1950–1980*

not a direct or immediate relationship between the decline of civil commitment and the imprisonment rates. The total confinement rate peaks in 1963 and then begins a steady decline. Thus, civil commitment drives general confinement trends during this era, and the prison does not take up the slack when civil commitment declines.

The other important finding highlighted by the comparison of civil commitment and incarceration in table 4.1 is the great difference in time served, which in turn accounts partially for the confined population differences. The average civil commitment period, according to the various reports published throughout the period, stayed between fifteen and eighteen months, decreasing slightly by the 1970s.[12] This can be compared to median time served for offenders first released on parole, which shows some variability between rape and lewd and lascivious offenders but both served much longer sentences. Overall, civil committees moved out of confinement after less than two years, while sex offenders in prison averaged between three and four years. Another trend to note is that child molesters (the bulk of the "other" offenders) usually received longer sentences than rapists, except during the mid-1960s.[13]

Harm, Danger, and Institutional Constraint

The sexual psychopath law passed in 1939 focused on civil commitment for early intervention, and as such it was conceived as a broadly based solution for sexual offending that included forms of sexual perversion, exhibitionism, and other noncontact offenses as well as perpetrators of sexual assault. But once in place, the staff assigned with fulfilling such a broad mandate soon realized they had neither the institutional capacity nor a therapeutic approach adequate for such a wide range of sexual deviants. By 1963 a cost-benefit analysis demanded Atascadero narrow its focus.[14]

As a result, the Department of Mental Hygiene proposed revisions to the civil commitment law to reduce admissions to the state hospital at Atascadero:

> In an interview Dr. Sandritter frankly admitted that, neither psychiatry nor any of the other more traditional ways of handling offenders—imprisonment, for example—is a complete solution. But, he added, the experience gained in handling sex offenders during the nine years of the hospital's existence has taught the staff that some kinds of offenders can be helped and others cannot. . . . "We are not as optimistic today as we were three years ago that we can help all offenders, but we are equally optimistic that we can help some of them," Dr. Sandritter said. Stated simply, the individuals who can be helped are those who have sympathy for their victims. The rest must be handled by other methods.[15]

Officials rejected jurisdiction of all people convicted of sex crimes, instead preferring a smaller number of offenders who could be helped. This highlights the intention to use civil commitment as a temporary hold while intense treatment is provided—not as an indeterminate incapacitation.[16] It also departs from the goal of the original sexual psychopath laws, promoted by psych experts as the way to capture all potential offenders before they progressed to sexual homicide. By the early 1960s, the experts implementing the law needed to limit the scope of their rehabilitative efforts. This constrained view of rehabilitation appears long before what is generally viewed as the failure of the rehabilitative project and in fact it is useful when viewed as both harbinger and explanation. Further, while public statements like Sandritter's suggest that empathy marked the treatable offender, examination of admissions data and other documentation of how civil commitment functioned show that the experts' and criminal justice actors' determinations of harm and dangerousness were determinative and that harmfulness was related to not only the offense, but to the social position of the offender and the institution's capacities.

Two studies at Atascadero show the differences in how offenses against children and adult women were constructed by practitioners. A snapshot of the civil commitment population in a 1952 sample shows 52% child molesters/pedophiles; 16% homosexuals; 14% exhibitionists; 5% rapists; and smaller numbers of incest perpetrators, voyeurs, fetishists, and those who practiced bestiality.[17] Of the 148 pedophiles in the sample, only ten were convicted of penetration offenses. That is, 94% of the child molesters committed acts described by the authors as "what is thought of as sex foreplay. Coitus was not usually a goal."[18] In the 1970s, criminologist George Dix compared random samples of commitments to California's Atascadero from 1967, 1972, and 1974. He paid special attention to the child molesters committed to the program to address the concern that civil commitment was unjustly used for nonviolent offenders—a widespread critique of preventive detention at the time. He found that child molestation accounted for 80% of the commitments in 1967, remaining the most common act in subsequent years but declining (to 68% in 1972 and 66% in 1974) while commitments for rape increased. Dix explains this as "an increasing willingness to use the program to deal with violent offenders."[19] These commitment trends and their interpretation, similar despite a twenty-year divide, reflect the belief that child molestation was largely not a crime of violence.

Dix describes the child-molesting offenders by including the sex of their victim, the activity involved (slightly more physical touching than genital contact or penetration), and the means of implementation (most often no force or threats were used). Dix's data show that Atascadero served as a receptacle for what might have been classified as mid-range offenders—they were considered reformable but were serious enough to merit confinement for at least fifteen months in order to provide treatment. The reported context of these offenses typically did not involve force, thus calling child molesters "nonviolent" and construing the harm of their offenses as compared to violent, forcible assault was literally accurate.

Similar to "harm," the concept of "danger" was also operationalized in a circumscribed way. Although "dangerousness" was written into law as a predicate for civil commitment, Atascadero staff had to keep their institution functional. They often viewed violent or otherwise unruly offenders as security risks, given their relatively open facility designed to foster a therapeutic community. In an Atascadero publication (likely from the early 1960s), the superintendent emphasizes that they did "not accept for treatment any sane patient who would be hostile or disruptive."[20] This security concern is echoed in another report, which explains that the earlier civil commitment program had transferred disruptive patients to the hospital ward of the Department of Corrections.[21] It appears that menace or dangerousness adequate to qualify an offender for civil commitment under the law would also have to be benign enough not to be disruptive.

In addition, finding "dangerousness" was largely tautological—past conduct is seen as evidence of future dangerousness.[22] Displaying some parallels to evolving definitions of child molestation as harmful, psychiatric experts have been even more reluctant to treat violent rapists—such rapists do not seem to be candidates for therapeutic intervention and their conduct does not have a clear relationship to a mental disorder. As an evaluation of sexual psychopath commitment in the early 1950s explained,

> Very few cases of physical sex violence, such as forcible rape, or sadism, are admitted to the hospital for the 90-day observation period. The few that were admitted were subsequently rejected for treatment at the hospital by the staff or the court. This course of action did not imply that this type of individual was not a psychiatrically deviated sex offender, but indicated that the state hospital program was not structured to accept him for treatment.[23]

A 1972 report on the Mentally Disordered Sex Offender program confirms this perspective, based on statewide data comparing the sex convictions that could have led to referral for civil commitment with those that were actually referred. While there is some variation by offense across counties, the two major offense categories—lewd and lascivious conduct with a child and forcible rape—show remarkable similarity across the state. Almost 60% of the lewd and lascivious convictions in Los Angeles County were referred for civil commitment from 1966 to 1970, compared with 18.6% of the offenders convicted for forcible rape.[24] Child-molesting behavior was far more likely to result in referral for civil commitment by lawyers and judges who simply did not classify forcible rape as potentially psychiatric—the Atascadero staff then continued this differentiation by preferring to recommend child molesters for indefinite commitment while returning rapists to court. When rapists were civilly committed, they were far more likely to be released because they were not amenable to treatment.[25]

This has two important implications. First, it shows how the law's implementation narrowed its scope for largely practical reasons: violent offenders were too problematic, and this took preference over their potential needs as psychiatric patients. Rather than tailor a separate program with more restrictions in order to balance the security problems posed by the more difficult offenders (often the rapists), the program rejected them. This then reinforced a popular notion held by those at the front end of the system that such offenders did not belong in civil commitment. This selection operated in conflict with the stated purposes of the law, denying treatment to offenders for reasons of institutional constraint, thus perpetuating the divide that continues today in how different kinds of sexual offending are perceived. Second, this rejection enshrined practitioner preference, shaping the field of sex offender therapy for years to come. In some ways, this is an expected implementation transformation. Those who work within state agencies and who straddle treatment and criminal justice know that there are competing imperatives and that the law as written must be interpreted in a way that "works" for the involved institutions. That is, while there is something offensive about the kind of filtering Atascadero staff did to create a treatable population they found desirable, it is naïve and perhaps unfair to expect otherwise. All programs function with limited resources and staff expertise. Nonetheless, whether the filtering was right or wrong, it had disparate effects on particular subgroups.

In California, it appears that institutional factors shaped psychiatric recommendations from the very beginning. At the front end, the recommendation to evaluate an offender as a sexual psychopath or MDSO was written after the parties had agreed to the plea. The probation department collected the data for the recommendation, and the psychiatrists wrote it up. Release decisions were also rather formulaic—a variety of sources show that there was a typical, expected length of commitment for offenders, enabling judges to perceive control of the length of time served: Atascadero staff released offenders after about eighteen months in order to conform to judicial expectations and to make room for the incoming patients. The Kinsey materials confirm that the staff working with sexual psychopaths fully understood the role that civil commitment played as diversion. A fact sheet dated 1953 states that "staff often hold men longer than they need to be held so that when they return to court, the court will put them on probation rather than give them additional time."[26] Individualized decisions related to their mental disorders were rarely significant.

Other factors, for which race and status may have served as proxies, may offer additional explanations for why some offenders were civilly committed and others were sent to prison. Based on his evaluation of the sex offender diagnosis and treatment program at Avenel in New Jersey, Simon Cole emphasizes that mid-range sexual deviance was viewed as more treatable than violence: "Psychiatric hospitalization, therefore, was reserved for petty sex offenders who seemed likely to escalate their crimes. Serious sex offenders were almost invariably returned to the criminal justice system for punishment."[27] California civil commitments tended to follow this pattern—most referrals to civil commitment were for nonpenetrating child molesters. Available data on probation (described in greater detail in this chapter) also support this notion. Rapists who qualified were given conditional probation with jail terms while most other sex offenders were given straight probation or fines.[28]

But while differentiation took place, the evidence in California for a more punitive approach to certain kinds of deviant offenders contradicts the conventional wisdom. While child molesters dominated the sex offender population in civil commitment, they also dominated the sex offender population in prison. From 1940 to 1969, more child molesters than rapists were admitted to prison each year, and child molesters served longer terms before first release on parole. Very few offenders were civilly committed for "sexual perversion" or for consensual homosexual activity among adults.[29]

Rather than being a crackdown on "perversion," Martin Forst's study of three counties in California finds that homosexual offenders almost always received probation rather than commitment or prison sentences.[30] An in-depth examination of Los Angeles County charging practices conducted by UCLA law students produced similar findings in the mid-1960s:

> Less than 1% of those who were originally charged with felonious homosexual activity ultimately received felony dispositions. The remaining 99% were disposed of as misdemeanants, either by conviction, by sentence, or by judicial declaration. The systematic disposition of adult consensual homosexual offenders as misdemeanants by sentence can be attributed to three factors: (1) Judicial recognition of the inefficacy of the criminal law as applied to adult consensual homosexuality; (2) Judicial acknowledgment of the inappropriateness of incarceration as a technique for proscribing homosexual behavior; and (3) Judicial evaluation of public consensual homosexual activity as a nuisance rather than as a menace to the community.[31]

In addition, Forst's study provides an important window into why civil commitment was used for those convicted of what we might consider mid-range criminal sexual deviance: offenders who committed serious crimes like child molestation or who were repeat exhibitionists but were not violent sexual aggressors or homosexual transgressors. After observing court proceedings, interviewing legal actors, and sampling from all the sex-related cases on the criminal docket, Forst found that the legal actor's perception of the harm caused to the victim largely determined the perceived seriousness of the offense. That is, a child molester whose victim gave no testimony of coercion or for whom there was no evidence of injury was not viewed as seriously as an offender who caused injury.

This is reflected in other contemporaneous studies as well. For example, in a work published in 1966, Jonas Robitscher, a professor of law and psychiatry, describes a case in which a judge sentenced an offender in Philadelphia to outpatient counseling over the objections of the prosecutor, who noted that the victims had suffered a traumatic experience when the offender kidnapped and molested them. "The girls will get over it" the judge declared at sentencing.[32] An offender charged with sodomy or sex perversion whose partner was also an adult was viewed as less serious than one whose consensual partner was under the age of eighteen. Forst also finds that civil commitment at Atascadero was viewed as the mid-range sentence for serious sex offenders: It was a more severe sentence than jail time but was less severe than prison for serious cases.[33] But for misdemeanors, for which offenders would typically serve six months, civil commitment was viewed as significantly *more* severe, though it also made sense when offenders needed to be protected from the general population.[34]

Comparing imprisonment and civil commitment for various offenses reinforces the conclusion that Atascadero tended to receive mid-range child molesters, as opposed to the most violent or even the most deviant of offenders. Though the data are incomplete for the civil commitment population, the snapshots from available studies support the conclusion that civil commitment tended to be reserved for a certain class of child molesters who for one reason or another did not demonstrate sufficient dangerousness for prison, whether because of their status or because of details of the offense (e.g., same-sex victims). Perhaps many of them would have received probation if there were no law authorizing civil commitment. Overall, civil commitment probably served more as a diversion from prison for the less violent of the serious offenders, especially since Forst's study shows that civil commitment was generally part of plea agreements and thus often served as an additional tool for negotiation.

This leads us to expect that as civil commitment declined, these child molesters would go to prison—yet this is not evident. Civil commitment was both a means of widening the net for the misdemeanants and a means of diversion for the felons. It turns out that a three-track system was in place for sex offenders.

Treatment and Its Limits

On the surface, the content of sex offender correctional treatment remains the same across the decades. One important feature, lurking beneath this surface, however, is the gap between academic psychiatry and the practice of sex offender treatment even at the most optimistic moment: the early years of the Atascadero program throughout the peak years of its use in the 1960s. Researchers in academic psychiatry were so focused on diagnosis, etiology, and classification, with some attention to risk prediction, that they experimented with treatment in very limited ways. Instead, innovation in sex offender treatment was pioneered by the patients themselves.[35] Offenders civilly committed before Atascadero opened received little therapeutic intervention from the "overworked hospital staff," so they decided to meet in groups to discuss their problems and their progress, and they held one another accountable.[36] By the 1960s, the Atascadero staff had made this group therapy approach their own, referring to it as a "therapeutic community."[37]

Sex offender treatment developed from a modification of Alcoholics Anonymous (AA), with its focus on accountability, and from the view of sexual deviation as a compulsion or addiction to be managed. This is evident in the language used in the Emotional Security Program materials, which explicitly states the connection, as well as in materials written by Norwalk State Hospital's Dr. Geddes.[38] Perhaps most important, this AA influence is seen in the goal of sex offender treatment. As others at Norwalk and Atascadero echo, the goal is not a cure but "rendering the man more safe." Geddes declares the success of this approach by claiming a 2–4% recidivism rate for those who complete treatment, as contrasted with an 8–15% rate for those who failed treatment.[39]

Kinsey's interviews with Atascadero staff show the importance of the staff's isolation from the field of academic psychiatry. Kinsey wrote that Dr. John C. Wrye "disregards most research published" about sexual offending because of its irrelevance: "Most published research is Ford quality when it should be Cadillac quality; he's never read the California Sex Deviation Study and has no interest in reading it."[40] Similarly, the first director of Atascadero, Dr. Gore, retired from an Army career and took a hard-line against most sex offenders, saying explicitly that their problems are "a matter of will."[41]

Just as the content of treatment evolved from the ground up rather than from expert theory and experimentation, reality confounded potential when it came to the quantity of therapy as well. An assembly subcommittee report on the sexual psychopath law in California concluded that

> much research is needed as to what constitutes treatment before large facilities or excess personnel could be used profitably. Psychiatrists in state institutions are underpaid and have too great a caseload. In the light of this evidence the subcommittee concluded that "there is very little in the way of successful treatment available for persons who are committed as 'sexual psychopaths.'"[42]

A few years later, a report on Atascadero argued that the empirical gap was probably irrelevant: The mere experience of being hospitalized was "an effective therapeutic device."[43] Atascadero was therapeutic because the hospital environment was a "community in miniature," which modeled healthy and socially appropriate relationships without removing the offender from the stressors of interpersonal living.[44] This was an attempt to rationalize the benefits of hospitalization despite extremely limited formal therapy:

> Because of the heavy work-load and limited staff, intensive individual psychotherapy was limited; group therapy was the favored technique. The aim was to have each patient in a small group for at least 1 hour per week with individual therapy as an adjunct. About one-half could be provided with this treatment during the bulk of the 2-year period. In addition to the number of small therapy groups, all the treatment patients met once a week for an hour in what was described as the "big class." About 70–80 patients convened regularly to hear discussions on mental hygiene, to listen to guest speakers, and to ventilate their feelings.[45]

Group therapy, then as now, was used because it was more efficient than individual psychoanalysis.[46] But despite the fact that the legal purpose of civil commitment was to provide treatment, very little time was allocated for any therapy at all—typically only one or two hours per week. Even in the early years, before the hospital population exploded, this therapy was usually provided by a psychiatric social worker, not by someone with a Ph.D. or M.D.[47] This left the rest of the offenders' time for the "recreation" described glowingly in the offenders' pamphlet, such as "wholesome satisfying" work on the hog ranch.[48] The bulk of "treatment" for civilly committed sexual deviants consisted of this therapeutic recreation, such as "stamp, astronomy, prospector and dance clubs" as well as musical and dramatic activities, all intended to "aid the men in . . . enhancing partially learned or forgotten acceptable leisure time habits."[49] "Patients" were also encouraged to interact with outsiders, so young female volunteers from the community were welcomed into the hospital to play cards and lead some of the recreational activities. Further, "those patients who [had] responded to treatment and [were] considered harmless—Peeping Toms, exhibitionists—[were] given gate passes to attend dances and other functions in nearby towns."[50] In addition to augmenting the services the understaffed program could provide, these interactions also modeled heteronormative relationships. Perhaps unsurprisingly, given this paucity of formal treatment, no offenders were released from civil commitment as "cured"—instead they were either deemed no longer a menace or not amenable to further treatment.

> It is difficult to evaluate the content or the availability of treatment for sex offenders in prison rather than in civil commitment, though we can contrast public statements from prison officials with those made in official proceedings. As a prison psychiatrist, Dr. Kellogg, reported in the Los Angeles Times in 1959, psychiatrists "try to get [patients] to understand why they're the way they are, accept it, and talk freely about it. The trouble is, many of them simply don't have the intelligence to grasp it." Most doctors have rejected the notion that emasculation by surgery suppresses sexual desire. [Kellogg declared,] "The drive originates in the brain."[51]

This implies that prison officials had the time and the resources to address the inmates' excessive sexual drives. But a statement presented to the Assembly Subcommittee on Sex Crimes a few years earlier contradicted this optimistic view. Dr. David G. Schmidt, the chief psychiatrist at San Quentin, described the treatment available to sex offenders: "Unfortunately we have not had sufficient staff to give each offender more than approximately two hours of individual treatment or an hour and a half of individual and approximately 10 hours of group therapy *each year*."[52] He went on to declare that "prison is a poor place to treat sick patients. . . . Civilian personnel may castigate these patients that have emotional problems, as nuts, and fruits, and sex fiends," and "one sadistic official often destroys the work of a dozen officers."[53] Thus, despite efforts to present social control through civil commitment or imprisonment as an opportunity for therapeutic intervention, image and implementation were far apart even at the height of optimism about rehabilitation.

The Indefinite Confinement of Nuisances

The Feagley case provided the starting point for this institutional analysis. After looking at the big picture, I now return to Feagley's fate. Feagley pled to misdemeanor battery for his deviant hair touching, but, despite the sentence authorized by statute, the prosecutor called for and received a judge's sanction for a different disposition: commitment to Atascadero State Hospital for observation. Evaluators disagreed about whether or not Feagley's compulsive desire to touch hair qualified him as an MDSO, but they did agree that they did not know how to treat him. As a result, they took advantage of the 1963 revision of the California law, which allowed people who were considered to be MDSOs but *not* found to be amenable to treatment to be transferred from Atascadero to a medical facility within the Department of Corrections. Thus, Feagley was technically held through civil commitment, but since his qualifying disorder could not be treated, the hospital sent him to prison. Without the MDSO designation, he would have remained in prison for a short term on the battery charge.

Feagley was not an anomaly. As Dr. Sterling W. Morgan, the medical director of Atascadero State Hospital, explained under subpoena in another case, it was policy:

> A person determined to be a mentally disordered sex offender is considered to be amenable to treatment within the facilities of the Department of Mental Hygiene if he recognizes that he has a problem, indicates a desire for help, and cooperates in treatment programs offered at Atascadero. Such persons are retained at Atascadero State Hospital for treatment of their disorder. Conversely, someone who does not think that he has a problem, or who does not want help, or who cannot participate in or benefit from our treatment program because his predisposition towards violence renders him primarily a custodial problem, is not considered amenable. He is sent back to the superior court as a person who is a mentally disordered sex offender but not amenable to treatment in order that he may either be sentenced as a felony offender or placed in a treatment unit within some facility of the Department of Corrections as a mentally disordered sex offender.[54]

Feagley thus represented the kind of offender who was more than a nuisance: He was not the type of psychiatric subject Atascadero wanted, but he was still someone who should be confined longer than criminal justice alone would allow.

The justices of the Supreme Court of California did their own investigations and found that this was not unusual—hundreds of offenders, almost all of them convicted for very minor misdemeanors, were confined within the prison system in California despite their status as civil committees.[55] This contradicts the official account but is in line with other cases of similar sex offenders in states like Michigan and Maryland who were caught in the limbo between psychiatric and legal categories.[56]

A special government report on the MDSOs in California acknowledges that some MDSOs were transferred out of Atascadero but claims that they were deemed "security risks" better suited to treatment within prison. These MDSOs served longer in prison than the typical MDSO who stayed at Atascadero: more than forty months for the transfers as opposed to about fifteen months for the "amenable" MDSOs.[57] Of the 2,073 offenders civilly committed for treatment and then discharged between 1966 to 1970, 14% were confined in the prison system like Feagley (n = 296).[58] There are no available data to determine how many of these were confined for conduct like Feagley's, but it appears that almost all were misdemeanants. This might be reasonable if these sick misdemeanants were actually receiving treatment during their extended stays in prison. But the *Feagley* opinion suggests otherwise:

> In response to our request for supplemental briefing of the issue whether such confinement is penal in nature, Feagley advised the court that he was housed in a cell in "D Quad" of the California Men's Colony, East Facility; that he mingled freely with the general prison population, wore standard prison clothing, worked for wages of a few cents an hour in the prison shop, submitted to full censorship of his mail, and was subject to all prison regulations concerning security.[59]

These misdemeanants were viewed as being too difficult for psychiatrists to treat, but as deserving more punishment than their convictions provided. In fact, the Atascadero staff had a preprinted form, used in the diagnosis of Feagley and for uncounted others, which made this clear:

> This man cannot utilize treatment but is still a danger to society and should not be provided additional opportunity to victimize others. He should be returned to the criminal court for action. We recommend that he be sentenced for the criminal act if sentencing is mandatory or if he is charged with a felony. If he is charged with a misdemeanor, I recommend that he be committed to the Department of Mental Hygiene for an indeterminate period and sent to the Reception and Guidance Center, California Medical Facility, Vacaville.[60]

The willingness of psychiatrists to relinquish jurisdiction of these offenders in everything but formal title is crucial to understanding the containment era, in which "sexually violent predators" are identified by extremely broadly defined mental disorders and are then indefinitely civilly committed even if they refuse treatment. In this situation, as in that of the unamenable misdemeanant MDSOs, psych expertise provides a veneer of justification for a social control mechanism that utilizes very little psychiatry in practice.

While individual cases of likely injustice such as Feagley's are important, they must also be considered in light of much larger trends. It turns out that while hundreds of people like Feagley were detained for lengthy periods, civil commitment appears to have provided diversion from hard time for many more.

Rehabilitation as an Instrument

Rehabilitative frames enabled the state of California to move offenders between the Department of Mental Health and the Department of Corrections under the guise of individualized treatment. But as has been discussed, little treatment took place, and the civil commitment laws really functioned more as instruments for achieving the institutional goals of the criminal justice and hospital systems. The next section will describe the other ways in which rehabilitative rhetoric served instrumental goals of control and diversion.

Two Tracks of Criminal Justice Control

First, while the focus thus far has been on civil commitment for sex offenders because it was the keystone of California's approach to the sex crime problem, the criminal justice share of sex offenders was always much larger, although not in the form of incarceration. That is, civil commitment and prison admissions in California during this period never rose above 700 per year for each category; the highest total is in 1965, when 883 were admitted to both systems (the highest civil commitments were in 1963, with 580). When viewed as rates of confinement, these numbers look even less significant. In contrast, most sex offenses were handled as "nuisances."

The Dominance of Misdemeanor Dispositions
Despite popular, official, and critical interest in civil commitment during this era, and regardless of whether viewed as a rehabilitative ideal or as veiled social control, the criminal justice system enjoyed numeric dominance pri-

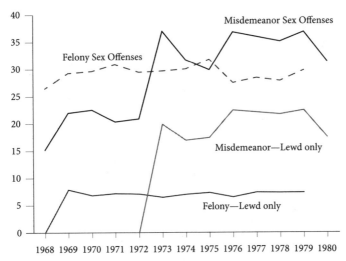

FIGURE 4.3. *Misdemeanor and Felony Sex Arrest Rates in California, 1968–1980*

Source: See Crime and Delinquency in California and California Criminal Justice Profile Series, California Bureau of Criminal Statistics and Special Services.

marily because of the number of people convicted of misdemeanors. Historical data about jail populations are well known to be skimpy, largely because responsibility for jail administration belongs to county-level government and has no centralized repository. Information about lower courts is also spotty, but fortunately statewide misdemeanor arrest information by offense is available for part of this period. When we combine special reports on probation, the law review series on homosexual prosecutions, and Martin Forst's study of three counties, we can piece together a general picture of the importance of the misdemeanor and probation systems for dealing with sex criminals.

The state began asking local authorities to report their misdemeanor arrest data in the 1950s. But data are not available for sex offenses until 1968 (prior offense breakdowns didn't separate sex offenses from public order and other offenses). Figure 4.3 takes the arrests reported in the annual publications of *Crime and Delinquency in California* and the California *Criminal Justice Profile* to show the importance of misdemeanors.

The figure shows that as the rehabilitative era drew to a close, the rate of arrests for sex offenses was typically higher for misdemeanors than for felonies[61] and that charges for lewd and lascivious conduct dominated those numbers after 1972. This was a result of a legislative change: Beginning in

1973, lewd and lascivious conduct could be charged as a misdemeanor as well as a felony. This was a legislative fix enacted after the state's lewd vagrancy statute was overturned (part of a national movement driven by the courts). This creation of a lewd "wobbler" was likely made in order to prevent the complete dismissal of charges for conduct or offenders not deemed worthy of a felony. Apart from the arrest patterns themselves, this is also an indication that many more sex offenders came through the precinct doors than made it to prison. As soon as this dual charging was available, misdemeanor lewd arrests began to outpace felony lewd arrests, just as misdemeanors account for more sex arrests than felonies throughout most of the period. The earliest statewide misdemeanor data show more than 3,000 sex arrests in 1968, dominated by indecent exposure. By 1979, more than 8,500 misdemeanor sex offense arrests were recorded, 60% of which were for lewd and lascivious conduct.

These numbers, while incomplete, show that the scale at the front end of the criminal justice system dramatically outpaced both prison and civil commitment combined throughout the era. In 1968, while fewer than eight hundred adults were admitted to prison and Atascadero, more than four times as many misdemeanant sex offenders passed through the system that year. In 1979, only about one thousand offenders entered confinement, but misdemeanants accounted for more than eight times as many sex offenders under state supervision and control.

We would expect the front end to be much larger than the back end, but most of these offenders were not screened out after arrest. For example, the UCLA Project shows that the vast majority of homosexual arrests proceeded through the system to sentencing. To get a sense of outcomes for misdemeanant sex offenders in the 1950s we can also look at the snapshot provided by fifteen counties that reported lower court dispositions to the California Bureau of Statistics for 1958: 95 of the 125 eligible sex offenders received probation (with seventeen counties reporting for 1959, 148 out of 185 sex offenders got probation).[62]

In addition to the large size of the misdemeanor system, felony probation also accounted for a larger number of sex offenders during the 1950s and 1960s than the prison system. About 950 felony sex offenders were on probation in 1955, compared to about 700 in both prison and civil commitment combined; in 1959 there were about 1,900 sex offender probationers compared to fewer than 850 in confinement.[63]

The other important pattern to note from these data is that the criminal justice approach to rape is different when compared with decisions for "other" sex offenses. Consider, for example, the 1959 report on those sex offenders recommended for probation (and not therefore the offenders charged under statutes that provided for a year or more of prison): "Excluding rapists, sex offenders seldom were jailed conditionally. The various courts and probation departments of California tend to favor straight probation for many of these probationers, and, in the case of those convicted of sex offenses other than lewd and lascivious conduct and rape, the majority were ordered to pay a fine."[64] The going rate for "minor" sex offenses was a fine, while convictions involving a child tended to get probation, and rapists were the most likely to serve some jail time. There was a reversal between 1955 and 1959—by the end of the 1950s, more rapists were on probation than child molesters or other offenders.

Another snapshot provides a view of the on-the-ground functioning of sex crime law in the rehabilitative era. The UCLA Law Review sampled every second felony prosecution and every fifth misdemeanor prosecution for the charges used for homosexual conduct during a single year in Los Angeles County.[65] One of the study's most important findings involved the broadly written sex crime statutes and the discretion these gave to police officers, prosecutors, and judges. The UCLA study found that the great majority of offenders investigated for homosexual sex crimes were convicted of misdemeanors and were very often sentenced to probation, largely because of "judicial evaluation of public consensual homosexual activity as a nuisance rather than as a menace to the community."[66] The UCLA study did not include the entire range of sex crimes, so its findings cannot prove that 99% of "other" sex offenses were reduced to misdemeanors. But the study supports the importance of misdemeanors for understanding the punishment of sex crime and emphasizes that criminal justice dominated civil commitment.

In addition to numerically overshadowing civil commitment, the criminal justice system was also a necessary precondition to the civil system, because arrest and referral through the criminal courts almost always preceded civil commitment.[67] During this period, civil commitment was a form of diversion rather than a separate system. This meant that criminal prosecutors had to be invested in such diversion for some sex offenders; that is, in differentiating among offenders as deserving probation, commitment, or prison.

Differentiating by Race and Class

A large body of research supports the contention that black and Hispanic defendants have historically been targeted disproportionately by the criminal justice system for arrest and prosecution and that they have often served harsher sentences; this has been especially true for black men accused of sex crimes against white victims. Several scholars have also claimed that it has been characteristic to treat white offenders in institutions and to send people of color to prison for the same crimes. Stephen Robertson argues that there was an intentional difference in the construction of what I call the "patient":

> The concept of psychosexual development also allowed psychiatrists to effectively whitewash the sexual psychopath, to ensure that he did not undermine the figure of the bestial black rapist that justified the incarceration or killing of African-American offenders. An immature sexuality was a normal characteristic of African-Americans, psychiatrists argued, a product of their race, rather than of arrested development. As a result, African-American offenders could not respond to the psychiatric therapies that, by helping sexual psychopaths complete their sexual development, ensured that such men would not again commit further sex crimes.[68]

Simon Cole sees some evidence of this in the 1990s in New Jersey. In practice, such whitewashing is more likely to occur earlier in the process—a result of forces that shape reporting practices as well as determine how offenders will be charged (e.g., black or Hispanic victims of sexual assault have been less likely to be known to the criminal justice system).[69] Available sources do not allow us to fully investigate these issues—we would need better data about the front end of the system—but there are snapshots of data about the use of different kinds of punishment for black and Hispanic sex offenders (often labeled "Negro" and "Mexican" by the data collectors), which suggest less disparity than we might have expected but some support for the view that race may be coded as a danger rather than a disease.

At the front end of the system, the UCLA Project found "no apparent differences in police practices based on the defendant's race."[70] White offenders are arrested for the majority of offenses overall, though more nonwhite offenders are arrested for misdemeanor sex offenses. Just as underreporting by black victims may influence the data, it is likely that patterns of homosexual activity and the relative publicity associated with these patterns varied by race and socioeconomic status. Perhaps most important, it may be that police officers did not enter the neighborhoods of people of color in order to identify violators or enforce the law. Regardless, this is one window into police practices that shows that people of color were not disproportionately subject to police crackdowns, at least for these kinds of sexual offending.

The probation report for 1957 does show some disparity in dispositions for sex offenses, but because the offense categories include such different kinds of offending—statutory rape counted along with forcible rape, we cannot reach any conclusions. In 1957, 63% of white rapists, 61% of Mexican rapists and 64% of Negro rapists were granted probation, while of those granted probation for "other sex offenses" 77% of offenders were white, 66% were Mexican, and 61% were Negro.[71] Looking at the data further, the report's authors write, "An offense showing a disproportionate relationship is that of rape. Only 3% of the total whites referred for probation were convicted of this particular offense as opposed to 5% for both Negro and Mexican defendants. Closer examination reveals that most of the rapes committed by the latter two groups were statutory rapes rather than violent rapes."[72]

These limited disparities can be read in several ways, all of which are probably part of the explanation. The general tendency for assault to occur within racial and ethnic groups is well established. Therefore, the tendency for rapists to assault victims of their own race, combined with the greater use of the criminal justice system by white victims, meant that more white forcible rapists were available for sentencing. In addition, it may be that people of color would be more likely to come to criminal justice attention because of reporting by white parents of statutory rape as a way of maintaining racial boundaries[73] or because they were already part of the juvenile justice system and thus more likely to be detected. These factors may have combined to mean that Negro and Mexican offenders received higher punishments than the going rate; for example, they may have been given probation for lesser offenses like statutory rape, an offense for which white offenders may only have been fined. Unfortunately, the data for probationers are incomplete and only suggestive.

However, prison admission data broken down into offense categories by race are available for 1949, 1955, and yearly beginning in 1963, helping to evaluate the claim that black offenders go to prison while whites are civilly committed. This picture of admissions shows that there is more disproportion by race in prison admissions for rape than for what are typically child molesting and deviance offenses. That is, although incarcerated rapists are mostly white, the number of rapists who are described as Mexican and Negro are higher than their actual share of the population. Child molesters and other deviant offenders are predominantly white across the decades. In addition, data for offenders first released on parole show that white offenders of both categories actually served slightly longer prison sentences in the late 1940s. This may be because the qualifying conduct had to be more serious for white offenders to be sent to prison, but we cannot draw firm conclusions.

In a study of rape incidents in Philadelphia widely cited as empirical proof that the myth of the black rapist was unfounded, Mehachem Amir found that the vast majority of rapes occur between members of the same racial groups.[74] While this kind of analysis does not allow us to see differences in how offenses were tracked by justice systems, it is important to keep in mind as it highlights the gap between true prevalence, systemic responses, and popular beliefs: all issues that the studies following Amir have also emphasized.[75]

A window into differentiation by race for civil commitment can be found in the commitments between 1966 and 1970, which received special scrutiny in a 1972 government report. The authors noted that Mexican Americans were more likely to be referred for civil commitment based on misdemeanor convictions than for felonies.[76] This suggests that the Mexican American misdemeanant was more likely to be deemed deserving of longer confinement for minor offenses (like Feagley) and that the Mexican American felon was deemed to be worthy of prison rather than of receiving psychiatric help. The same report also notes that, after referral, a higher proportion of the Mexican American misdemeanants were committed.[77]

An additional study about Atascadero was published in 1975, reporting on the differences by race and offense of sex offenders committed in 1965. Published in the Archives of Sexual Behavior by a social worker who went on to become a prominent critic of the *DSM*, Stuart Kirk, it found that the civilly committed blacks were more likely to have committed sexual penetration, tended to have older victims, and used force.[78] An additional analysis of the relative occupations of the offenders finds that class explains the offense differences more powerfully than race: Unskilled offenders of both races were more likely to have committed the rape of an adult by force than their blue-collar and white-collar counterparts.[79] Kirk posits, "Whites may have to engage in more 'unusual acts' in order to get convicted and committed to the hospital, while blacks are committed for less 'deviant' behavior."[80]

Altogether, these bare but suggestive data show less disparity in sex offense enforcement by race than the literature might have led us to expect. But there is some evidence for "whitewashing" of sexual offending in the civil commitment and criminal justice systems. Certainly, the back end of the system reflects assumptions about force, harm, and danger, filtered through the lenses of race and class by decision makers at the front end. The possibility that Mexican American sex offenders were more likely to be confined for misdemeanors is deeply troubling, and it points to the pitfalls of differentiation when left unguided and unchallenged.

Net Widening or Diversion?

Simon Cole interprets the greater likelihood for violent sex crimes to result in prison sentences as support for arguments made by other scholars (like Estelle Freedman and George Chauncey—see appendix A) that sexual psychopath laws used violence as a pretext for cracking down on deviants. The rhetoric in support of early civil commitment laws was actually quite transparent—commentators were explicit about the hope that minor offenders could be identified and treated, thereby preventing future violence. As this discussion has shown, however, that rhetoric did not correspond with usage of the civil commitment law in California, which operated the nation's largest civil commitment program. The Freedman and Chauncey arguments rightly bring our attention to a limited expansion of formal social control on the front end—that is, these laws may have justified police sting operations like the ones documented in the UCLA report—but those offenders were not civilly committed. Judges knew psychiatrists would not find consensual homosexual activity to constitute the "menace" required under the law.[81] It is possible that the statutory rape or child molestation offenders in civil commitment were more likely to be there because of same-sex activity, but this is not known. Thus, according to the available California data, the conclusion that these civil commitments were a "crackdown" is unfounded. In fact, compared to the typical time served in prison in the 1950s (between three and four years for both rapists and child molesters), civil commitment was clearly preferable, because commitments averaged from between fifteen and eighteen months in order to keep up with the incoming flow of new committees as well as to meet judicial expectations of the "going rate."

There was typically more interest in using psych expertise to cure criminality than there was actual therapy.[82] But despite the lack of actual therapeutic intervention, the sex offender as a "patient" or treatable subject remained central to psychiatry's identity throughout this era. The Atascadero director quoted by Slater also stated, "It is our responsibility, then, to be ready to accept these patients as worthy of improvement. Without this there can be no treatment. Without treatment, we no longer would have a hospital."[83] Without the premise of sex offender treatment, the psych experts would lose the shining beacon of their ability to solve a crucial crime problem: sexual violence.

Nonetheless, while far less therapy ever took place than was planned by proponents, the availability and usage of civil commitment prioritized psychiatric notions in correctional policy in California and in other states as well. Evidence also shows that court actors and legislators responded to the recommendations of the staff who oversaw the civil commitment program.[84] In these ways, treatment professionals had a tangible impact. But the importance of psych expertise was also constrained. Individual dispositions for sex offenders were based on formulas and institutional pressures rather than on psychiatric assessment. Instead, public and political support for rehabilitation allowed diverting some offenders from hard time under the guise of individualized treatment.

Civil commitment was not a mechanism for expanding formal social control over homosexuals. Instead, civil commitment focused on nonviolent child molesters and other offenders who would have served short jail terms without the psychiatric option. Crackdowns on deviance were prevented by predominant construction of harm as physical wounding, not as the experience of nonviolent touching, coerced or otherwise. Discretion dominated, though it may not have been individualized. Judgments about the going rate and relative harm were determinant—punishment judgments always came before psychiatric diagnoses. This created a divide between child molesters and rapists because the accepted belief was that rapists deserved punishment. Psychiatric judgments supported the nonpathology of rape so this distinction was not due to prosecutorial discretion alone.

The systems' emphases on child molesters over rapists may help explain why rape prison admissions remain low when "other" sex admissions go up; it appears that changes in rape law and in public awareness do not translate into more rapists going to prison. Instead, punitiveness retains its original target—child molesters—and sends more of those to prison as the general incarceration rate increases. The underrepresentation of rapists in civil commitment also suggests that the feminist interpretation of rape as normal rather than pathological (and of objections to inclusion of rape behavior as part of evidence of paraphilia in the *DSM*) dovetailed with what criminal justice and psychiatric experts already believed about sexual deviance—rather than this being an example of feminist victory as feminists themselves and historians like Jenkins have claimed, it looks more like a happy coincidence.

The aggregate picture of the period from 1950 to 1980 shows the rise and fall of civil commitment as the primary strategy for sex offenders within an overall stability of social control. Civil commitment drops in the early 1970s and within a decade of this drop the prison rate increases. Is this a case of delayed reaction (the child molesters that are not committed by the mid-1970s go to prison)? Or is this substantial independence of the two systems?

The data discussed in this chapter argue against the theory of delayed reaction. The prison population was evenly divided between other sex offenders and rapists until rape incarcerations rose notably in the early 1970s.[85] Compare the rapist to child molester ratios in civil commitment of 1:10 and later of 1:6: civil commitment is always mostly child molesters. There is no delayed reaction—for that, we would have seen child molestation rates of imprisonment rise after civil commitment admissions declined. Instead, admissions for rapists rose, showing there is no discrete correlation.

But it is also reasonable to ask whether the civil commitment cases are the result of net widening or of diversion (this question prompted Forst's study). In one sense, it cannot be net widening because arrest always precedes civil commitment. But if the question is of more or less formal social control, then there may have been some net widening in the 1960s because of the influence of ideas about signs of future dangerousness (e.g., escalation from exhibitionism and peeping to violent offenses). Some offenders spent longer in confinement because of the availability of civil commitment.[86] Offenders who did not look like "patients" would end up serving a shorter amount of time in jail, while offenders who did look "dangerous" would serve longer sentences in civil commitment than if disposed as a misdemeanant, but less than they would have with a prison sentence (and the time at Atascadero was widely viewed as a "softer" way to serve time).[87] The fact that imprisonment rates of child molesters do not jump higher in the 1970s when civil commitment drops off is strong evidence of net widening.

In general, the three-track system is controlled by prosecutorial vetoes and punitive priorities but with a role for psych experts. Widespread support for rehabilitation made the civil commitment option a viable one, especially because the psychiatric track provided punishment of certain duration (almost always eighteen months) in an era of indeterminate prison sentences. If court actors distrusted the motives of psychiatrists, they knew the sentencing outcome for civil commitment was reliable. Had punitive considerations ruled exclusively, there would never have been the option, let alone the high usage of civil commitment seen in the 1960s. ·

But the most important implication of the data presented here may be that the decline of sex offender civil commitment in California was a leading indicator of the decline of rehabilitation, one that has not been acknowledged before. Even while public faith in expert ability and in the potential for offenders to reform was at its peak, concerns about discretion and limitations on rehabilitation in practice led to the early decline of the rehabilitative ideal for sex offenders. All available evidence about the criminal justice response to sex crime during the rehabilitative era points to a surprising finding—faith in rehabilitation peaked and declined much earlier than we would have expected, given the overall correctional climate and the 1976 determinate sentencing revolution.

By the mid-1970s, Atascadero staff were receiving far fewer referrals and committing far fewer sex offenders than in the heyday of the civil commitment experiment of the 1960s. Their selectivity in refusing to recommend commitment for offenders likely contributed to the perception that their rehabilitative abilities were limited. While it may have been sensible to restrict civil commitment to those most likely to benefit, over time this practice undermined faith in the ability for treatment to work for any sex offenders. Along with the national publicity that highlighted examples of the program's failures to cure, Atascadero staff contributed to their own decline, first by claiming broad capacities, then by quickly circumscribing those claims, without ever offering much evidence of success. In contrast, contemporary civil commitment's focus on management over treatment for SVPs appears much savvier, as it sets a lower and more measurable bar for success, a feature of contemporary penality in general, which Jonathan Simon has emphasized.[88]

Another important lesson from this research is the mediating effect of discretion. The penal code offered wide latitude for selecting arrest charges. Prosecutors and defense attorneys could negotiate a variety of issues before pleas. Judges could impose indeterminate sentences to prison, the more determinate term in confinement typically produced by civil commitment or, as they did most often, judges could sentence sex offenders to probation or jail. But who benefited most from this mediation? Psych experts, judges, and correctional officials all tended to prioritize harm over deviance. Rapists were more often viewed as nonpsychiatric, while child molesters might receive probation, prison terms, or civil commitment dispositions. The bare arrest data suggest that police officers were more likely to arrest blacks for rape. Insights from the Atascadero staff suggest that disposition decisions about child molesters were driven by notions of treatability, shaped by race and class. So decisions at both the arrest and the disposition stage usually meant prison time for offenders of color.

Given the much higher stakes that accompany sex offender status today, and given the continued domination of notions of black dangerousness, it is likely that decisions about treatment amenability are continuing to concentrate inequality. Further research needs to document how sex offenders are selected for arrest and prosecution and to explain why there are variations by race and socioeconomic status at each stage of the criminal justice process. Care should be taken that diversion is not driven by unchallenged notions of "treatability" that are not grounded in empirical realities.

Sex Offender Policy in the Containment Era

1980–Present

Last month Illinois Criminal Judge Berkos gave a lenient sentence to notorious plumber-rapist Brad Lieberman, who, on top
of prior rape convictions, pleaded guilty to five rape charges.
In an interview, the judge explained his sentence: "Lieberman
had done things that did hurt the women, but fortunately he
did not hurt the women physically by breaking their heads or
other things we see. He didn't cut their breasts off, for instance."
   The fact that a state judge could seem almost casual about
rape shows that beneath the new surface sensitivity, many of the
cultural prejudices linger. "What we do in our society, whether
it's in photography, films or language, is devalue sex," says Psychologist Groth, "and that gives the message that sex can become
a weapon to degrade somebody." Such moral carelessness is what
has made the U.S. violent in private, as well as in public.

—Dowd 1983

In the containment era, the public would rather hear about fantastic
accusations of satanic ritual abuse of children than address the more common incidents of sexual violence. In addition, child abuse is now viewed as
inherently more harmful because typically its victims are inarguably inno-
cent, while violence against women is complicated by persistent beliefs
regarding the complicity of adult victims. This is evident in the McMartin
preschool hysteria that dominated the 1980s and 1990s, which I discuss in
detail in this chapter, and that eventually resulted in seven arrests and the
longest-running and most expensive criminal trial in history. The pretrial
investigation ran from 1984 to 1987, and the trial itself extended from 1987
to 1990.

This chapter covers the era from 1980 to the present, which I call the "containment era." "Containment" is the designation for a prominent model for managing sex offenders in the community; it also refers to the rhetoric of pollution often used to describe the problem of sex offenders.[1] The containment era features many continuities with the past, including the focus on monstrous offenders rather than the far more typical abuse by familiars. But there is expanded responsiveness from government officials to sexual violence against women that does not involve harm conceived of as mutilation—by the end of the era, fewer judges would make statements like Judge Berkos above, although they can still be heard.[2]

Chapter 2 described the strictly incapacitative strategies that yielded to include research and treatment in the sexual psychopath era; chapters 3 and 4 demonstrated the importance of civil commitment, variously conceived as incapacitation, rehabilitation, and prevention. But since 1980, rehabilitation is rarely promoted, while strategies to prevent and punish have grown exponentially. Unlike earlier diversity and divergences in the discourse, penalty enhancements in the containment era are more uniformly promoted across fields and constituencies. In addition, most of these new laws have affected a large number of offenders, rather than remaining at the level of rhetoric or token application.

Talk about the Problem of Sex Crime and Sex Criminals
The McMartin Preschool Panic

> I believe we are dealing with no less than conspiracies in these cases, organized operations of child predators. . . . Preschools in this country in some instances have become a ruse for larger unthinkable networks of crime against children. If pornography and prostitution are involved, which is sometimes the case, those networks may have greater financial, legal, and community resources than any of the agencies trying to uncover them. . . . We have in most communities plans for dealing with fires, floods. California has earthquake descriptions in all their phone books; the federal government is even developing plans for emergency response to nuclear war. . . . We need a community disaster model to combat this kind of thing.
>
> —Testimony of Kee MacFarlane, Hearing before the House and Senate Children's Caucus of the Senate Committee on the Judiciary in conjunction with the Third National Conference on Sexual Victimization of Children, April 26, 1984

Accusations of satanic abuse at the McMartin preschool came to public attention in early 1984, when a local news anchor announced that children at the preschool in Manhattan Beach, California, "had been keeping a grotesque secret of being sexually abused and made to appear in pornographic films while in the preschool's care—and of having been forced to witness the mutilation and killing of animals to scare the kids into staying silent."[3] By the time that news broke, Virginia McMartin's family-run school had already been forced to close its doors—California's Department of Social Services had suspended the preschool's license based on its own conclusion that abuse had occurred, despite the uncertain outcome of the ongoing criminal investigation. But even after retrial no one was ever convicted of actually harming any children, let alone of perpetrating the kinds of horrific abuses that were widely reported in the media. The media circus surrounding McMartin was not only national but also international in scope.[4] In retrospect, McMartin has often been compared to the Salem witch trials. But as fruitful as that analogy may be, it also is worth comparing McMartin to the sensational coverage of sexual psychopaths in the 1930s and 1940s. Both eras are characterized by parental and community pressure to respond, the media offering sensational accounts of monstrous offending, experts eager to offer their services, and police and prosecutors ready to call on the public to help in law enforcement.

There are many "lessons" to learn from McMartin. As one commentator, who testified in many of these types of cases, wrote in 1995,

> Today, most professionals understand that there is no compelling evidence supporting the belief in a worldwide conspiracy of pornographers and ritual abusers who infiltrate day care centers. Most understand that the children in the McMartin, Scott County, Edenton, Martinsville, Michaels, Akiki, Fijnje, and hundreds, if not thousands, of similar but smaller and less publicized cases were not horribly abused in bizarre, sadistic rituals involving animal torture, graveyards, and infanticide. Most now understand the vulnerability of young children to suggestive, leading interviews, coercive adult behaviors, and "disclosure-based" play therapy.[5]

The McMartin legacy also includes profound changes in the implementation of sex crime policy: loosening the laws of statutory limitation and trial evidence and nationalizing the mandatory reporting of child abuse. It also illustrates the continuing use of sex crime as a symbol for social and governmental failure and as a vehicle for officials to demonstrate their concern. In fact, the most interesting aspects of the McMartin story may be the way various officials responded to the crisis and the shifts and continuities from previous panics we can identify here.

Just as De River, Hoover, and many others took advantage of sexual psychopath fears decades earlier, certain opportunistic experts and officials made the most of the hysteria prompted by the McMartin accusations.[6] The journalist John Earl has written incisively about the role played by Kee MacFarlane, a social worker who led the Children's Institute in fomenting and benefiting from the McMartin sensation. After MacFarlane's testimony (excerpted above), her organization received millions of dollars in federal grant money.[7] Many others came to prominence and financial benefit as well at the expense of the McMartin defendants, who were eventually released from prison, vindicated but impoverished.[8]

As with other media sensations, the McMartin case led to increased scrutiny of the government's response to sex crime. Most initial responses to the accusations focused on the problems of preschools, putting part of the blame on women in the workplace.[9] Colleen Mooney, the spokeswoman for parents of McMartin schoolchildren, released a statement when the arrests were announced: "This case is another example of how social agencies, as well as law enforcement, have not kept pace with a society where the two-income family has become the rule, not the exception."[10] Several articles in the wake of the accusations also focused on licensing and social service agencies. But within two months, the state senate displayed the new-law fallacy, which had dominated previous eras. Legislators proposed a variety of new laws aimed at making it easier to convict child molesters and harder to release them on parole. The bills were described in the *Los Angeles Times* as intended to prevent the incidence of child molestation, though the content actually addressed evidentiary, sentencing, and release issues.[11] As with prior laws, these focused on identified offenders, rather than on true prevention.

Jenkins writes about the satanic abuse panics as occurring just at the right time to benefit from a strange coincidence of goals and timing: the feminist campaign to recognize sexual assault combined with the medical and social welfare movements organized to recognize physical abuse of children as well as conservatives' concerns about "unrestrained sexual license."[12] This political and social power was supported by many experts, though largely not ones affiliated with mainstream academia. By the 1970s, "something approaching a freestanding child abuse profession developed out of existing traditions in social work, therapy and counseling, and the associated societies, conferences and journals soon emerged."[13]

But the fervent belief in child victims, and in adults who reported their recovered memories of abuse, gave way to skepticism and scandal, which in turn exposed the coercive qualities of the therapy that produced such reports. Social scientists such as Richard Ofshe and Elizabeth Loftus helped to shift the tide against recovered memory.[14] Jenkins sees this recovered memory backlash as a turning away from willingness to take child abuse within the family seriously, leaving an opening for a return to the focus on strangers as predators.[15]

The Bogeyman Takes Over

While satanic abuse hysteria dominated the 1980s and early 1990s, the "sexual predator" eventually became the focus of the containment era. The paradigmatic "sexual predator" is a sexual murderer of a child, much like the sexual psychopaths and fiends of the 1930s and 1940s. Multiple nationally publicized cases have dominated the airwaves, including the murder of Megan Kanka in New Jersey (which led to the community notification laws described later in this chapter).[16] Contrasting two works of fiction that are emblematic of their eras shows that this undifferentiated image of the sex offender as bogeyman has taken over: There is far less contradiction and uncertainty in the containment era. In the 1950s and 1960s there was interest in understanding what was normal as well as what was horrible about child molesters, as evident in *The Mark* as described in chapter 3. By 2004 the goal was to gain insight into a monster so that it could be contained.

The Woodsman

Four decades after Israel wrote the screenplay for *The Mark*, in 2000, the playwright Steven Fechter wrote another account of a released sex offender attempting to make it on the outside.[17] *The Woodsman* takes a very different tone. Rather than granting the possibility of normalcy and therapeutic rehabilitation, this film is about an essentially bad guy and the temptations he faces.

In the film adaptation, released in 2004, Walter, played by Kevin Bacon, spent twelve years in prison for molesting young girls. On conditional release, Walter rents an apartment and takes a job with a boss who knows about his record—all echoes of Jim in *The Mark*. Sergeant Lucas (played by Mos Def) lets Walter know that he is being watched and goes further than the police in *The Mark*, who only contacted Jim in connection with an unsolved crime. While in *The Mark* this was presented as police harassment, in *The Woodsman* it is presented as productive. It serves notice to Walter that he can be returned to prison at any time, a surveillance-as-deterrent belief that is typical of containment.[18]

As in *The Mark*, Walter is shown to be struggling, but his struggles are against deep urges that suggest he is specifically sexually attracted to girls. The two turning points in the film are ones in which Walter realizes the evil of his past conduct and shows some empathy for victims. First, while watching schoolgirls from his window, he sees a suspicious man trying to lure little boys. This observation of another makes his own fault clear. His subsequent conversation with Robin, a girl he encounters in the park, facilitates further realization. When Robin tells him that her father sexually abuses her, he feels both sympathy and empathy for her, finally recognizing molestation as harmful. This kind of realization is entirely absent from either the book or film version of *The Mark*, in which Jim's victim is never presented as a character. Thus, *The Woodsman* departs dramatically from *The Mark's* project of humanizing the offender. It dramatizes the belief that sex offenders cannot be cured of their obsessions but that they can learn to view women and girls without the distortions that obscure the harms of sexual assault.

Rather than a man who acted out in ways we can understand, Walter is a separate type. But, like *The Mark*, *The Woodsman* raised issues regarding the obstacles placed in front of sex offenders and attempted empathy for the sex offender protagonist, but not empathy borne of similarity. While Jim is a regular guy gone wrong, Walter is subject to compulsive urges and probably cannot be healed. *The Woodsman* ends with Walter assaulting the perpetrator he had seen picking up little boys, badly beating him and thus trying to "beat" the badness out of himself. The message is that the best we can hope for is that monsters will recognize themselves and will be recognized by others, another theme of the containment era.

The Mark and *The Woodsman* are outliers, but they are revealing breaks in the dominant discourse about pedophiles, as portrayed in popular fiction and film. Far more common are stories about staking the monster. Television crime dramas may give us some personal details about the monsters before they are staked, but they do little to humanize. In a few cases the audience may feel sorry for pathetic molesters that cannot succeed with women of their own ages, but viewers generally also accept the need to prevent further conduct that would stem inevitably from compulsions.

Thus, when the neighborhood executes the pervert, as in Hubert Selby's *Last Exit to Brooklyn* (a novel published in 1964 and adapted into a film in 1989), or the cops beat the molester into confession (as in countless crime dramas from *NYPD Blue* to *Law and Order*), it is the appropriate resolution to the conflict between good versus evil.

Sometimes these films do call forth some mixed feelings or moral ambiguities. Often these are addressed in the glimpses the audience gets into the making of the molesters. For example, in *Hard Candy*, a 2006 psychological drama, the child pornographer tells a story from his childhood about how his brain became wired to find children, pain, and sex aphrodisiacal. But the teen who is confronting him with his adult crimes finds this explanation laughable and in fact would find any explanation irrelevant. *Hard Candy* is the ultimate revenge drama and highlights how satisfying we find punishment.[19] During one of the climaxes of the film, the heroine appears to castrate the offender. As the avenger, she claims to be acting on behalf of victims—"I am every little girl you ever watched, touched, screwed, killed"—and there is something universally appealing to her retribution. Overall, the audience sides with her and takes pleasure in her power. These kinds of punishment stories are simplistic but satisfying.

Expanding the Toolkit: What to Do with Sex Offenders
Public Panic, Penal Enthusiasm, and Expressions of Disgust

At least two features of the sensationalized public and expert response to child murders in the sexual psychopath era rule out moral panic as exclusive explanation, and the same is true of the containment era. The murder of Polly Klaas, discussed at length in chapter 6, clearly helped galvanize media attention and probably accelerated the rise of a variety of sex offense laws on the legislative agenda. But we should look to other explanations of the particular salience of new laws beyond that of public panic.

Examining the way in which sex crime seemed to be the "issue of the year" for legislators throughout the 1990s, Mona Lynch identifies expressions of disgust, fear of contagion, and pollution avoidance in federal legislative rhetoric about sex offenders.[20] Lynch studies the legislative fervor over sex offenders, focusing especially on the Omnibus Crime Bill of 1994. Enhancing Freedman's and Jenkins's historical studies, Lynch finds that policy making for sex offenders continues to serve a Durkheimian function. She argues that laws about sex offenders play a role in constructing and preserving boundaries between the pure and the dangerous, and reflect on socio-cultural anxieties and discomforts surrounding sexuality, family, and gender roles: "The sex offender is essentially supernaturally dangerous and contaminating to the idealized social body."[21] This construction of the sex offender as monstrous, mortally dangerous, and polluting supports an "anything goes" approach to the problem of sex crime. Many of the features of the responses are not new but rather show continuity with past eras. Their practically unanimous support and their widespread implementation are, however, remarkable.

Containment

The strategy that best exemplifies the contemporary focus is the containment model, a synthesis of "best practices" selected from a survey of parole and probation officers who manage sex offenders and promoted by the American Parole and Probation Association and the Center for Sex Offender Management. No state has fully implemented it, though most have adopted some of its principles, especially in sex offender treatment programs in state hospitals and prisons.[22]

The original containment model contained five, mutually reinforcing components:

1. A philosophy that values public safety, victim protection, and reparation for victims as the paramount objectives of sex offender management;
2. Implementation strategies that rely on agency coordination, multidisciplinary partnerships, and job specialization;
3. A containment approach that seeks to hold sex offenders accountable through the combined use of both the offenders' internal controls and external criminal justice measures, and the use of the polygraph to monitor internal controls and compliance with external controls;
4. Development and implementation of informed public policies to create and support consistent practices; and
5. Quality control mechanisms, including program monitoring and evaluation, that ensure prescribed policies and procedures are delivered as planned.[23]

The model succeeds most in assuring the public that safety and collaboration are top priorities. The third component is the most specific, requiring some form of risk assessment to track deviant interest and program compliance.

Though vague, the containment model succeeds in institutionalizing jurisdiction sharing between correctional officers and treatment practitioners and signals the quasi-professional status of sex offender treatment. Assumptions about therapy and about the behavior and character of sex offenders make it very difficult for treatment practitioners to be acknowledged as "professionals." The field of sex offender therapy lacks a licensing program, professional examinations, university-based professional education, or an ethics code—all traditional markers of professions.[24] General training for practitioners in social work and other psychiatric fields rarely focuses on sexual offending, leaving it instead to a paraprofession.[25] Though clinical assessments for accused sex offenders and for those facing civil commitment may be administered by psychologists or psychiatrists, treatment programs often employ lower-status personnel such as social workers, marriage and family therapists, and polygraph administrators.[26] But despite these complications, sex offender treatment is a growing field, in part because states that authorize the containment model and its variants also contract for assessment and treatment services. While professional status may be elusive, government funding is increasingly available.

"Containment" dominates the shape of sex offender treatment and correctional strategies nationwide. The elements of the model remain central. An emergent emphasis is the importance of sharing jurisdiction not only between corrections and treatment, but with victim advocacy groups as well.[27]

Other Containment Policies since the 1990s

In addition to the general management model mentioned above, in the 1990s sex offenders brought under criminal justice control became subject to a new breed of policies, as well as the augmentation of older policies. In this section I discuss laws passed nationwide in response to fears about sexual predators—in prior chapters I also offered California's law making as representative, but in the containment era there is even more uniformity across the country through the federalization of criminal law and policy. Though most of these laws originated in the states, eventually federal laws mandated compliance if states wanted to continue to receive federal money for criminal justice (for example, through Byrne grants). In contrast to the 1950s, when fears of sexual psychopaths led some states to invest in rehabilitative incapacitation and research, the majority of responses to sex offender laws in the containment era are similar across the country.

Castration and Execution

Incapacitation through castration and execution continues be part of symbolic law making in the containment era. Although California's civil commitment program was abolished in 1982 when the practice fell out of favor nationwide, a doctor who conducted research at Atascadero reported that 270 MDSOs still remained in 1984. The doctor, using a surprisingly colloquial designation that may have been his own, explains that the remaining offenders were "hard-core," defined as "repeat offenders or patients who had not achieved a recommendation for outpatient treatment after more than two-and-a-half years in the hospital."[28] Volunteers from the hard-core MDSOs were used as subjects for a double-blind evaluation of the effectiveness of chemical castration compared to saline injections. The study found a striking placebo effect, although the authors put it more gingerly: "Favorable results were obtained with either injected substance."[29] Reluctant to conclude that chemical castration does not work, the doctor interprets the findings as tainted by the subjects: "Almost all hard core incarcerated MDSO patients have as their primary concern release" from confinement. "There seems little doubt that our subjects generally self-reported what they felt were desirable responses."[30]

This lack of empirical support did not stop the castration experiment. California legislators passed a law in 1996 requiring chemical castration for certain sex offenders released on parole. Citing concerns about long-term effects on organ function, several sex offenders seeking release have since volunteered for and paid for their own *surgical* castration.[31] There are no national data on the number of chemical castrations or on the surgical castrations that take place under the threat of laws mandating the chemical form, but we can assume that, numerically, castration is probably not a wide-spread component of sex offender management.

To date, the death penalty remains constitutional only for murderers except in the military, which still includes rape as a capital offense. However since the mid-1990s a handful of states—Oklahoma, South Carolina, Montana, Louisiana, and Florida—have authorized death sentences for certain sex offenders, focusing especially on child molesters. The U.S. Supreme Court ruled in 1977 that the death penalty could not be used for rapists,[32] and in 2008 it overturned Louisiana's version of this new generation of death statutes for punishing sex crimes. State courts had upheld the child molester statutes on the grounds that children, unlike adult women, are special classes in need of protection,[33] but this argument ultimately failed.

Exceptional Policies

The Omnibus Crime Bill of 1994, already mentioned as a significant rhetorical event for politicians, included some dramatic departures from our centuries-old Anglo-Saxon principles of due process. The bill was a harbinger for the containment approach to sex offenders as a less-deserving class. In this instance, it expanded the tools for prosecutors in federal sex trials, allowing evidence of prior sex offenses by defendants, even if there was no conviction or even a charge related to the prior accusations. These so-called lustful disposition exceptions to the rules of evidence were subsequently enacted in several other states, but as yet remain in the minority.[34] Nonetheless, these evidentiary exceptions are similar to a variety of other legal changes made by state and federal legislatures and sanctioned by the courts that treat sex offenders as a group whose degraded status and assumed characteristics justify its designation as a different class. Propensity evidence is just one example of the perpetuation of the bogeyman fallacy, particularly the belief that sex offenders are uniquely likely to commit offenses out of a biologically based compulsion. In reality, decades of solid recidivism research proves that whatever causes sexual offending, re-offense rates are very low compared to every other kind of crime except for murder.[35] But my own experience testifying on this issue in a challenge to Louisiana's lustful disposition rule demonstrates disinterest in challenging this premise empirically,[36] and other examples show similar disinterest.

Expansion of Registerable Offenses

In California, some classes of sex offenders had been required to register with local law enforcement since 1947. But the new wave of policies in the containment era included a drastic expansion of qualifying offenses. By the end of the century, people with convictions for noncontact offenses such as indecent exposure and possession of child pornography were required to register for life as sex offenders.[37]

Across the country, states have varied widely in whom they require to register and for how long. Persons moving across state lines may find themselves becoming "sex offenders" when they move, as in the case of Ryan Johnson, whose story is featured in the last chapter of this book. In short, he was cited for public urination in Florida in the 1980s, and although Florida law has never required him to register, Arkansas authorities arrested him for failing to register when he moved there. To address these kinds of gaps and inconsistencies, a section of the Adam Walsh Child Protection and Safety Act (2006) created a national database, under the Sex Offender Registration and Notification Act (SORNA).[38] This federalization of sex crime law requires each state to update their registries with information on offenders extending back through crimes committed in the 1970s, and these registries must include juveniles as well.[39]

In addition to its other uses, registration continues to function as another layer of police and prosecutorial discretion. Failure to register is a felony,[40] giving police and correctional officers even more power over released offenders in the community. The nationalization of registration and notification through the Adam Walsh Act has added significant new burdens on sex offenders in terms of registration requirements, notification policies, and restrictions on travel. A proposed federal bill, the International Megan's Law, would require U.S. citizens to notify other countries of their sex offender status before traveling, likely leading to numerous rejected visas.[41]

Corrections officers themselves may have trouble keeping up with the latest requirements under the law, and they cannot be expected to accurately advise offenders about how to ensure strict compliance. In a recent case I witnessed personally, a sex offender on probation in New York who completed treatment, as well as bachelor's and master's degrees, lost his fully funded place in a doctoral program because of misunderstanding the registration requirements related to school attendance. He filed an amendment to his New York registration information, believing it would be entered in the national database and forwarded to all the right places. Instead, state law required him to register in person as well, and when his information was forwarded as expected, the result was an arrest and banishment from campus.[42]

While the national registry was intended to streamline requirements and increase compliance, its implementation thus far has proven opposite. Other problems with the complicated web of obligations under the Walsh Act also are related to new federal powers that invade state and tribal sovereignty. In practice, these registration laws have shown numerous unintended consequences for offenders as well as communities.[43]

After the widely publicized murder of seven-year-old Megan Kanka in 1994 by a convicted sex offender, Congress passed legislation that required states to release information concerning registered sex offenders.[44] The novelty was the authorized release of such information to the public, in order to allow communities to protect themselves by disallowing known offenders the opportunity to commit more sex crimes—the knowledge-is-power fallacy. Previously, registries were for law enforcement use only and functioned more often as a shortcut for selecting suspects for unsolved crimes.[45]

The classification and notification systems vary from state to state, and even from county to county.[46] Many departments originally established their registration systems in response to the 1994 Jacob Wetterling Crimes Against Children and Sexually Violent Offender Act,[47] and the federal law passed in 1996 that conditioned federal grants to police departments in compliance with Megan's Law. By the mid-1990s, most jurisdictions maintained a database of local offenders that members of the public could view by appointment and after promising not to share the information. By the early 2000s, most jurisdictions also posted names and other information on a public Web site. In California, more than 75,000 offenders are included in the online Megan's Law database.[48] With a population of about 28 million, 1 out of approximately every 375 adults in California is a registered sex offender, demonstrating the broad reach of the law. Notifications by real estate agents and schools also magnify our awareness of the sex offenders in our midst.

But despite the realities of sexual offending patterns and of the inclusion of broad categories of offenders in the registry, community notification laws are premised on sex offenders as strangers—they assume that with the proper information, parents can protect children from unknown predators. These laws have come under criticism for their infringement on civil liberties and have been included in the overall trend toward government delegating the responsibility for public safety.[49] While the Supreme Court invalidated some state laws during the initial period of experiment with community notification, by 2006 all fifty states had functioning notification laws that met constitutional approval; SORNA's requirements have been tested in the courts as well and remain largely in effect as passed.

The Gap between Intention and Impact

A rapidly expanding body of policy evaluation research shows that these new sex offender laws are not supported by evidence of impact on recidivism.[50] While it is generally difficult to prove such impacts because the real world of crime and punishment is not a sterile experimental lab, the available research disputes even a correlation between the laws and recidivism rates.

One of the more problematic attempts to contain sex offenders has been the use of banishment zones, created when local municipalities or states enact residency restrictions that prevent persons designated as sex offenders under state laws from living within a specified distance (often 1,500 feet) of places where we expect children to congregate, such as playgrounds and daycare centers.

Part of the problem with these restrictions is their application to a broad group of offenders who include many convicted of crimes unrelated to children or who are themselves children. For example, the federal Adam Walsh Act assigns people convicted of sex offenses to one of three tiers. Tier assignment determines inclusion in the community notification database and, by extension, the impact of residency restrictions on offenders. In the federal approach and in many states, the tier level is established by the offense; without consideration of the particular individual's risk of re-offense.[51] Thus if an individual with a long history of violent offenses pleads down to a minor sex offense, he will automatically be deemed "low to moderate risk." In contrast, an individual with no previous criminal justice contacts and no other warning signs in his background who pleads to a charge of unlawful sexual contact will automatically be in the higher-risk tier.

This approach to sex offender risk determination and registry placement, although statutorily mislabeled "risk-based" in many states, is actually conviction-based. Recent analysis of the impact of Adam Walsh Act shows that registrants are reclassified into higher-risk categories not supported by known risk factors.[52] This ignores a deep research base that provides the basis for individualized risk predictions.[53] Some states, such as New Jersey and Washington, do use risk assessment tools to classify sex offenders. In these states, experts use factors associated with future sexual offending to place individuals along a continuum of low to high risk of future dangerousness. These assessments inform placement into the sex offender registry, as well as treatment and supervision decisions for the offender when released in the community. They create a smaller, more targeted group of offenders whose housing would be restricted under residency laws. But unfortunately, this selection is not the norm.[54]

By early 2007, residency restrictions were either enacted or under consideration in dozens of states, and they had already come under harsh criticism. For example, the Minnesota Department of Corrections found that sex offenders tended to be more likely to move *out* of the range of surveillance due to restrictions (Iowa, Oklahoma, and Georgia, citing problems like those in Minnesota, are among the other states that may rescind their residency restrictions).[55] Local ordinances restricting sex offenders from coming within certain distances of parks and schools have suffered from constitutional flaws (e.g., *Doe v Lafayette*). But just two years after passage in California, the Department of Corrections and Rehabilitations itself pointed out the misallocation of resources and other unintended harms. Sex offenders released on parole cannot find their own housing because their families' homes are often within restricted areas, so the state is forced to place them "in motels or halfway-house settings where multiple sex offenders live" at a cost of almost $25 million annually.[56] In Florida, national attention has focused on sex offenders forced to live under a bridge because they cannot find legal housing. Approximately seventy men live there because the "bridge is one of the few places in the county outside the 2,500-foot (760-meter) limit, aside from wealthy areas where the offenders could not afford to live, and has been approved by state officials, [ACLU] attorneys for the men said."[57]

Numerous studies published since 2004 confirm the problems. Sex offenders forced out of urban neighborhoods may be less likely to find employment and may have to live farther from treatment centers and public transportation options.[58] Several recent studies have found that residence restrictions reduce affordable housing options so that offenders lived in unrestricted housing mainly in high poverty areas.[59] This concentrates offenders in areas that are already vulnerable to crime and other social problems, and therefore there is less surveillance and support for sex offenders.

Most important, research shows that the goal of these laws, reducing recidivism, is not achieved. Minnesota concluded that "over the last 16 years, not one sex offender released from a [Minnesota Correctional Facility] has been reincarcerated for a sex offense in which he made contact with a juvenile victim near a school, park, or daycare center close to his home."[60] Another study in Minnesota found that failure to register was unrelated to either sexual or general recidivism for sex offenders who were released from prison from 2000 to 2004.[61] Findings from an Iowa study based on data from three years after residency restriction implementation indicated that child molestation offenses did not decrease. The most productive criminologist in this area, Jill Levenson,[62] describes many other related findings that also question the efficacy of these laws.

Civil Commitment of Sexually Violent Predators

Although less uniformly popular, civil commitment for sex offenders has been reborn in many states. Washington enacted the first of the new post-prison civil commitment laws in 1990 after two sensational sex crimes; California followed in 1996 along with a handful of other states. By 2007, twenty states plus the federal government had enacted new civil commitment provisions for sex offenders—all of which followed the pattern approved by the state courts following Washington.[63]

These civil commitment laws allow the state to keep prisoners who have served their full sentences in protective custody for as long as they are deemed dangerous. While civil commitment during the rehabilitative era often functioned as diversion from prison, "sexually violent predator" laws, as they are known, indefinitely confine offenders in a treatment facility after they have served their prison sentence.[64] The U.S. Supreme Court ruled against challenges to these laws, upholding the Kansas statute in *Kansas v. Hendricks* (1997) and refusing later claims that civil commitment is inherently punitive in *Seling v. Young* (2001).

While there is some continuity with prior commitment enterprises, sexually violent predator commitment is different in two important ways. First, it is not a separate track for sex offenders but rather is a tool for extending the confinement of sex offenders who would otherwise be released from correctional control. It does not bring more offenders into the system but keeps offenders longer. Second, confinement as an SVP is much more uncertain than it was in the past. During the rehabilitative era it may have served the interest of some defendants to seek referral to civil commitment over traditional confinement because it resulted in a shorter confinement under more comfortable conditions than that experienced by child molesters and rapists sent to prison. But today, confinement as an SVP is usually truly indefinite—the *New York Times* reported in 2007 that of approximately 3,000 sex offenders civilly committed nationwide since 1990, only about 250 have been released, most for technicalities rather than for treatment completion.[65]

The *Los Angeles Times* series on the rehabilitative goals of California's approach to crime described in the last chapter uncritically reproduced the official rhetoric about the correctional and civil commitment systems, including the fiction that civil commitment as a sexual psychopath differed only slightly from imprisonment for a criminal sex conviction. This view suggested that placement is more or less capricious but that this is inconsequential because efforts in both systems are focused on individualized treatment.

Many readers at the time would have challenged this portrayal even then. Contemporaneous critics of civil commitment and of indeterminate sentencing (largely located in critical criminology) saw the overall medicalization of criminality as a veil for increasing social control over certain deviant behaviors and of certain offenders.[66] This critical view emphasized the inequality of outcome for different groups of offenders—critics of indeterminate sentences pointed out the systematically longer sentences served by black offenders, while critics of civil commitment declared that it led to the extensive confinement of nonviolent offenders and was used to express anxieties about particular kinds of threatening deviance.[67]

Annual admissions for civilly committed sex offenders reached their height during the years of rehabilitative optimism, which peaked for sex offenders in the 1960s. In the contemporary era, civil commitment peaked in 2000 at a rate of just 0.24 out of 100,000 persons. As figure 5.1 shows, using the California

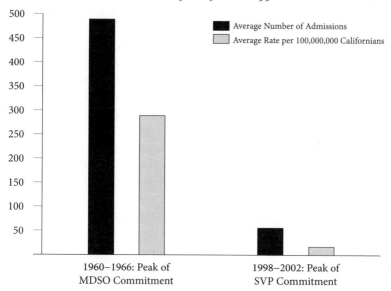

FIGURE 5.1. *California's Sex Offender Civil Commitment in Two Periods: 1960–1966 and 1998–2002*

Source: Commitment admissions for the period 1998-2009 derived from the data provided by the California Department of Mental Health, available online at http://www. dmh.ca.gov/Services_and_Programs/Forensic_Services/Sex_Offender_Commitment_ Program/Facts_&_Figures.asp Historical data compiled from Frisbie and the California Statistical abstract.

example (which maintains the largest SVP program), admissions are far fewer in number and in rate in the containment era—the average rate from 1960 to 1966 is seventeen times the average for 1998–2003. The scale of social control through civil commitment is insignificant when compared to the earlier era. Civil commitment in both eras has more ideological weight than practical impact—unless we include in that calculation the fiscal impact of SVP programs.

Civil commitment is an expensive endeavor. In 2007, California spent far more than any other state on its civil commitment program, budgeting more than $147 million, compared to about $40 million for Washington and about $5 million for Kansas (California's larger budget may be justified by its larger commitment population, but New Jersey, which has only 100 fewer committees, budgets only about $22 million per year).[68] California's total outlay includes the building of a new hospital at Coalinga, which is largely unstaffed and which resembles a shopping mall in some of its patient facilities. By 2010,

New York was spending $175,000 per inmate, and the national average was $96,000 a year. As the Associated Press described it, this average is "about double what it would cost to send [an inmate] to an Ivy League university. In some states, like Minnesota, sex offender treatment costs more than five times more than keeping offenders in prison. And those estimates do not include the considerable legal expenses necessary to commit someone."[69]

These costs are especially striking because, nationally, most offenders who complete treatment are not truly released. The great majority of the approximately two hundred offenders released from California's civil commitment program since 1996 were released on "technicalities," including findings of innocence. Public protests and continued supervision have resulted in no true successes—of the handful of men who have "graduated," one lived in a trailer on prison grounds, one moved out of state, and a third violated release conditions and was returned to Atascadero in 2006.[70]

However, there is some good news evident in the California program. Under contemporary law, the initial SVP referrals are standardized and the majority of cases are screened out. The initial referral net is very wide— all sex offenders released from prison who meet the law's conditions are automatically sent for a record review, and large numbers of offenders are screened out at each phase of the process. Since 1998, just over 2% of the initial referrals have been civilly committed. This is far lower than during the earlier phase of civil commitment, when between 50% and 63% of initial referrals were committed. The data also show most screening out by Department of Mental Health staff, showing some continuity with the previous era in the exercise of discretion by psych experts.[71]

This screening out is especially significant in terms of the continuing role of expert discretion, both from criminal justice and psych experts. In California, while judges tend to be wary about finding against SVP determinations, psychiatric evaluators apply the law's criteria with significantly more rigor. As of 2009, DMH record reviews rejected 68% of referrals and another 24% of the remaining pool through clinical evaluations. In contrast, prosecutors rejected only 12% of cases they received, and judges found only 13% of cases lacked probable cause for SVP status. This insulated discretion to differentiate has continued even after a 2007 revision to the law by popular ballot initiative, which expanded SVP eligibility to an even broader pool, including persons with just one victim. Thus, civil commitment provides a model of how public sentiment translated into broad laws can be mediated by experts whose decisions are not as strictly scrutinized as those made by those held more directly accountable by voters.

Experts and Governance

Shifting Politics and Disappearing Strategies

> The problem before us as psychiatrists interested in sex offenders
> as patients and as members of society is to clarify as best we can
> our concepts of sexual abnormality and the psychological deter-
> minants of antisocial behavior and to adjust our terminology to
> conform with the true state of our knowledge of personality pat-
> tern disorders. Most important of all, we must be constantly aware
> of our limitations as well as our potentialities as we endeavor to
> put our understanding and our techniques to the use of society
> by informing the lawmakers and carrying out their provision for
> psychiatric management of dangerous, antisocial offenders.
> —Bowman 1951, 181

In 1951, Dr. Karl Bowman, the psychiatric expert described at length
in the sexual psychopath chapter, knew he was swimming upstream. Simple
concepts from psychiatry and criminology had made their way into the public's toolkit, but nuance and complexity did not. While the attributes of the
public's image of the sex offender as bogeyman have not changed much over
time, the salience of that monster has dramatically increased for policy makers and has pushed aside competing images. Further, the assumptions associated most strongly with the bogeyman have provided a convenient rationale
for increased incarceration, and experts have failed to effectively contradict
those assumptions or provide reasons to differentiate among sexual offenders. In part, this is because experts themselves may believe the fallacies or
lack consensus; in other cases it is because they have no status or credibility.

The Sex Offender Knowledge Base

In a historical review of the relationship between psychiatry and the criminal law published in the *American Journal of Psychiatry* [*AJP*]) in 1965, Dr.

Seymour Halleck provided a timeline of the major events in the field he describes as "psychiatric criminology" (meant to distinguish theory and research-based interest in the criminal from "forensic psychiatry," which Halleck used to describe the psych experts within criminal justice and correctional systems).[1] Halleck's survey of the first hundred years of the *American Journal of Insanity* (which became *AJP*) finds a great deal of interest in the offender but also a rigid dichotomy between the mentally ill offender and the culpable criminal who was unworthy of medical attention.[2] The consequences of this dichotomy combined with the increased political vulnerability of the field have meant that little research on sexual offending has been conducted by the academy. A contemporary researcher concludes that "it may, by now, simply be impossible to do the type of research that will help solve important social problems dealing with sexual behavior."[3] Similarly, the *New York Times* opined in a title from a 2004 article, "Long After Kinsey, Only the Brave Study Sex."[4]

The State of the Art

As explained in chapters 3 and 4, even during an optimistic period for correctional rehabilitation, 1950 to 1980, institutional constraints prevented widespread therapeutic intervention for offenders in general and sex offenders in particular. But beyond the constraints particular to California, it appears that American academic psychiatry has had very limited interest in sexual offending. From 1950 to 1980, the *AJP* published only thirty-five articles relating to sexual offending in 360 issues.[5] Forensic psychiatrists focused on the classification of sex offenders rather than etiology or treatment and moved from the study of the offender to the study of victims by the end of the period. Only one article about treating offenders appeared in the *AJP* during this era (it was a review of the Atascadero program published in 1957); however, most of the articles about victims also include victim treatment. This foreshadows the dominant approach of the containment era: "Punish the offender and treat the victim." The empirical basis for claims during this period was largely record reviews and case studies, from either correctional or clinical samples (no random selection or controls). Recidivism research conducted by the Atascadero staff was published in professional rather than academic journals. This, along with the very managerial focus of the 1957 article, reflects the delegation of the sex offender from the psychiatric academics to the workhorses even at the height of rehabilitation. This conforms to Halleck's depiction of the rise and fall of forensic psychiatry in general.

As the California assembly concluded in 1950 (and as the 1975 *Feagley* opinion emphasized), not nearly enough was scientifically established to justify sex offender confinement for treatment: "The demand for treatment of these violators has been relatively sterile because there is no unanimity of thought within the professional groups normally engaged in the treatment of personal and social ills. Within the framework of existing knowledge there are many recommendations but few conclusive or verified assertions."[6] Sixty years later, there is little to suggest that this has changed.

Psychological experts in the area of sexual offending are aware of the status of their own knowledge, echoing Bowman in several ways. In the mid-1990s, as states and the federal government feverishly passed new sex offender laws, a federal clearinghouse for information, the Center for Sex Offender Management, solicited input for new sex offender management strategies. The experts who responded rated "knowledge development" as a high priority.[7] Jim Breiling, at the National Institutes of Mental Health, has referred repeatedly to sex offender knowledge as a "young science"; Robert Prentky, a contemporary psych expert on par with the Bowmans of the past, reviewed fifteen years of clinical literature on sexual offending and concluded that the field must import methods from more "mature" disciplines.[8]

Some experts believe that comparatively little grant money is available for this research in the containment era because society is still so uncomfortable with the topic.[9] But even though the research that does take place tends to depend on public funds, the research has not tracked legislative interest. Prentky's retrospective shows that research on recidivism, arguably the hottest topic in the public and political arena during this time, accounted for only 2.4% (n = 16) of published papers during the period he surveys.[10] Of the 177 recidivism studies used in an oft-cited 1998 meta-analysis, which is widely viewed as the best benchmark for understanding sex offender recidivism, more than 50% were unpublished, and the bulk of the remainder appeared in obscure and non-peer-reviewed journals; some dated back to 1943.[11] Prentky also found that most of the clinical literature in the field focused on case description or victim impact; the latter a topic that loomed large on the public agenda, which marks a significant departure from the decades prior to Prentky's review.[12]

The Kinsey research remains, to date, the largest and most detailed study of sexual behavior of a sample of the general population. While more recent research includes treatment efficacy as a variable, it also usually samples from people in treatment at a particular location (clinical samples) or from those arrested, convicted, or incarcerated for sex offenses (criminal justice or correctional samples). These provide useful information but are severely limited in their generalizability. As a result, what we know about who sexually offends, and what works to stop their future offending, is limited to the groups who have already entered either treatment or the justice system. Because the vast majority of sexual offending is not detected by either of these groups, we cannot make solid claims about what would work with most offenders.

In California, early use of sexual psychopath laws to civilly commit certain sexual offenders allowed clinical studies that showed small successes for treatment. A clinical sample at Norwalk State Hospital claimed a 2–4% recidivism rate for those who completed treatment, as contrasted with an 8–15% rate for those who failed treatment.[13] Later research at California's Atascadero State Hospital found similar results. But nationally, very few follow-up studies were conducted. More commonly, offenders undergoing treatment would have their prior records investigated for a retrospective measure. This is not a true measure of recidivism but was often conducted as a substitute (and continues to be today). For example, in Baltimore, Manfred Guttmacher found that a very small correctional sample of sex offenders referred for therapy between 1939 and 1949 had a recidivism rate of 5%.[14]

Research began to increase in the 1980s. In 1996, the United States General Accounting Office published an examination of the literature that found twenty-two published articles on the effectiveness of sexual offending treatment programs.[15] The review was inconclusive, because methodological limitations prevented any determinations of the impact of treatment on recidivism.

The subclass of cognitive behavioral treatment pioneered in California, relapse prevention, remains prevalent nationwide, despite a rigorous follow-up study released in 2005 that found no treatment effect.[16] A randomized clinical study of California's relapse prevention program compared the re-offense rates of offenders treated in an inpatient program with the rates of offenders in two untreated prison-control groups. No significant differences were found among the three groups in their rates of sexual or violent reoffending over an eight-year follow-up period.

Meta-analytic reviews of multiple sex offender treatment studies attempt to control for the various design and other methodological problems that have plagued evaluation research. In 2002, Dr. Karl Hanson examined forty-three studies on psychological sex offender treatment, finding an average sex offense recidivism rate of 12.3% for treatment groups and 16.8% for comparison groups.[17] Most recently, the Campbell Collaboration Group on Crime and Justice has begun a systematic review in this area. Their first publication included a meta-analysis, which found sixty-nine studies with adequate information for review, including both published and unpublished research in English, German, French, Dutch, or Swedish, and including a wide range of treatment interventions.[18] The meta-analysis found sexual recidivism of 11.1% for the treated group and 17.5% for the comparison group over an average follow-up period of five years. As the authors point out, this seems like a modest effect, but given the low base rate of sexual recidivism, treatment creates a reduction of nearly 37%. However, more research must be conducted to determine which treatments are most successful and to isolate how and why they succeed.

There is also a lagged effect in communicating state-of-the-art knowledge and practice to the practitioners who work with sex offenders. In the 1970s, the Quaker prison reformer Fay Honey Knopp became concerned by the lack of specialized treatment services available for sexual abusers. In 1976, her organization, the Safer Society Foundation, began tracking the development of specialized sex offender treatment programs. Safer Society has periodically conducted national surveys, which are the single best source of information about current practice in the United States. The interpretation of their 2002 results makes it clear that "what is common practice is not always best practice,"[19] in part because clinicians trained in the past will need time to incorporate new knowledge into what they do.

Thus, the knowledges and practices around sexual offending fail to fully reflect a vibrant body of research. The knowledge base is neither deep nor wide.[20] The medicalization of formal social control in the previous era might have provided the opportunity to remedy this, but rehabilitative experts yielded too much ground too soon and found themselves demonized. In place of medicalization, management seems to rule.

In 2003, the Annals of the New York Academy of Sciences devoted a special issue to sexual offending. Among the expected articles on etiology, treatment, and legal reform was an article that further demonstrates the unique position of psych experts in the containment era. Laurie O. Robinson, a U.S. Department of Justice official, wrote "Sex Offender Management: The Public Policy Challenges." It is essentially a plea for giving experts a place at the policy-making table.[21] Robinson describes the "knowledge gap" between experts and everyone else.[22] But, recalling Bowman, Robinson underplays the uncertainty among experts in favor of advocating for better "translation" of what experts already know: "The response by government officials is still too often driven by anecdote and rhetoric rather than by facts, research, and successful practice"—the monster obscures the ability to view some sex offenders as reformable deviants.

Challenging Psych Expertise

While psychiatrists might tell the public and policy makers that therapeutic interventions could be justified for the undifferentiated mass of "sex offenders," in practice, the offenders selected for treatment have always been a much smaller pool who fit the treatment being offered. Two contemporary examples also highlight the problems psychiatrists face in protecting the boundaries of their own jurisdiction—first, involving attempts to redefine mental disorders in the *DSM*, and, second, involving the prerogative to empirically test popular orthodoxies.

DSM Contestations

The *DSM* has moved from an internal document to one that is publicly scrutinized, especially as it changes definitions of disorders related to sexuality. Previous chapters described debates about whether homosexuality and rape were properly included in diagnostic criteria—a 1995 outcry shows the increasing accountability of psychiatry to nonexperts. Revisions to *DSM-IV* attempted to correct a general problem that members of the American Psychological Association had identified with the prior version. *DSM-IV* applied a new way of describing mental disorders to almost all of its diagnostic criteria—the finding of "clinical significance."[23] This phrasing was intended to help clinicians distinguish between what society or others might perceive as deviance or disorder, but which did not disrupt or disturb the subject.

The uniformly applied "clinical significance" language meant that the definition of paraphilia in *DSM-IV* included the phrase "the fantasies, sexual urges, or behaviors cause clinically significant distress or impairment in social, occupational, or other important areas of functioning."[24] This definitional change was perceived by the public as "normalizing pedophilia" because it appeared to exclude child molesters, for example, who suffered no distress or regret.[25]

The significance of all this is that psychiatry's internal attempts to resolve a definitional problem left the discipline open to policy criticism. One review of the misunderstanding stated, "Admittedly, it is difficult to know how to draw a boundary between variations in normative sexual fantasies and behavior and clearly pathological sexual behavior."[26] But the reaction to this boundary drawing suggested that psych experts had better choose a very inclusive boundary in the future.

The APA is taking a very long time to implement revisions in *DSM-V*, which is scheduled for final release in 2012, but the proposed revisions reflect the influence of both of these past controversies. The proposed revision to the paraphilia criteria is a carefully calculated move, which acknowledges that the psychiatric field does not exist in a vacuum but shapes and is shaped by legal and social norms and uses. Part of the revision restates the claim made by experts in the sexual psychopath era regarding the separation of diagnostic terms and popular understandings. Just as many disputed the relevance of the "sexual psychopath" and its ilk as a term of art, the current revision attempts to take back "paraphilia":

> The Paraphilias Subworkgroup is proposing two broad changes that affect all or several of the paraphilia diagnoses, in addition to various amendments to specific diagnoses. The first broad change follows from our consensus that paraphilias are not ipso facto psychiatric disorders. We are proposing that the DSM-V make a distinction between paraphilias and paraphilic disorders. A paraphilia by itself would not automatically justify or require psychiatric intervention. A paraphilic disorder is a paraphilia that causes distress or impairment to the individual or harm to others. . . . This approach leaves intact the distinction between normative and non-normative sexual behavior, which could be important to researchers, but without automatically labeling non-normative sexual behavior as psychopathological.[27]

This distinction is a sensible one and seems to strike against the subjection of psychiatric tools to legal and social requirements. The language that specifies "harm to others" is an important addition, and it may protect the profession from new accusations of "normalizing" pedophilia. But this remains to be seen.

In addition, the new *DSM* will specify a new disorder, explained as a response to the overuse of the previously vague criteria: "There has been an unfortunate tendency to over-diagnose Paraphilic Coercive Disorder (usually under Paraphilia NOS) simply on the basis of repeated coercive sexual behavior. Care must be taken, in using patterns of behavior, that these are truly indicative of sexual coercion being a source of arousal. . . . The diagnostic criteria proposed here make this clearer and should lead to less frequent but more appropriate diagnosis."[28] This is another sensible move, especially as it relates to the arousal-action nexus, a prominent feature of current sex offender practitioners' discourse and practice (see later in this chapter). Most important, it is a clear attempt to wrest control over legal uses of psychiatric terms back from the workhorses—the section cites a 2008 article that describes how civil commitment proceedings utilize *DSM* diagnoses. The committee knows how *DSM* terms are used in practice and is attempting to control that usage more directly. Finally, it maintains the distinction between rape in the legal definition and the smaller subcategory of rapists that are sexually motivated.

"Harm" Orthodoxies and the Limits of a Discipline

The 1995 semantics debate about *DSM* terms was only a precursor to the controversy surrounding an article published a few years later in a journal of the American Psychological Association, and that reaction showed that psychology as a discipline was also extremely sensitive to external critique. The 1998 article in the *Psychological Bulletin* argued: "Many lay persons and professionals believe that child sexual abuse (CSA) causes intense harm, regardless of gender, pervasively in the general population. . . . Self-reported reactions to and effects from CSA indicated that negative effects were neither pervasive nor typically intense, and that men reacted much less negatively than women. The college data were completely consistent with data from national samples. Basic beliefs about CSA in the general population were not supported."[29]

Condemnation came from all over, including from the U.S. House of Representatives where one congressman called the study "the emancipation proclamation of pedophiles"; the talk show pundit Dr. Laura Schlessinger said, "The point of the article is to allow men to rape male children."[30] The APA moved to distance itself from the authors, as did the authors' institutions. Despite the fact that the article's methodology had survived peer review, the APA invited the American Association for the Advancement of Science (AAAS) to conduct an additional review in order to appease Congress and the public—but the AAAS, perhaps more secure in its status, refused and rebuked the APA for its capitulations.[31]

These controversies reveal the near-holy status of popular beliefs about sexual offending and about the tenuous position of psych experts. Experts have become politically suspect—internal decisions are now subject to public scrutiny, especially for their policy implications. This collapses the separate endeavors of scientific inquiry with normative, social policy making. While there may be room to criticize psych experts for failing to take up the challenge of research and experimentation surrounding sexual offending in the past, in the containment era it is clear that certain orthodoxies are largely off-limits to empirical testing.

Debates about the etiology of sexual offending deserve their own book. As I have shown in various chapters, the public's tolerance for psychiatric explanations of sexual violence has waned, in part because of the tendency to view sickness as an excuse. This concept of what it means to be "sick" and whether this excludes any personal responsibility is tied to larger social debates about the role of psychiatry in criminal law. The advances and retreats in the psychiatric construction of paraphilia are examples of this. But these changes also reflect a wider conflict in contemporary ideas about rational choice, social structure, and personal psychology as related to criminal conduct. The present gestalt reflects the paradoxical notion that sex offenders are mentally abnormal, having an uncontrollable urge to offend, but that they also should be held accountable as if they had freely chosen to commit their crimes.

Knowledge and Practice

Dangerous deviants seldom may make themselves as obvious as the offenders in De River's psychoanalytic study of the sexual criminal.[32] De River's construction of the extreme deviant was somewhat unique—most psych experts offered more nuanced accounts. But because officials like police and prosecutors, as well as policy makers, are pressured by the public to do something about sex crimes, there is something very appealing about finding a visible marker of deviance that would allow targeted intervention. Thus, while the academic Dr. Nathan Sidley, quoted in chapter 3, could declare, "If it is impossible to predict reliably, we psychiatrists shouldn't try," the reality was that practitioners like his respondent, Dr. Manus, were "frequently called upon to render opinions as to the 'dangerousness' of sex offenders."[33] In the face of the criminal justice system's insistence that psych expertise provide some basis for distinguishing among dangerous sex offenders, a body of clinical and professional literature has developed, which largely supports popular assumptions about sex offenders.

Policy in the containment era reflects the legacy of several related ways of thinking about sexual offending, which have characterized popular discourse since the 1930s: an individual's identifiable sexual deviance, separate from any conduct, as itself signaling danger; the certainty of sex offense escalation; the inability of the sex deviant to control impulses; high recidivism rates; and sexual deviance as being resistant to therapeutic intervention.

The assumption that sex crime is caused by pathology, whether willfully chosen and indulged or compelled, is in marked contrast with the framing of other crime problems—we generally do not think robbery is caused by a mental abnormality and it certainly doesn't have its own *DSM* designation. This constellation of assumptions, believed by the public and largely unchallenged publicly by psych experts, combined with the "nothing works" frame, which is nearly universally applied to criminality, results in an "anything goes, nothing works" system of sex offender "management," which creates power without accountability.

The connection between arousal and action is assumed for sex offenders, even when experimental research suggests otherwise.[34] This connection is described in the sex offender treatment literature as the "sexual preference hypothesis."[35] The research record by the mid-1980s already contradicted this belief (or at best was inconclusive).[36] But sex offender treatment practitioners have been so invested in modifying arousal and developing impulse management therapy that they strain interpretations of the data to support the continued use of the arousal-action nexus, largely because of its "commonsense" appeal.[37] The measurement of deviant arousal features prominently in almost every risk assessment and in several actuarial instruments, as well as in correctional evaluations of compliance with release conditions. After describing the contemporary field of sex offender practitioners, I will deconstruct the use of one such measurement tool.

Uneasy Bedfellows:
Treatment Professionals and Correctional Officers

Over the twentieth century, academic psychiatry and psychology (hereinafter psych fields) have largely abandoned the criminal subject, leaving the work of correctional treatment to practitioners. This is not to say that the psych fields are no longer prominent in corrections; in fact, the opposite may be true. As American incarcerated populations expand, so do the treatment needs, both medical and psychological. But the connections between the psych fields and the correctional systems have moved from being scholarly to practice-based.

In the containment era, the demand for sex offender evaluators has created a separate "paraprofession" represented nationally by the Association for the Treatment of Sexual Abusers (ATSA) and described in the periodic survey of treatment providers conducted by the Safer Society Press.[38] Several states have active chapters of the ATSA, and California has an active group of its own: the California Coalition on Sexual Offending (CCOSO). Both the ATSA and CCOSO bring together correctional officers and treatment practitioners in need of continuing education credits or needing help with their sex offender caseloads. Most of the members of these paraprofessional groups have bachelor's or master's degrees; very few conduct research and even fewer have academic affiliations. The leading figures, the ones most often recruited to lead training sessions at the annual conferences, are the handful of clinical researchers working in private practice or with state corrections on risk assessment and, to a lesser extent, treatment issues. In an era in which treatment for criminal offenders is generally denigrated, sex offender treatment maintains a limited stronghold through its collaboration with and subjugation to corrections.

At this point, it would be easy to lambaste the treatment practitioners and leave it at that. But one of the most challenging aspects of the research that produced this work has been my exposure to the hard-working people who do the on-the-ground work of sex offender management (see appendix A). Despite the historical context and the larger political and professional factors that limit what we currently know about sex offenders and that constrain the translation of that knowledge at the policy and public levels, the people who work with sex offenders, in correctional and therapeutic capacities, do not deserve our criticism, they deserve our praise and support. The remainder of this chapter is informed by my participant observation in the world of sex offender management, carried out over several years, in two geographically distinct jurisdictions. This section therefore takes my analysis of discourse and policy and grounds it in my personal observations and the insights of the people who have spoken with me and shown me their work.[39]

Recall the "containment model" introduced in chapter 5: a strategy that exemplifies the practical management focus characteristic of the sex offender field. The rhetoric of the model is aimed at reassuring an anxious public, with vague assurances about safety and collaboration. The only clearly defined component is the third, which builds in surveillance methods such as polygraph monitoring to measure deviant interest and compliance with offense-avoidance plans. Because tests for compliance common in other corrections contexts such as urine tests for drug usage are not available, a tool like the polygraph is used by a trained or licensed specialist to measure whether offenders are complying. On the one hand, the containment model therefore signals the quasi-professional status of sex offender assessment and its necessary specialization. But it also highlights the treatment field's subservience to assessment.

The structure of criminal justice, as well as popular support, has shifted away from prioritizing subjective judgments in punishment practice.[40] Instead, we want something concrete, something measurable, something that we can call objective, to justify the sorting of sex offenders and to account for the progress of rehabilitation. We no longer want to measure bumps on heads, but we want an equivalent. Two measurement tools, the polygraph and the PRV-3, can be used by decision makers to sort sex offenders into risk categories and to account for treatment compliance, analogous to drug testing. For example, a probation department must decide how many of their sex offenders will get GPS monitoring versus the cheaper, more traditional methods—or which offenders get to be on the special sex offender caseload of fifteen, and which can be managed by an officer overseeing one hundred offenders. For certain cases, they may contract for a deviance measurement, such as a polygraph or PRV-3, to justify their allocation of resources.

This is important because assessment accounts for the largest share of mental health resources for sex offenders. For example, South Carolina reports that 98% of sex offenders under community corrections receive assessments from their Department of Mental Health, but only 44% receive any treatment or therapy.[41] Assessment in this sense includes both the specialized arousal assessment described here as well as actuarial tools that can be administered by officers or the lowest levels of case worker—assessment has become the primary mode of mental health services for sex offenders.

Deviance Assessment Tools: The Polygraph and the PRV-3

Various sex offender polygraph tests may be used. The first is the simple, incident-specific test, such as, "Did you touch the child sexually?" This is the question that the polygraph is designed for—knowing whether a simple yes or no is truthful. The question is buried among other benign questions so that the body's response to the meaningful one can be compared to the others—the theory is that a person's anxiety or other emotion surrounding a lie will cause a measurable difference in bodily responses. For example, if you answer, "No, I have not been to the moon" *and* you say, "No, I have not touched the child," and the polygraph creates similar readings for both of your no answers, then you pass.

Single incident polygraphs may be given pretrial, but the more common sex offender polygraphs cover a suspect's lifetime sexual history as well as recent conduct, so they include incidents, thoughts, and feelings covering from anywhere from six months to fifty years or more. For these, the subject fills out an exhaustive questionnaire, and then the polygraphist follows up on the truthfulness of answers when the subject is hooked up to the machine. The subject is asked not just "did you . . . ?" but "have you ever . . . ?" This range of time and included conduct introduces great complexity—the framing of the numerous deviance questions and how they are ordered among the benign or control questions become a matter of art for the polygraph administrator.

The PRV-3 is a conceptually similar tool that was developed to substitute for the polygraph and the penile plethysmograph.[42] The PRV-3 is less intrusive, has withstood scrutiny under Daubert questioning so that (unlike the polygraph) it is credible in court, and standardizes some of the most open-ended aspects of other deviance assessments. Both the polygraph and the PRV-3 are used to get the offender to admit to his deviant desires, as well as his past conduct. As one assessor explains to test takers, "I've been doing work with sex offenders for more than twenty years, but I can't see what's rattling around in your head." The implication, of course, is that the machines can.

The PRV-3 test subject is told he will take a two-part test: subjective and objective. Crucially, before the test begins, test takers are told that their answers to the sexual history questions constitute the "subjective" part of the test—meaning they can control their answers, but that these answers will be tested against an unexplained "objective" measure, so they had better tell the truth. Beyond comparing their admitted sexual interests with what is measured unwittingly, test takers are also warned that their answers will be compared with the profile of a "refuter-deceiver"—another check on their honesty.

After a suspect answers sexual history questions (this takes from one to three hours), he spends about thirty minutes looking at slides on the computer and is asked to rank his sexual interest in each pictured subject. He looks at over one hundred images of various Caucasian and African American men, women, boys, and girls, as well as slides meant to illustrate a few other noncontact deviant behaviors, including exhibitionism and transvestism, and some slides that picture sadomasochism and frottage. For each slide, he ranks the image from 1 to 7; 1 translates roughly as whether he would "try to kill the subject for coming on to them," 5 is accept the advances in a lukewarm way (e.g., "not kick them out of bed") to 7, "do whatever they can to hit that." This is not my language and it is not formally what the PRV-3 "script" calls for, but it is more or less what an assessor I observed said in order to explain the task to the test taker. Putting the ranking into colloquial language is perceived as key to getting good responses. Further, offenders are encouraged to believe that the computer is objectively measuring their deviance by how they are told to sit and where they are told to put their hand.

Since the PRV-3's creators believe the test's reliability could be deeply affected by the context of the test, assessors are trained to administer it in a private, darkened room, without the assessor present except to advance the test and to orient the test taker.[43] Surprisingly, while there is standardized language about how to conduct the test, the individual assessor is on his or her own in terms of explaining the relationship between the three aspects of the test.[44] This is potentially very troublesome, as a particular assessor observed uses this freedom to provide several examples to direct subjects toward the kinds of answers he feels will provide the most accurate data, including the colloquial language aimed to reduce the cold, clinical nature of the tool's official directions, as well as hypothetical situations such as public masturbation, which are intended to illustrate the definitions of "deviance" and "sexual interest."

Perhaps more troublesome is the implication built into the PRV-3 that if test takers are not honest in how they answer the self-reporting questions, the "objective" component and the refuter comparison will "discover" an inconsistency and show that they are lying.[45] Thus the actual workings of the test and its measurement of sexual interest may be far less important than the threat of being revealed as a liar. For subjects who are under the watchful eye of a probation officer, any indication of deceit could be grounds for violation of probation and a return to prison or, at best, a poisoning of the client-officer relationship. This creates a strong incentive to answer "correctly" on both the questionnaire and in the portion that uses visual stimuli. As a result, the PRV-3 proprietors indicate that their questionnaire produces more and better information about sexual conduct and interests than clinical interviews or other assessments.

Thus it turns out that in practice, the self-report may be the more meaningful measure, for which the visual stimuli and refuter comparison serve as triangulation as well as coercion. This is also characteristic of the sex offender polygraph and is likely common to assessments in other quasi-therapeutic and correctional contexts as well, in which consent and freely given information are compromised by the power imbalance and the high stakes for the person being assessed.

There is much to say about the unclear empirical support for these tests, but this is less interesting than how the tests are used.[46] The key to the meaning these deviance measures produce is distinct from the technical aspects of the way they acquire raw data. Rather, what is important is what comes before and after: The framing of the test so it creates true knowledge and the assessor's choices in interpreting the raw data and declaring deviance or normality, deceit or truth. But once the data are produced, they still require interpretation.

The PRV-3 proprietors go to great lengths to ensure uniformity in how the test is administered and in how the report they send to assessors is used in creating an individualized report. In particular, the example of how to prepare a summary evaluation, based on the test administrator's own use of the tool, showed the best possible use of the tool and its framing. The language was careful and limited, and the tool was just one source of information, along with a lengthy in-person clinical interview, multiple legal documents, and multiple other psychometric assessments. An assessor I observed showed me samples of the summary evaluations he provides, and they also reflected this level of care and context.

But the kinds of data the PRV-3 provide make this clinical interpretation especially open to abuse. While some of the questions on the self-report and some of the images elicit responses that are clearly problematic, others must be carefully interpreted in light of the particular individual. Specifically, whether someone has frequent fantasies about sex with strangers may impact his social desirability score but should not be used as indicative of significant deviance on its own—this is likely a common fantasy in the general population, as is the use of pornography. An assessor should only use that kind of response to draw conclusions about risk or treatment need if the individual has a history of stranger rape. This is just one example of many. In terms of individual assessment, the clinician must be careful to frame a subject's visual interest in teens or preteens with the subject's own age (e.g., there is much less reason to call an eighteen-year-old's sexual interest in a fourteen-year-old deviant, however illegal it may be, than a forty-year-old's interest).

The assessor mentioned above was very careful to put results in context, to the point of often receiving negative comments from the correctional supervisors who referred cases to him for assessment: They did not appreciate his tendency to say positive as well as negative things about each subject.[47] The most regular source of referrals for assessments comes from criminal justice agencies, which have an understandable preference for assessments that are not unduly helpful to defense attorneys. As therapists may charge $150 per assessment, on top of what the proprietors receive, the pressure to produce helpful reports based on the tool is therefore a combination of financial pressure as well as the kind of workgroup pressure well-documented elsewhere in the criminal justice system.[48] Over time, the assessor is likely to feel more allegiance to his colleagues in probation and parole than to an individual test taker who he may see only once. As in all cases of expert assessment or testimony, real-world pressures and relationships can potentially erode independent judgment and objectivity.

While these assessors are independent in the sense that they own their own businesses—named innocuously "Johnson Security" or "Neighborhood

Advisors"—and they may do other kinds of work, they earn a significant portion of their income from state contracts to assess sex offenders.[49] The assessors I have known demonstrate great integrity in resisting the pressure to tailor their reports to the preferences of the agency paying their bills. But they operate under only informal constraints (there are no national standards or required licenses for these assessors, no code of ethics to help them resist the pressures to conform and no university-based programs). The embeddedness of forensic evaluators within or adjacent to the state agencies they report to has merited attention from the National Academy of Sciences and hopefully will lead to more independent crime labs. Similarly, sex offender clinicians may own their own businesses but typically compete for contracts with state agencies and are thus tied to them for income (they may be thought of as hybrids, and thus as organizations that challenge traditional regulatory frameworks).

As a probation officer explains about the value of the deviance assessment, "we want to know if the guy is safe." The beauty of these tests is that it does not matter whether they function in the technical way they claim—whether the physiological measures provide an accurate means of distinguishing liars from truth-tellers or deviants from people with normal desires. Rather, the tests "work" because we believe they work, regardless of the numerical output. They work because offenders are fearful of being caught lying, so they will admit to problematic desires or deviant conduct before or after the test. They work because probation officers want proof that their offenders are not violating, and the test's output, interpreted by the assessor, gives that proof.

Perhaps unexpectedly, most often, both of these tests can "benefit"[50] probationers—the PRV-3 especially is sufficiently fine-tuned so that the raw data the tool can produce do not tend to show very many "deviants" among the standard pool of probationers I saw it used with; other studies, although limited, also confirm the PRV-3 as reliable in terms of sorting deviants in a limited way. This meant most of the probationers qualified for lessening of their restrictions or did not get priority for the scarce treatment spots—thus, a finding of no or limited deviance was very helpful to them.[51] Other offenders who have complied with treatment and changed their behaviors may also be able to "prove" this with a repeat polygraph or PRV-3.

Therefore, while there are gaps in the empirical testing and validation of those tools, these are irrelevant to their use. Because the tests require specialized access and skill—not just anyone can administer a polygraph or a PRV-3—the clinicians who use the tests operate under a cloud of mystery. Mystery provides cover for clinical expertise. Rather than a detached calculation of risk probability used to mete out the appropriate punishment for individuals, this is discretion under the guise of objectivity. The sex offender field has embraced the workhorse function debated in the prior era, with all the constraints and complications that go with it.

Much of the new legislation passed since the 1990s requires someone to make a clinical determination of the treatment amenability or future dangerousness of convicted offenders.[52] This demand has created a separate "quasi profession," a field organized through state and national voluntary associations that brings together correctional officers and treatment practitioners in need of continuing education credits or information about how to manage their sex offender caseloads. The workers that present sex offenders punishment, those Geoff Ward refers to as "task executors," have also shaped the task.[53] Specifically, they have shaped policy in many states, with the assistance of the national clearinghouse, the Center for Sex Offender Management (CSOM), itself a collaborative effort of the U.S. Department of Justice and the American Association of Probation and Parole.

The discretion is not unique to deviance measurements. Sex offender civil commitment legislation creates a wide net for the state to keep and control potential "predators." While there is limited variation in the legal proceedings for establishing and maintaining an offender in civil commitment, most of the actual variation occurs at the risk assessment stage, beyond the bounds of legislative or judicial frameworks. Though statutes prescribe certain elements that must be considered such as actuarial predictions in practice, the clinicians who make the recommendations often have complete leeway to include any and all information they deem relevant.

Though actuarial predictions proclaim objectivity, most risk assessments seem to be "adjusted actuarial," what the leading scholar on risk prediction calls the procedure of amending an actuarial score with clinical judgment.[54] For example, in Minnesota, the initial screening process is based upon the MnSOST, an instrument that rates an offender based on his or her history of sexual and nonsexual offenses, number of victims, presence of "paraphilias," chemical dependency, and victim characteristics.[55] But this limited set of factors is then expanded to include the clinician's assessment of the offender's mental state, the offender's own stated beliefs about his or her risk (both admission and resistance or denial seem to be read as indicating risk), treatment history, empathy for victims, and release plans.[56] Evaluators I interviewed in California revealed that almost all adjustments made to actuarial scores for SVPs are upward, thus screening in many additional offenders that the tool alone would have screened out. In New Jersey as well, psychologists and psychiatrists employed by the state blend actuarial tests with their own "clinical" assessments.[57] While actuarial instruments like the MnSOST or the more widely used RRASOR and STATIC-99 include factors proven to have some empirical correlation with sexual recidivism, many of the additional factors that clinicians consider have been proven irrelevant.[58]

Much of the broader contemporary approach to sex offender management rests on two assumptions: First, the best way to stop future offending is to focus on identified suspects or past offenders, and, second, deviant sexual interest predicts actual conduct. For example, most in the sex offender field are deeply entrenched in clinical perspectives, and therefore they primarily listen to what the already-identified child molesters say about their past conduct. Unfortunately, the best research on new sex offenses shows that this is mistaken—that only a very small fraction of known offenders go on to commit new sex offenses and that, in contrast, people with no sex offense history are far more likely to commit sex offenses.[59] Therefore, focusing on what the small group of known offenders can tell us about their pasts is not likely to reveal information that will help us identify the majority of future offenders. This may be the single largest problem in criminology more broadly but has been especially problematic for sexual offending given the low base rates as well as the lack of broad social surveys that ask representative samples about their sexual interests and criminal sexual conduct.

Further, other research into sexual interest, outside the sphere of the specialized world of sexual offending, demonstrates the inadequacy of present theorizing. Meredith Chivers, a clinical psychologist whose research is in some ways a continuation of Alfred Kinsey's open investigation of sexuality in all its permutations, has documented the untethered nature of arousal and prior conduct. She has published many articles related to sexual psychophysiology. In a 2007 article co-authored with two other scholars whose work is often more focused on sexual offending, Chivers compared the self-reported arousal and the plethysmographic arousal measurements of heterosexual and homosexual men and women to a variety of sexual activity. Specifically, the subjects viewed short film clips with a variety of human sexual partnerings (male-male, male-female, female-female, etc.), as well as clips depicting bonobo sexual activity. They found that heterosexual women's responses were correlated with depictions of sexual activity, and as such responded to women exercising and to bonobos having intercourse. They also found that men were more cued to gender in their responses. This study does not in itself undermine tools like the PRV-3, but it shows how we need to learn much more about how humans respond to visual sexual stimuli. If "normal" heterosexual women are turned on by bonobo pornography, then our assumptions about the meanings of men's reactions to pictures of various sexual stimuli are thrown into some doubt, along with the larger issue of what constitutes "deviant sexual interest."

Regardless, in terms of the current law, once you are categorized as a sex offender, it is a permanent master status, so a great deal rests on the measurement of deviance. It is the offender's one chance to challenge the determinism; it is the dynamic factor in an otherwise static equation. For decision makers, deviance measurement gives insight into the essentially different other, which we require in order to manage his risk. These decisions are not made about a small number of people, but rather take place for tens of thousands each year. Beneath the surface of the apparently fair and objective determinations of deviance and risk, subjectivity is not only possible but necessary. Perhaps more important, the apparent existence of a measure that reveals the deviant other allows us to continue believing the deviant is an "other," and not us. Even though the assessors themselves know better, do differentiate among offenders, and may actually view offenders more humanistically, the fact that they provide the assessment maintains the monster status quo.

Chilling Effects

From anti-crime petitions circulating in the pews to a direct appeal for "long and overdue changes in our judicial system," the family of Polly Klaas sounded a call for legislative action last night—and politicians were only too ready to heed it. In one of the most amazing political and media spectacles ever to mark a child's memorial service, Governor Wilson spent part of his time addressing mourners by calling for life imprisonment for rapists and child molesters. Senator Dianne Feinstein did her part by reiterating her position about putting more police on the street. . . . The fact that California's governor and senior senator traveled all the way to Petaluma to eulogize a 12-year-old girl that they had never met underscores not only the way the kidnapping and death of Polly Klaas touched a state and a nation but how the issue of crime will be a key factor in driving the political agenda for 1994.

—Lucas 1994

In contrast to the overlapping but often distinct fields that shaped ideas about sex offenders in the past, by the containment era the experts are rarely heard challenging the dominant monster construction. This is evident in the Polly Klaas case, which received a blitz of national attention from the media and from elected officials, and it in many ways paralleled Linda Joyce Glucoft's murder forty-five years prior in its policy impacts. In this chapter I examine such changes in policy since the grieving Glucoft parents were featured in national coverage and turned that kind of public attention into a force for particular policies.

Polly Klaas's abduction from her Northern California home during a slumber party received widespread attention because of her parents' savvy use of the media and because Winona Ryder, a celebrity from the same town, offered a large reward for the capture of the kidnapper. More than 4,000 volunteers joined the search for Klaas, recalling the manhunt for the Glucoft murderer in 1949. A handprint left in the Klaas home eventually led to the arrest of Richard Allen Davis, who guided police to her body. After Davis was found to be a "career criminal" with prior convictions for sex offenses, Polly's case became emblematic of the need to get tough on recidivists and on sex offenders in particular.

If the McMartin case served as a platform for experts concerned about the recognition of child sex abuse, the Klaas case provided an unprecedented forum, as the opening quote demonstrates. Reactive statements and policies contain all of the basic themes associated with "calls to arms" against sexual predators that have characterized the years since Klaas's murder: failures of the "system," the need for increased policing, and the get-tough approach to known offenders.

In an op-ed in support of his proposal to impose life sentences on sex offenders, Governor Wilson reflects the bogeyman fallacy in all its features, echoing the purely incapacitative rhetoric of the early 1930s:

> Critics of our "one-strike" law, and the "three-strikes" law for career criminals I signed two weeks ago, say we can't afford to spend money for the high cost of keeping criminals locked up for life. I say we can't afford not to. After all, what price could we possibly put on preventing another woman from becoming a victim of rape?
>
> Rape is a heinous crime. Even when victims escape lasting physical trauma, the psychological scars can last a lifetime. Robbed of her most basic sense of security and privacy, a rape victim lives in fear, especially when her assailant is, as the law now stands, inevitably released from prison.[1]

While the problem of sex crime has long provided opportunities for politicians to demonstrate their commitment to community safety, Wilson, California's state and national legislators and President Clinton all used the Klaas murder and the specter of sexual assault to prove their zero tolerance for criminals.[2]

Political discussions of sexual predators commonly sanctify the victims, reflecting what Simon has described as the rise of the victim as the ideal subject of government.[3] When President Clinton signed the 1994 crime bill into law, he made repeated reference to Klaas, as well as to Judy Sposato and James Darby, two other victims of crime during 1994 whose cases received public attention. "Their deaths," Clinton said, "galvanized this nation and shamed our political system into action. It is in their memories that I dedi-

cate this bill. I hope this law will always be remembered in their names."[4]
This political rhetoric included gestures toward feminists and advocates for
women but was really built on fears of threatened children. Little changed on
the ground in terms of the enforcement of rape law, and much suggests that
social beliefs changed either. Commentator Maureen Dowd noted this in
1983, using a judge's minimization of a rape without mutilation as a sign that
"cultural prejudices linger." The selection of valorized victims signals this as
well: It may be easiest for society and politicians to rally around the cases
of murdered young girls, who everyone could respond to both because they
were inarguably "innocents" and because we are all deeply terrified of losing
our children.

But the persistent fixation on beautiful child victims not only makes sense
because of the "proximity" we feel toward those victims[5] but also because we
are conflicted about how to view sexual assault. Maureen Dowd may have
overreacted in her reading of the judge's statement described in the containment chapter: Rape without mutilation *is* less harmful than rape with mutilation, and judges are in the business of making punishments fit crimes in
terms of relative harm. But she was right to remind us that American culture has not really shifted significantly, despite promising signs in law and
politics. The roots of this reticence can be found in the institutionalization of
differentiation.

Addressing the Legacy of Underreacting

In chapter 3 I described cases that today would be portrayed as involving
monstrous offenders, but at the time the offenders were viewed as nuisances.
If prosecuted, these nuisance offenses were often settled by misdemeanor
pleas with probation or short jail sentences. Such outcomes held no shame
for prosecutors in 1947; instead, a case brought to that sort of quick conclusion was admired as speedy justice.[6]

For example, the Los Angeles district attorney, who pledged the "full
power of his office in stamping out sex crimes upon women" in a speech
to a ladies' club, was also lauded as bringing quick resolution to the case of
Henry Paulette, accused of coercing several young girls into his car.[7] Paulette's repeated crimes made him worthy of criminal justice attention, but he
was not depicted as a menacing serial predator who must be incapacitated.
Instead, the "full power" of the DA's office could justifiably result in probation.
As Paulette told the judge when he pled guilty, "Something came over me, I
don't know what it was . . . I didn't mean any harm to anyone."[8] Described

as prey to his own urges, this offender could be pitied and slapped on the wrist rather than severely sanctioned. As the next chapters will show, this is largely related to the criminal justice system's preference for noncarceral punishments for many offenders until the containment era. Sex offenders of this type were not unique enough to merit more than a standard sentence.

But often the criminal justice system never addressed these kinds of offenders; either they remained unreported or were diverted. A vast number of offenders were not criminal justice problems until at least the 1960s, when reporting laws and broadening notions of harm began to upgrade offenders from the nuisance category. Prior to this, families were more likely to deal themselves with the problems of the dirty old uncles who fondled the children or with the adolescents who engaged in sex play or even with offenders like Bernard Stringfellow (mentioned in chapter 1) and Paulette who molested children in public places. But these kinds of "internal" problems have come under the purview of the state over the last fifty years, and part of that process has included the criminalization of this kind of "nuisance" offending as both dangerous and harmful.

Victims and Governance: Shifting Politics and Disappearing Strategies

The McMartin preschool accusations described in chapter 4 became shorthand for responsiveness to victims, a constituency that has risen in importance since the 1980s.[9] For example, California Attorney General John Van De Kamp referred to McMartin repeatedly during his public appearances in 1984, despite having no role whatsoever in the case. Voter opinion polling had identified child abuse as a hot issue before the McMartin scandal broke[10]—so rather than driving public and political interest, McMartin may have simply provided a useful vehicle. It is interesting to see that reporting in 1984 explicitly tied the electoral race for district attorney with the prosecutions in the McMartin case and with public statements about child abuse. But early in the era, the orthodoxy had not yet taken hold. At a Los Angeles news conference to kick off National Victims' Rights Week, Van de Kamp said, "We need to look beyond burglaries and property crimes to the protection of our most precious resource—our children" and went on to voice support for sex crime legislation.[11] However, Van De Kamp supported an effort to convert Neighborhood Watch into a broader watchdog function that would include reporting child abuse within communities. As he explained to an audience of sheriffs,

Van de Kamp said that he was "shocked" on a recent visit to San Quentin state prison to learn of the high percentage of convicts who were abused or molested as children. By homing in on child abusers, the community can aid in getting the criminal off the street and in the long run may reduce the number of criminals, he said. "We need to make sure we are our brother's keeper . . . and our children's guardian—then we will be doing something important to prevent crime," Van de Kamp said.[12]

In a break from the new-law fallacy, Van De Kamp focuses on community crime prevention—he suggests that by catching child sexual abuse in our communities we can break "the cycle." This focus of political will is especially instructive because it demonstrates that despite the sensational fears of the early 1980s, the victim-or-offender fallacy had not taken over: Acceptable discourse could still deviate from the "aid the victims, punish the offenders" rhetoric, which later dominated.

Demonstrating responsiveness to an "increasing" sex crime problem has been a measure of good governing in each era I have discussed, and the sexual monster has been especially useful to prosecutors. In the sexual psychopath era, California Attorney General Howser referred to "nine murders of women by sex fiends in the last few weeks'" in Los Angeles alone as a preface to his call for increased use of registration laws.[13] During the era of rehabilitative debate, Los Angeles County District Attorney Evelle Younger called for the death penalty for rapists as part of his general plan to reduce crime.[14] In the containment era, the value of convicting an offender who represents this "increasing" problem cannot be overstated. The Web site of the Alameda County District Attorney, which is arguably its most important public "face," prominently features the Burton Abbott execution for the murder of Stephanie Bryan in 1955 as one of the key events in the history of the office.[15] This execution has had a shelf life of more than fifty years!

When the death penalty is not possible, prosecutors today have little to lose in advocating for prison as the one and only strategy for managing sex offenders. This is in part because victim advocacy organizations moved from the fringes to the mainstream in the decade just prior to the containment era. Since 1980, many victim advocates took up the zero-sum mantra—treat the victim, punish the offender.

Prosecutors get the best of all possible worlds in supporting this approach—they call for a strategy that is within their purview as justice officials (as treatment really is not) but which they lack the responsibility for overseeing in practice. As Frank Zimring and Gordon Hawkins noted in their 1992 report on prison policy, the U.S. approach to criminal justice means that prison input is locally determined, while prisons themselves are a state responsibility—prosecutors neither feel responsible for prison populations nor does their local electorate connect these decisions with the costs incurred by sending these prisoners to the State Department of Corrections.

The Victim or Offender Orthodoxy

While the images of victim family members have held saliency in public since at least the nineteenth century, victim advocates have not always been universally accepted. The McMartin case again serves as an important example. From 1976 to 1984, victim advocates went from the margins to the mainstream. Victims protesting sex offender punishment went from extreme to central, and during this time their efforts helped exclude rehabilitation from the prosecutors' repertoire.

For example, in 1976, feminists who protested the use of civil commitment in sexual assault cases are held at arm's length by both the judiciary and the media covering their efforts and certainly are not considered an asset by the prosecution. After deciding to civilly commit an offender, in part to ensure longer confinement that the criminal sentence could promise, the judge reacted angrily to the National Organization for Women (NOW) members in the audience whom he referred to as "a bunch of deceived women."[16]

Just two years later, the *Los Angeles Times* was reporting regularly on the efforts of Gloria Allred, the local NOW chapter president, to secure the prosecutions of child molesters. Allred's efforts met with limited success in terms of case outcomes—in declining prosecution in one such case, the deputy DA explains that the alleged offender had no priors and no other victims, seeming to frame him as a nuisance rather than a priority.[17] But Allred succeeded in bring the pressure of her organization into the public view and, with it, more public approval.

By 1982, the drumbeat for the war on molesters was now pounded by "housewives" and "angry grandmothers" as well as by feminists, creating more palatable allies for law enforcement.[18] Among several cases that highlighted disputes over the acceptability of civil commitment as a sentence, the case of a released MDSO who murdered Amy Sue Seitz had special impact.

Theodore Frank was a former monk who served short prison terms during his twenties and thirties for a series of child molestation convictions. In 1974 he was civilly committed to Atascadero as an MDSO. Four years later, he was released "as a model of what could be done with modern psychiatry."[19] A year after that, voluminous evidence tied him to the torture and murder of Amy Sue Seitz, a toddler killed six weeks after Frank's release from Atascadero. During his trial, Frank was described as an "articulate, intelligent man who had been studying for a degree in sociology at California State University Northridge when he was arrested. He wore three-piece suits, well-trimmed gray beard and looked 'just like one of us.'"[20] Anger over the actions of this "monster among us" led not only to a jury's death sentence but to the formation of one of the first sexual assault victim advocate organizations and a successful campaign to repeal the MDSO law.

The prosecutor in the case, Irving Prager, and the girl's grandmother, Patti Linebaugh, formed Society's League Against Molestation (SLAM), an advocacy organization designed to use the media to pressure the government to punish, not treat, sex offenders.[21] A 1982 article about Linebaugh presciently declared that "the impact of Patti Linebaugh's anger has spread so far, it could well curtail the treatment of child molesters throughout the country."[22] The target of the angry grandmother's ire, as explained by the article, is the lenient view that state courts across the country display toward child molesters, as embodied by the availability of civil commitment instead of long prison terms.[23] SLAM sought to remove the nuisance and reformable deviant ways of thinking about sexual offending from use by the criminal justice system. While it may have taken another decade for victim groups to become the dominant force behind laws such as three strikes, in the early 1980s they foretold these broader impacts by signing the death knell for sex offender rehabilitation during confinement.[24]

In addition to this practical impact, the alliance of victim and prosecutorial interests during this period created a marked rhetorical shift that has since been dominant. Prager, by then retired as a prosecutor, put it this way in a 1984 feature article:

> There is no psychiatric treatment that can cure the urge to molest children. The answer, he says, is to put the convicted child abuser, particularly the molester, behind bars . . . the foremost obligation of the criminal justice system is not to help the molester, but to protect the victims and potential victims. "Incarceration is not good for the child molester, but it is good for the kids they would have molested," Prager said. Prager and his SLAM associates want legislators to abandon the notion that child molesters are "sexual psychopaths."[25]

An important shift took place between the late 1970s and the early 1980s, which made Prager and his organization extremely popular. Others have described this as a coincidence of goals among conservative, family-oriented movements with victim and feminist advocates. But it is important to distinguish the synchronicity of concern about child molesters from any such similar agreement about violence against women. Instead, child victimization has remained the focus of policy change, without the kinds of structural changes implicated by feminist critiques. Such efforts to use child victimization laws as symbolic achievements that emphasize punishment continue today, as embodied by the work of an organization that can be viewed as a direct descendant of SLAM.

Since the mid-1990s, several states have debated closing what is called an "incest loophole"—a phrase popularized by Andrew Vachss, an attorney and child advocate.[26] The proposed California legislation to close such a loophole would remove the discretion to handle certain kinds of sexual abuse within families or with the oversight of the Department of Children's and Family Services. This legislation argued against the discretion to differentiate the true monster from those who might previously have been dismissed as nuisance offenders but who could also be viewed as amenable to treatment. Such differentiation was viewed as unacceptable leniency.

> The loophole legislation was drafted by a national organization, PRO-TECT: PROTECT is a national pro-child, anti-crime membership association. We are founded on the belief that our first and most sacred obligation as parents, citizens, and members of the human species is the protection of children from harm. We are committed to building a powerful, non-partisan force for the protection of children from abuse, exploitation and neglect. We believe that this must be done through a determined single-issue focus, a meaningful mainstream agenda and the use of proven modern political strategies.[27]

This organization appears to be the product of the merging of the NOW legal advocacy efforts with the political mobilization of the "angry grandmothers" who succeeded in abolishing California's MDSO law. Allred herself is one of their supporters, as well as many local prosecutors and state and local law enforcement.[28] PROTECT and Allred epitomize the kind of single-issue advocate that Zimring and colleagues view as having central significance in current California criminal justice politics.[29]

Opponents in California included public defenders and judges, who objected to the removal of rehabilitative options. For example, California Attorneys for Criminal Justice (CACJ) argued,

> Under these extremely limited circumstances, offenders can be placed in treatment and maintained on probation in the community. No legitimate arguments exist to deprive trial courts of the discretion to allow family members to be treated in the community. No rational justification exists for categorically insisting that all sex offenders be sentenced to prison. An overwhelming experience of courts, probation officers, prosecutors, and defense attorneys is that the vast majority of family molests lead to successful treatment and favorable community management.[30]

In New York, District Attorney Robert M. Morgenthau opposed the law, citing the lack of evidence that any loophole existed.[31] But Morgenthau failed, and the New York legislature passed PROTECT's revision. Critics are swimming upstream—instead, "categorically insisting that all sex offenders be sentenced to prison" is the general trend since 1980, regardless of rationality.

The campaign to close the incest loophole also demonstrates the pressures single-issue advocacy groups can place on prosecutors. PROTECT lists as one of its goals "Demand Accountability for Prosecutorial and Judicial Practices," explaining that "too often . . . prosecutors turn away from child abuse cases they see as challenging, time-consuming and low-profile . . . and judges become callous and cynical. As public servants and elected officials, prosecutors—and judges—have a duty to give crimes against our children their utmost priority, expertise and effort."[32] This is no doubt accurate—sex cases remain difficult to pursue through to sentencing. But the problem is probably not sentencing flexibility, as appealing as this is as a vehicle for symbolic recognition. Feminists and child advocates must continue to push for recognition through the law, given the historical record and the contemporary plateau regarding the system's response to rapists. Unfortunately, the advocates most often heard in public arenas are the ones who call for undifferentiated, punitive responses.

The Politics of Sex Offender Punishment

Contemporary policy reflects the monster image, so, to apply it to more typical situations, the familiar offender, like Uncle Al, must be re-viewed as a monster. This involves explaining that nonviolent child molestation is as harmful as physical violence—a broadening recognition of trauma experience that can occur without physical injury. Police and prosecutors would have dismissed Uncle Al as a nuisance and psych experts might have treated him as a patient, but now the zero-sum approach to crime and punishment means giving all criminals the maximum punishment in order to prove we are doing right by victims. We need to provide whatever treatment and rehabilitation resources we may have to the victims who deserve such treatment.

There are two possible explanations for the rise and entrenchment of the monstrous image of the sex offender within decisions made by police officers and prosecutors. It is possible that the influence of the public's undifferentiated view, as promoted by some victim advocates, has increased the severity of those decisions without changing any underlying theory of sex offenders held by police, lawyers, and judges. This would be an effect of the de-insulation of these decision makers. It is also possible that there has been a change in decision makers' theory of sexual offending—Uncle Al now appears to the beat cop to be a potential monster, and the prosecutor agrees. Without more insight into how arrest and charging decisions are made, as well as those involving acceptable pleas, we cannot say which hypothesis best explains the narrowing. The archival evidence suggests that it may be some of both.

The Durkheimian desire to draw boundaries and designate monsters turns out to be hard-wired. Research using brain scanning shows that the same areas of the brain that release endorphins in response to pleasurable stimuli are also active when viewing scenes of punishment.[33] Law enforcement leaders facilitate staking the monster as well. For example, in a recent Philadelphia case, the police released a description of a suspected child rapist. The suspect was immediately identified by the community and beaten severely, while police officers stood by. In response, two of the citizens were awarded bounties. The president of the local Fraternal Order of Police explained, "We put out a call to bring this savage beast off the street, and they stepped up."[34] The video of the "angry mob beating rapist" was posted by the local news station and widely distributed online. While popular discourse has always contained an element of righteous vengeance against monsters, the government sanctioning is remarkable. It is also a vivid illustration of the general trend in the containment era toward passing law enforcement responsibilities back to communities.

Given the synchronicity between law and order and advocacy interests, alternative viewpoints are difficult to promote. Those who challenge the orthodoxy do so at the risk of appearing to "oppose" efforts to take sex crime seriously—a problem that similarly plagues other criminal justice reform efforts, including scaling back the drug laws. But sex offender reforms are particularly sensitive; there is no comparable "face" to the victim of drug laws to complicate drug law reforms.[35]

Attending to the Orthodoxy

> It is safe to say that men and women who have experienced sexual abuse have every reason to be skeptical about the sincerity of those who are involved in the offender program. I value their queries and find their perspective helpful. It is easy to become so focused on the pain of the offender that you lose the perspective of those affected by the abuse. . . . Despite the healthy skepticism, I have been told by various men and women who are survivors of sexual abuse that it gives them a "sense of hope" that things can change, when they have an opportunity to interact either directly or indirectly with those who have offended.
>
> —Yantzi 1996

The sociologist Robert Merton describes the tendency for social stress to create deep divisions between groups, creating privileged "insiders" whose voices we are more likely to listen to, in contrast with those of the under-valued "outsiders."[36] This process is visible in the historical context of our approach to sexual violence, as described throughout this book. But this polarization is also a feature of the broader field of penology, the sociological study of punishment.

At scholarly conferences, in community debates, and in the media, the topics of criminal offending and the criminal justice response tend to force parties into association with one of two possible perspectives, which are viewed as conflicting and mutually exclusive. For example, when critically examining the practice of nursing in prison, Katherine Maeve and Michael Vaughn preface their work with the following statement: "It has been our experience that discussing health care for prisoners is sometimes reacted to in ways that suggest we are anti–prison staff and pro-prisoner, or somehow endorsing or excusing criminal behaviors. Please be assured, we are not."[37] This binary approach is part of a larger tendency that prioritizes crime victims as authorities on questions of crime and punishment.[38] Elected officials are especially vulnerable to being labeled as either tough on crime (pro-victim) or soft on crime (pro-offender). This forced opposition has had a chilling effect on policy innovation in the crime control field; it has also severely limited the development of a robust critical analysis of criminal justice policy, either in theory testing or theory generating.

My own experience in attending conferences and in teaching both undergraduate and graduate students has put the existence of this binary within the sexual violence field into dramatic relief. For example, at a 2004 meeting of the Law and Society Association, a panel exploring the Catholic sexual abuse scandal led to emotional and antagonistic statements from researchers who studied the experience of victims and those who studied the impact of punishment policies, including the accusation "you don't care about my perspective as a female victim." While comments may become heated and overly personal whenever academics disagree, this was unusual in its level of personalization, in particular in the use of personal experience as the ultimate trump card in a scholarly debate: No reasoned response could match the invocation of victim status. At the American Society of Criminology meetings, even the presentation of papers now seems to be divided along this binary, with those covering sexual violence issues informally divided into panels that focus on either the "offender" or "victim" to attract like-minded attenders. This division was further illuminated during an exchange at the 2009 meetings when someone from the audience chastised a "pro-offender" panelist for being cavalier in her tone about the work of victim advocates. In this case, the comment led to a fruitful acknowledgment of the tendency to fall into adversarial habits.

This gap is also evident in other discussions, both academic and informal. Debbie Nathan, the author of a book discrediting the satanic cult child sex panic in the 1990s, has said, "I have often had a sense of being intellectually and professionally marginalized, and I have experienced instances of editors killing pieces I've written about sexual hysteria because they got cold feet, as well as refusals to assign such stories."[39] When presented with evidence about the empirical basis of claims about sex offender recidivism—the gap between what we expect to be true (high recidivism rates) and what numerous research studies have shown (low rates compared to other offenders)—most individuals have trouble addressing that cognitive dissonance. But those who have had careers or vocations in victim advocacy or family services have an especially difficult time accepting that high recidivism numbers are not necessary in order to bolster recognition of the problems of victimization— that is, most prefer the compelling argument that there are numerous repeat offenders to control, rather than the reality that most offenders are not easily identified by their past crimes.

For example, in 1996, when Pete Wilson, the then governor of California, signed a law authorizing chemical castration as a condition of release for certain offenders, he declared, "More than half of all paroled sex offenders will commit a new sex crime offense or parole violation less than a year after being released from prison, and . . . three out of four will commit a new offense or parole violation within two years." Surprised by these assertions, the criminologist Franklin Zimring discovered that the Department of Corrections' data reflected a 17% one-year recidivism or parole violation rate—one-third of the "more than half" that Wilson had claimed (two years after release, the rate it reported was 26%, also one-third of Wilson's 75% rate).[40] As he explains,

> The problem is that only a minority of offenders re-offends, but the number of sex crimes committed by that minority might still be quite large. But locking people up because 30% of them will offend sounds bad. But if we lock them all up under those circumstances, most of the people we incapacitate won't really be threats. We might owe them decent food, housing and maybe an apology. That makes us uncomfortable. So why not instead convince ourselves they are all going to rape children if we don't lock them up? Once we assume that, then it's their fault! My hypothesis is that we deliberately overstate the proportion of sex offenders who will re-offend so that we feel more comfortable punishing them in advance. And that is a comfort we will not give up without a fight.[41]

Zimring posits that the discrepancy between Wilson's rhetoric and the reality failed to distress the public because we simply cannot accept the implications of that those low sex offender re-offense statistics. What Zimring fails to account for is this particular context of the urge to overstate: the desire to rectify for past disrecognition of sexual violence by systems and societies. This righteous desire to use the law symbolically takes precedence over what empirical evidence requires.

The debate in the psychology community around the measurable harm of child molestation discussed in the previous chapter is another indicator of this problem: Scholars and advocates who worked to overcome biases against victims were unable to accept that one of their supporting arguments may not be as solidly grounded in empirical research as they assumed. As Hollida Wakefield writes, people tend to equate the harmfulness of an act with its moral wrongfulness: "Even though Rind et al. explicitly differentiated between these concepts, people think of child molesters as monsters who violate society's moral, legal and ethical codes. How could such terrible behavior not also be damaging?"[42]

Laurie Robinson, cited earlier for her work on the sex offender knowledge and translation gap, also emphasized that experts must be careful about how they frame their work:

> Language, too, is important: In encouraging treatment for sex offenders, for example, it is helpful to clarify its use as a tool to help reduce future victimization, and not to describe it as a therapeutic service to be provided to offenders.
>
> . . . . Because of their powerful voice in helping shape crime policy in this country, victims should be drawn into both policy formulation and planning for programs and research. When planning was underway for the Justice Department's 1996 Summit, the strategic and moral importance of making the victim advocate community a key ally and focusing on the goal of reducing victimization became evident. Groups like the National Center for Victims of Crime and the National Organization for Victim Assistance should be partners in this work. Equally important, state and local crime victim advocate groups can play a vital role."[43]

Treatment should not be promoted for its value to offenders but only as it relates to victims. This becomes deeply problematic for experts in this area, as evaluation research on treatment efficacy in reducing recidivism does not present a strong case. While many of us support access to treatment as a feature of humane correctional regimes, this is not an appealing argument on its own. Sexual offending cannot be governed without directly engaging victim groups.

The unfortunate opposition of "offender" and "victim" has persisted in part because of the changing politics of criminal justice and in part because of the special history and politics of sex offender policy innovation and its responding scholarship. The offender or victim dichotomy is also related to the larger tendency to view criminal justice through one or the other of Herbert Packer's two models: crime control, which can crudely be viewed as anti-offender and pro-victim, and due process, which could be similarly viewed as anti-victim and pro-offender.[44]

In addition to the particular historical circumstances that led to the rising influence of single-issue advocates like those who support sex crime victims, the dominant themes of scholarship that documented and often criticized sex offender policy making have entrenched the "either pro-victim or pro-offender" perspective.

Part of feminists' second wave efforts to achieve justice for victims of sexual violence included making sure that violence was taken seriously by the justice system and by experts. For example, Susan Brownmiller was at her most polemical when criticizing how criminology addressed sexual offending, and the heart of her critique was the "sickness excuse" she felt the criminologists of the 1950s offered. She claimed that Manfred Guttmacher, Alfred Kinsey and his colleagues, and Karl Bowman and others who published fairly large and detailed clinical studies were all essentially apologists for sex offenders.[45] But this was at best a misunderstanding. In fact, Brownmiller's sharpest critique is actually a misquote. She claimed that Karpman had written that "rapists . . . were 'victims of a disease from which many of them suffer more than their victims.' "[46] Karpman wrote the bulk of those words, but, crucially, did not write them about "rapists"—rather, that quote came from his chapter about the clinical and legal category of sexual psychopaths, a motley assortment of people who were arrested on sex charges but diverted into civil commitment. Karpman and the other "apologists" who Brownmiller criticized all actually opposed the use of the term "sexual psychopath" for precisely the reason Brownmiller did as well—it was a "junk" category that mixed very different types of offenders.[47] But what matters is not the accuracy of her claims but that she made them and that they held sway. Experts became the enemy, and criminological and psychiatric ways of knowing sex offenders became untenable.

The most recent version of the *Diagnostic and Statistical Manual* shows that she eventually won this point: Its diagnoses exclude adult rape (unless it meets very unusual criteria). Therefore, rape is not a sign of mental illness from legal or psychiatric perspectives but is constructed as psychiatrically "normal," as Brownmiller and others demanded. At least these aspects of our policy express that we take sex crime seriously, because we include more offenders under the umbrella, and we do not let them off as "sick."

The stakes are so high in debates about sexual offending, and the people who choose to engage with these issues are often so grounded in their own perspectives that dialogue between the poles rarely takes place. Those who question the punitive response to sexual offending are often oblivious to the ongoing need to address sexual violence. But even criticism of the policies that comes from more sensitive scholars is usually read as anti-victim. Then and now, questioning current approaches appears to dishonor or devalue victims.

Privileging Certain Victims

There are additional ways in which the orthodoxy that now surrounds sexual assault victimhood is limited and limiting. Not only is the preferred public image of a victim a child, but there are expectations about what "real" victims believe, which harms they will have experienced, and how they will feel toward their assailants. Victim groups that oppose the dominant approaches are sidelined. For example, one of California's victims' rights groups responded to residency restrictions by illustrating the absurdity of pushing sex offenders out of areas where they could be supervised: They created a map that showed the scarcity of legally located places for sex offenders to live in after the restrictions. When the group raised this concern with the legislative authors of the proposition, the authors described the group, the California Coalition Against Sexual Assault (CalCASA), as "the enemy." A victim advocacy group that presented a reasoned critique of the popular punitiveness could be dismissed—indicating the shallowness of political attention to victim concerns. Further, individuals who express alternate experiences, either in their continued and complicated feelings toward their assailants, or in their desire for rehabilitation as well as just deserts, are vulnerable to harsh critique.[48]

In my undergraduate teaching, I typically assign Pamela Schultz's account of her interviews with child molesters.[49] My thoughtful, sophisticated students, who become expert at arguing both sides of criminal justice controversies, are almost uniform in their inability to find Schultz credible when she frames these stories with the desire for rehabilitation in addition to incapacitation. Her status as a survivor does not overcome the incredulity created by her unorthodox position. We are simply conditioned to believe you cannot get over victimization and that you will always want retribution and retribution alone.

The rise of this particular strain of victim political advocacy is crucial to understanding the changing politics of criminal justice. In this chapter I focused on the rise of single-issue victim organizations that push for policy change and often push for punitive responses. But there is another way in which victims play a determinant role.

Sex offender management now gives a privileged position to victims and their representatives in individual cases as well as in policy making. The containment model, which used to have three prongs, has been adapted to include a fourth: "a unique collaboration exists among the probation office, a sex offender treatment provider, and a victim advocate, with the advocate actually playing an integral role on the supervision team."[50] This role for victims is in some ways related to the version of "restorative justice" co-opted by many criminal justice agencies, one that incorporates the idea of accountability in the restorative justice model without much else.[51] There are other models, including community movements to take restorative justice approaches and apply them to sex crime and punishment. While Americans are less open to incorporating restorative justice for sex crimes,[52] some experts and advocates have successfully implemented such programs with little fanfare. For example, in Arizona, the Centers for Disease Control and Prevention funded a violence prevention program for perpetrators called RESTORE.[53] The program applies a conferencing circle approach that can empower victims yet also divert first-time sex offenders who meet certain criteria from traditional criminal justice penalties. Offenders sign a redress plan and agree to twelve months of follow-up. The RESTORE effort is the most systematically and rigorously designed and evaluated program to date, but there are numerous variations. For example, jurisdictions may also employ "circles of concern" in which sex offenders are supported in the community by "stakeholders" who may include victim advocates.[54] These programs are very rare, but when created with broad support and ongoing supervision from a variety of stakeholders that include victim advocacy groups and law enforcement and corrections, they may offer an alternative to the management model of sex offender policy that is now widely entrenched.

National Sex Offender
Punishment Trends since 1920

The factors identified in previous chapters have joined with mass incarceration since the 1980s to create a prison population increasingly composed of sex offenders—in part this is because most sorting of sex offenders now takes place *after* incarceration. Nationwide, the general patterns of incarceration show trends for rape versus child molestation similar to those in California. According to the best sources of data we have on victimization, rape reporting rates have declined nationwide since 1972. Similarly, the best data on sexual victimization of children, although much less complete, do not show an increase in reporting or prosecution of child sexual assault that would correlate with or explain the long trend upward for other sex incarcerations nationwide. Instead, the monstrous image and related fallacies, supported by changes in the politics of criminal justice, mean far more nonrape, "other" sex offenses are fueling long prison sentences. In this chapter I discuss the impact of sex offender discourse as well as practice in order to show why and how the discussions of previous chapters matter.

The Explosion of Sex Offender Incarceration

One of the central mysteries of sex offender punishment in the twentieth century is the relative stability of sex offender imprisonment during the public panic of the sexual psychopath era, followed by dramatic increases beginning in 1980. There is no way to show national trends extending throughout this long historical period, but figure 1.1, shown in the first pages of this book, makes the trend clear: Prison admissions for sex offenses remained low throughout the 1960s. Shorter-term trends in a selection of other states where data have been compiled complement this picture.

2007-02-28. doi:10.3886/ICPSR04572. Complete series is available at http://www.icpsr. umich.edu/cocoon/NACJD/SERIES/00070.xml

FIGURE 8.1. *Sex Offenders in State Prison, 1974–2004*

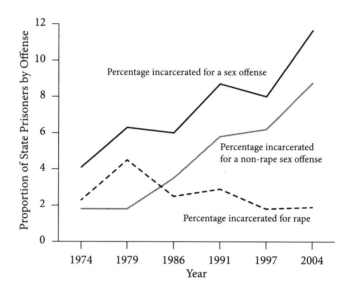

The trend line is interpolated from the available data points from the 1974, 1979, 1986, 1991, 1997, and 2004 surveys. Numbers used to calculate rates are the raw numbers, not the weighted estimates. Complete data are available from the author. Note that there is reason for increased oversampling of sex offenders, so this trend line through the raw data, not the weighted values, may overstate the proportion of certain offenders. But even if the percentage in 2004, for example, is inflated compared to real values, the difference between the rape and the "other" sex offense lines remains significant.

Source: U.S. Dept. of Justice, Bureau of Justice Statistics. "Survey of Inmates in State and Federal Correctional Facilities, 2004" [Computer file]. ICPSR04572-v1. Ann Arbor, MI: Inter-university Consortium for Political and Social Research [producer distributor],

The solid line in figure 8.1 represents the overall trend in sex offender incarceration, while the other lines portray rape and "other" sex offenses separately. Overall, the figure shows that growth through the 1970s and continuing through the twenty-first century is typical of the national trend as well as California's. Figures 1.1 and 8.1 show unprecedented and explosive growth of a magnitude that is almost entirely unrelated to crime rates or even to arrest rates (as the following series of figures in this chapter will show).

In addition to displaying the spectacular growth of sex offender incarceration beginning in the 1970s, these figures contrast with the impressive stability and even some decline during the preceding eras. The sexual psychopath era experienced at least as much public panic and governmental reaction as the containment era, and close readings of the FBI's Uniform Crime Reports (UCR) for this period show that there was a significant increase nationwide in reported rapes during the sexual psychopath era.[1] The criminologist Tamara Lave shows that between 1935 and 1955, rape received atypical notice by criminal justice agencies: During the same period, murder rates *decreased* nationwide by 22%, while reported rapes *increased* 83%. Yet incarceration rates for rape were stagnant. Similarly, the middle of the century was a time of widespread public support for rehabilitation in general and therapeutic confinement in particular. Nonetheless, neither public panic nor belief in the therapeutic possibilities of corrections led to the kind of prison expansion seen in the containment era. In order to understand these trends, the available data for the front end of the system can be examined. Unfortunately, these longitudinal statewide data are only available for reports and clearances for forcible rape, as the FBI does not ask states to provide reports and clearances for "other" sex offenses.

Rates and clearance rates for forcible rape in California peaked in 1980 and declined by 1999 to levels lower than the levels in 1970.[2] Other states, such as Washington, show similar patterns, which found a plateau in rape arrests from 1990 to 2004 and decreases in arrests for "other" sex offenses.[3] This trend is well known by scholars who study rape. It undermines the hypothesis that better reporting practices prompted by the feminist movement's attention to rape at the front end of the justice system explain the post-1980 increase. In fact, by the mid-1980s, the criminal justice system may have reached something of a stasis, having incarcerated much of the pool of previously unknown rapists that were convictable.

Comparable data for child molestation are not available, but recent work published by David Finkelhor shows that spikes in reporting cannot explain the "other" sex offense imprisonment boom either. Finkelhor and his colleagues measure a variety of kinds of harms to children, and found that "various forms of child maltreatment and child victimization declined as much as 40–70% from 1993 until 2004, including sexual abuse, physical abuse, sexual assault, homicide, aggravated assault, robbery, and larceny."[4] Finkelhor reports that available indicators show that sexual abuse of children climbed until 1990 (likely because of increased reporting and professional mobilization), when a decline began, which continues today. While Finkelhor posits a possible connection between increased imprisonment of sex offenders and reductions in reported sexual abuse of children, there is no evidence to sug-

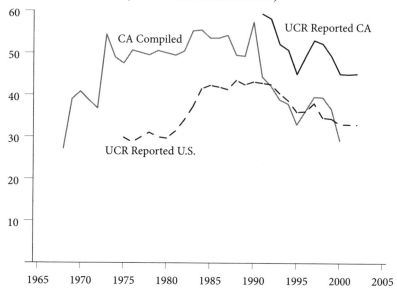

FIGURE 8.2. *California and U.S. "Other" Sex Arrest Rates*
(Felonies and Misdemeanors)

gest that increased criminal justice attention can account for the sustained increase in sex offenders in prison.

This picture of the front end of the criminal justice response to sex crime can be expanded by comparing California arrest rates for forcible rape, felony "other" sex offenses, and misdemeanor sex offenses. As discussed in chapter 3, misdemeanor arrests are more numerous than felony arrests. However, felony rape arrests outpace felony "other" sex offense arrests until the mid-1990s (when misdemeanor arrests begin to decline), suggesting that more offenses were being charged as felonies that might otherwise have been misdemeanors. But none of the trends in arrest rates correspond to the steady increase of sex offender incarceration after 1980.

Nationally, the UCR show a similar pattern for forcible rape arrests, but there are some differences for "other" sex offense rates. Rape arrests declined as expected because reports and clearances have also declined. Unfortunately, state and federal collection practices differ significantly for "other" sex offenses, making comparison more difficult. California reports distinguish misdemeanors from felony "other" sex offenses, while the UCR put them together into an "other" category. To allow a rough comparison, figure 8.2 combines the data from California into a combined felony-misdemeanor "other" category (while these UCR reports provide arrest data by state, the reports have only done so for non-index offenses since 1990; those data are included as well).

The trend in "other" sex offense rates shows a generally similar pattern of increase and decline in arrests, though California's increase begins earlier and both its increase and decline are steeper.[5] Despite the differences in the "other" sex category, known to be a catch-all category that is especially susceptible to changes in statutory definitions and charging decisions over time and across states, all California and national sex arrest rates eventually peak and decrease by the late 1980s.

Not all states show the same patterns of sex offender arrests. While I emphasize here the similarity between California's and the national patterns, this is not necessarily representative of the average trend across states because California accounts for a large share of the national criminal justice picture. Nonetheless, state trends do tend to show increases in "other" sex offense arrests over the 1990s. For example, Lloyd Klein conducted a time-series analysis of computed sex offender arrest rates from the UCR for state arrests from 1980 to 1997 as well as a selection of state arrests through 2003.[6] Klein finds that higher "other" sex offense arrests amid overall declining arrest rates is the typical pattern, but some states diverge from it. Specifically, Tennessee, Georgia, and New York exhibit an upward spike in sex offender arrests while Michigan, Minnesota, and Tennessee exhibit an upward spiral in forcible rape arrests only.[7] Klein emphasizes the importance of regionally and temporarily specific factors to explain this variation, including periods of intense media and political interest.

The key insight from these statistics is that, because the sex offender arrest rate decreases, the sustained incarceration boom cannot be attributed to increased law enforcement efforts on the front end, as one might have guessed based on the rape reform laws in the 1970s and 1980s and on the push to recognize and report child abuse (as scholars and advocates have claimed).[8]

The offense composition of the prison population illuminates the importance of nonrape sex offenses for most of these increases. The rate of both categories of sex offenders in California prisons increases when the determinate sentencing reform takes effect during the late 1970s. But while the rate of rapists in prison per 100,000 in the United States begins to increase in the mid-1970s, it levels off until a sharp increase in 2003. In contrast, "other" sex offenses continue to increase, skyrocketing up through 2006 (the last year

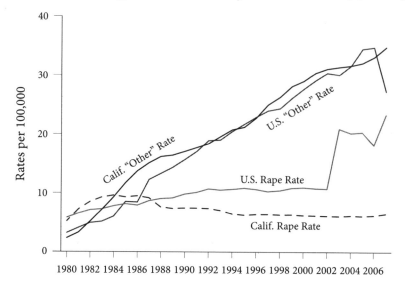

FIGURE 8.3. *Sex Offenders in Prison, California and U.S. Rates, 1980–2007*

with available data). Figure 8.3 focuses on the period since 1980, highlighting the similarity of California and national patterns.

Rape rates in California are also similar to the national pattern, though in 1987 the national rate increases slightly before leveling off, while the California rate decreases before leveling off. Most remarkably, the rate of "other" sex offenders in prison continues to increase through 2006, and in 2005 the U.S. rate[9] had passed California's, showing that other states were beginning to fuel the "other" sex incarceration boom as well.

Available state prison trends show a generally similar pattern, but with some variation according to state.[10] Even over the relatively short period that is easily available for comparison, modest increases are evident, such as in Illinois, which reported that the sex offender incarceration rose from 9% of the prison population in 1995 to almost 10% in 2005 and Georgia, which reported an increase from 12% in 1999 to 14% in 2008.[11] In Washington, the overall share of sex offenders in the prison population has decreased since determinate sentencing kicked in, but child sex offenders have become more numerous: increasing from only 28% of the sex offender in prison in 1998 to 73% by 2004.[12] South Carolina reported that of all sex offenders from 1996 to 2004 "criminal sexual conduct with a minor is the single most frequent type of sex crime for which individuals have been convicted."[13] Altogether, these trends establish that both in California and nationally, sex offender arrests are in decline, while sex offender prison populations tend to increase, driven by "other" sex offenses. Obviously, forces other than input from police officers, lawyers, and judges are at work.

Part of the explanation can be attributed to trends toward longer sentences for sex offenders (as for all prisoners). Time served for sex offenders first released from California prisons on parole demonstrates increases since 1980.[14] Sentences for both forcible rape and lewd and lascivious conduct with a child[15] show the effects of significant changes in statutory construction and legal interpretation over time, but the sentences for lewd conduct are especially variable because such a category can also include a variety of other offenses. Therefore, the variation in police and prosecutorial practices in charging "other" sex offenses (practices that we lack the ability to compare thoroughly over time), makes longitudinal comparison somewhat suspect but still highly suggestive. The sentences for both categories generally track each other, rising and falling similarly. The median time served for a child sex offender released in 1980 was thirty-three months, similar to thirty-seven months for rapists. By 2004, time served for released child sex offenders had nearly doubled at sixty-two months and time served for rapists had increased more modestly to fifty-three months. These sentence increases are not unique to California. Washington State reports that sex offenders average the longest time in prison, second only to murderers.[16] Thus, the effects of sex offenders on prison populations may have a very long lagged effect, showing more impact on the yearly total population of prisoners even as the number of new offenders admitted to the prison decreases.

Explaining the Sex Offender Punishment Boom

In the containment era, numerous ideas, strategies, and influences swirl around the subject of sexual offending. Decades of sustained public anxiety about sexual assault have left their mark, most notably in policy implementation driven by the concept of the predatory stranger sex offender, but also in acknowledgment of assault by familiars. Beginning in the late 1970s and 1980s, the rate of sex offenders sent to prison increased at an unprecedented rate, and it continued to climb for those convicted of "other" sex offenses at a rapid pace. Legislative interest in sex offenders also rose to new heights, with the proliferation of national policies like Megan's Law and Jessica's Law, as well as numerous other experiments at the state level, including the sexually violent predator civil commitment regimes.

In California, the explosive carceral responses to sex offenders are accompanied by enormous state population growth, as well as an explosive focus on incarceration at the national level, which actually preceded California's imprisonment boom. Changes in the structures of criminal justice decision making also take effect during this time, removing layers of insulation between policy makers and the public and reducing the discretion of police and judges in favor of prosecutors.

This multiplicity of possible causes to explain the quantitative and qualitative explosion in the punishment of sex offenders results in the dilemma of isolating the most plausible among them. Individually, there are plenty of necessary but insufficient conditions; the task becomes how to describe their interaction and relative rankings as potential causes. By lengthening the view to include patterns of punishment before the boom, we can better determine which conditions may have causal significance.

In chapter 2 I described the 1930s and 1940s as a time in which public outcry surrounding the perceived "increasing problem" of sex crime led legislators and executives to create and support new laws, including the laws that created the sexual psychopath civil commitment apparatus. This apparatus did not take full effect until the 1950s and 1960s, after most of the panic had receded. But although that bundle of laws also included penalty enhancements, the criminal justice system did not pick up on the cue from policy makers to prioritize sex crime by increasing arrests, and the courts did not send more sex offenders to prison. Thus, these public panics and new laws did not strongly affect criminal justice.

A vast literature in the sociology and political science of law casts doubt on the direct relationship between legal change and policy impact.[17] Zimring and colleagues have shown that, in California, legal innovations like the three strikes law have been mediated by other pressures that prevent short-term incarceration increases, although increases will likely be observed in the long term.[18] In the sex offender context, Jenkins and others have suggested that lawmakers who passed sexual psychopath laws may have known at the time that the new laws were not likely to address the sex crime problem, but they could not resist the public pressure to do something, demonstrating the kind of arousal and soothing that Murray Edelman described as a feature of symbolic politics.[19] But these same authors also tend to argue that there was a real impact on sexual criminals, just not the violent criminals the laws were promoted as targeting.[20] But the evidence does not support either increased social control and confinement of homosexuals or general increases in any categories of sex offenders admitted to prison.[21]

The insufficiency of moral panic for explaining levels of social control is especially important in light of the explosion—both quantitative and qualitative—of sex offender punishment since 1980. Commentators have focused on what the contemporary cycle of law making and public panic has in common with the past, describing it as a new wave or cycle in a longer historical trend.[22]

Certainly, intense public fear about sex crime has come in waves and laws have been passed in response to those fears. This aspect of the comparison is valid. But the comparison blithely overlooks what distinguishes the containment era: Not only are some new strategies in use, such as community notification and residency restrictions, but the older strategies of incapacitation are being used at much greater rates. The sex offender prison population was stable during the sexual psychopath era, and it remained stable throughout the next era, when faith in correctional rehabilitation might have rationalized some increased numbers of prisoners in addition to the commitments to state hospitals, which did increase. Instead, the sex offender prison population rate remained stable from 1940 to 1980, despite changes in the magnitude of public fears as expressed in the media and as acknowledged by policy makers. It also remained stable despite the rise and fall of the belief in the capacity of experts to rehabilitate. Then this long period of stability was shattered by an enormous increase around 1980. Prison admission rates show a similar trend—in California, from 1940 to 1971, there is actually a 48% decrease for sex offenders, and then from 1971 to 1984, there is a 486% increase!

One lesson from this long-term perspective is that the combination of a panicky public with pandering law makers is only one necessary condition—to truly account for the dramatic expansion of sex offender punishment since 1980, it is necessary to isolate and rank other conditions as well. Other scholars' analysis of the 1994 three strikes bill supported this contention, and this analysis of sex offender law confirms it.[23]

To identify other necessary conditions, we should abandon one of the underlying assumptions about sexual criminality that has appeared throughout the twentieth century and persists into the twenty-first: the assumption that sex crime is unique and that therefore punishment strategies and patterns of punishment should be different for sex offenders than they are for other criminal offenders. Instead, quantitative trends in sex offender punishment are better understood as part of a tailwind effect caused by general increases in punishment.

Data Supporting the Tailwind Theory of Sex Offender Imprisonment

Comparing Incarceration Rates

Zimring and Hawkins have previously demonstrated that California penal trends bear little relationship to crime trends,[24] and this holds true for sex offender punishment as well. Neither reported crime nor front-end input in the form of arrests explains the prison increases. This is especially clear with regard to "other" sex offenses, for which reporting and arrest rate trends bear little relationship to imprisonment trends.

In contrast, there is a criminal justice trend that does track California's sex offender incarceration rate: California's general incarceration rate, the total rate of prisoners admitted to California prisons for all offenses. California's incarceration rate is roughly similar to the overall U.S. imprisonment rate. In 2005, the California rate was just below the U.S. average.[25] Trends over time are also similar, though the U.S. rate increased before the California rate.[26] Rates of incarceration for "other" sex offenses, forcible rape, and other general offenses show remarkably similar trends until the mid-1980s. At that point the rate of prisoners admitted for forcible rape peaks and begins to drop, while rates for offenders of "other" sex offense and general crimes continue to increase in lockstep until the late 1990s, when they finally diverge.

The scale of sex offender incarceration pales over the long term compared to the general growth of prison populations, as figure 8.4 illustrates, with a longer span of data available for California. The general increase involved much larger numbers of offenders and higher rates of incarceration. In order to show the relationship between sex offender incarceration and general incarceration, the first year with somewhat reliable data for all three categories is provided as the baseline, that is, data for 1953 are normed to 100 to illustrate the variation in subsequent years.

The three rates show similar trends until 1980, when forcible rape increases. "Other" sex offense rates continue to increase with the general incarceration rate until the mid-1990s, when "other" sex offense incarceration continues to increase as general incarceration begins a modest decline. So while the increase in sex offenders in prison may be related to general trends in incarceration, those incarceration trends were clearly not driven by sex offenders until very recently.

Simple statistical tests confirm the explanatory power of general imprisonment trends in California for explaining sex offender imprisonment. Linear regression of the data for 1950–1980 (data are incomplete prior to 1950) shows that general incarceration explains more than 45% of the variation in

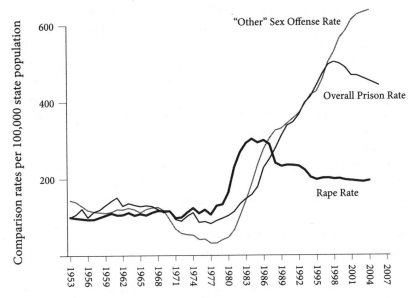

FIGURE 8.4. *California Prison Growth Compared to General U.S. Sex Offender Confinement, 1953 to 2007*

sex offender incarceration (R^2 = .452, p = .000). Correlating the two shows significance (Pearson's = .672, p = .01). These two analyses show that prior to 1980 and the major penal expansion, general prison population rates are a powerful influence on sex offender population rates.

The same tests show an even more powerful relationship over the long term—a linear regression shows that general incarceration explains more than 92% of the variation in sex offender incarceration between 1950 and 2006 (R^2 =.92, p = .000), while correlating the variables also shows significance (Pearson's = .961, p = .01).

Given the generally low values that these kinds of tests usually produce in social science contexts, these high levels of prediction and correlation are even more noteworthy.

Penal Change before Legal Change

Altogether, this quantitative analysis is strong evidence of a close relationship, which is especially significant because it shows that *the relationship existed before the factors commonly used to explain the 1980 sex offender increase were in play*. Moreover, it helps explain the stability of sex offender incarceration prior to 1980 as well—the factors that restrained general prison growth during this time were apparently stronger than the public panic and other factors that might have increased sex offender imprisonment. Incarcerations for sex offenses are not special cases but are subject to general penal trends.

While there is much to marvel at in terms of the changes in kinds of sex offender punishment in the containment era, all were independent of the numerical increases in incarceration. All of the new and enhanced sex offender laws, including community notification and sexually violent predator laws, followed increases in incarceration in the 1980s, rather than driving those increases, because the important legal changes are concentrated in the 1990s and continue into the 2000s.

More conclusively, even if we were to find a relationship between the timing of California's sex offender laws and increased incarceration, the nature of the most dramatic new policies excludes them from relevance. Civil commitment for sexually violent predators and community notification are both policies that affect offenders after incarceration, and therefore they cannot contribute to increases in incarceration.

Institutional Change: The New Politics of Criminal Justice

The third source of evidence of a tailwind effect on sex offender incarceration is an institutional one—the same actors at the same levels of government can be attributed responsibility for increases for both the general prison population and for the sex offender population in prison. Both the institutional location and the mechanisms appear to be the same. To describe this institutional story requires a brief detour into the new politics of criminal justice in California.

Zimring and colleagues argued that the 1994 three strikes initiative descended from California's 1976 shift in punishment from indeterminate to largely determinate sentencing, related as well to other changes that removed the power to apply general rules from insulated decision makers.[27] I make a similar claim for the punishment of sex offenders in the containment era— rather than serving as a special example of our extreme and particular hatred of sex offenders, these new laws capitalized on public concern about sex offenders but were facilitated largely by the same forces that allowed the passage of measures like three strikes: distrust of government, the decline of experts and lost faith in rehabilitation, the rise of harm over dangerousness as a valuation of offending, victim valorization, and the rise of single-issue advocates.[28]

Throughout the three eras I describe, covering 1930 to the present, government failure to protect potential victims from the perceived problem of rising sex crime has been a common theme. The public has not only been concerned about sex crime for much of the twentieth century but has placed a portion of the blame for the incidence of sex crime on failed criminal justice and social service institutions, from the probation system blasted in the 1940s to the inadequate child-care licensing decried in the 1980s, and the many failures of policing, prosecution, and rehabilitation criticized throughout the century.[29]

This particular distrust of the government's ability to address the sex crime problem exacerbates the general distrust of "big" government and of a "pro-offender" judiciary fostered by neoconservatives, and capitalized upon by single-issue advocates. These are all developments in the politics of criminal justice since the 1970s. Barker, who analyzed two snapshots in the victim's movements, a Washington initiative and one in California, writes,

> For many crime victim groups, a "good" and "just" society was a society in which the experience of victimization was regarded as significant, traumatic, and legitimate: a good and just society acknowledged that victimization could be a life-altering experience and one that deserved social recognition and official compensation. . . . To crime victim advocates, cold correctionalism not only failed to recognize the brutality of crime, but it also excluded the experience of crime victims, the "real" victims, altogether. By focusing nearly all of its attention, care, and expertise on the needs of the offender, correctionalism seemed to value criminal offenders as objects of study and projects for improvement more than it recognized or valued the painful experience of crime victims.[30]

The victim-or-offender fallacy therefore grows from a well-intentioned effort to bring justice to the wronged. But however just the underlying goals, there are numerous examples of the relentless pursuit of punitive policy in order to make meaning of a terrible victimization. This kind of punitive and single-minded focus may most often correspond with the politically savvy family members of child victims.[31]

The Polly Klaas case described in chapter 7 provides just one example of this wider phenomenon: Polly's father, Mark Klaas, became a regular advocate in the legislature after his daughter's murder. He remains to this day a self-made expert on child abductions and sex offenders, offering commentary on every related case and legislative proposal to receive public attention. He and other national figures such as Mark Lunsford, whose daughter Jessica is the namesake of many residency restrictions, are examples of the kinds of single-issue advocates who have changed the politics of criminal justice in California and nationwide.[32] In a recent example, Lunsford attacked the Georgia legislature for scaling back its residency restrictions, a story of reform described in my conclusion. Lunsford objected by essentially claiming that there is no such thing as a low-risk sex offender and that "no one in the history of mankind has ever been reformed."[33] He has previously declared, "I can't get my hands on the guy that murdered my daughter so I've made it my job to make the rest of these sexual offenders and predators' lives miserable, as miserable as I can."[34] These advocates are devoted to using their notoriety to pass more and tougher sex crime laws.

Another shift marked by laws similar to the three strikes law is the provision of more power to social actors that best represent public sentiment—that is, prosecutors—and removal of power from judges, who have held an objective perspective, at least theoretically. The mandatory sentencing component of three strikes and other similar laws takes discretionary power away from judges and hands it to prosecutors: These provisions remove judicial power to choose among penalties, giving far more impact to prosecutors' charging decisions.[35]

Jonathan Simon has written extensively about the role of the prosecutor in both state and national politics:

> The prosecutor has long been a unique and important office holder within the American systems of justice and government, with deep but limited powers and a special claim to represent the local community as a whole. In the last decades of the twentieth century however, the war on crime reshaped the American prosecutor into an important model for political authority while also giving real prosecutors enormous jurisdiction over the welfare of communities with little attention to the lack of democratic accountability.[36]

Prosecutors not only determine whether and how to bring charges, they often drive the location of the hearing, the sentence sought, and whether parole or civil commitment would be pursued.

While Simon focuses on the importance of the prosecutor for understanding shifts in governing styles, other scholars who look at the workings of prosecutors emphasize decision making such as nonprosecution or plea-bargaining, with some of these scholars focusing on decisions not to pursue sexual assault charges.[37] But little recent research in the United States has examined the prosecutorial function in total, therefore failing to measure

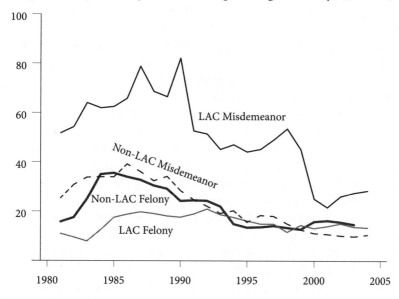

FIGURE 8.5. *California Lewd and Lascivious Arrest Rates—Los Angeles County and California, Excluding Los Angeles County, 1976–2004*

Note that the arrest rates in the figure are calculated per 100,000 adults rather than per 100,000 Californians as most other figures in this book are calculated. This is because adult population data for California are harder to obtain for the period before 1976, so for figures showing trends over longer periods, the total population data must be used.

the impact of the structural changes that have moved power from judges to prosecutors.[38] I focus here on the importance of how prosecutors charge sex offenses that could be either misdemeanors or felonies. I refer both to choosing how to classify conduct that could fit within several possible offense categories, and to "wobblers" (single-offense categories like "lewd and lascivious conduct," which in California can be considered either a felony or a misdemeanor). This kind of charging decision has a crucial impact on the sex offender prison population.

In contrasting the civil commitment procedure with the other tracks for sex offenders during the rehabilitative era, I have showed the importance of a "third track" in addition to prison or hospitalization—the misdemeanor track. While "wobbler" offenses that can be charged as either felonies or misdemeanors have become a feature of many criminal codes, it is clear that sex crime has always itself functioned as a "wobbler" category of crime,[39] even before and aside from the legislature's explicit provision for this. Recall the

California arrest data presented earlier. By 2004, misdemeanor arrest rates are still higher than felony "other" sex offense rates. But the gap was much greater in the 1980s, beginning to close in the early 1990s as the misdemeanor rate decreased.[40]

Figure 8.5 presents the arrest rate trends in another way—distinguishing the Los Angeles county share of the arrest rates from the state rates. These trends confirm the continuing importance of misdemeanor arrests as well as the closing gap between misdemeanor and felony sex offenses. More specifically, there are three features of sex offender criminal justice that can be isolated by looking at the impact of California's most prolific county. First, Los Angeles County drives the state's misdemeanor lewd arrests—the Los Angeles rate is much higher, and the state rate follows the same trend. Many things could account for this, perhaps including the Los Angeles Police Department's long tradition of pursuing sex crimes all the way back to De River's Sex Offense Bureau and its improved access to the resources to enable this. Second, Los Angeles County does not drive the felony lewd arrests as clearly—in this case, the state rate is higher, but both rise and fall more or less together. Finally, all the rates generally decrease by the mid-1980s and are in 2004 significantly lower than their highest peaks during the 1970s and 1980s.

This explication of sex offender arrest rates in one county emphasizes the importance of local decision making on the criminal justice and correctional systems. Local decision makers determine the input into the state corrections system with little pressure to control that input.[41] The arrest rates shown in figure 8.5 confirm the determinative role that local criminal justice decisions play in California's punishment of sex offenders.

Civil commitments also varied by county, both in number and in the offenses that led to commitment. For example, from 1966 to 1970, Los Angeles County referred only 7% of the offenders convicted of sex perversion in their jurisdiction for civil commitment, while statewide, excluding L.A. County, more than 20% of perversion convictions were referred for commitment.[42] Similarly, Los Angeles County referred only 14% of the indecent exposure convictions for commitment, while the non–Los Angeles counties together referred 30% of their exhibitionists for civil commitment.[43] Prison admissions also show local variation, which changes over time as well. In 1973, Los Angeles County contributed 30% of the rapists sent to state prison and 28% of the lewd and lascivious offenders, compared to San Francisco County's contribution of 11% of the rapists and about 2% of the lewd offenders. By 1983, Los Angeles County was responsible for 38% of the rapists admitted to prison that year and 23% of the lewd offenders, compared to San Francisco's 2% of the rapists and just 1% of the lewd offenders.[44]

The variation in arrest, commitment referral, and imprisonment by county as well as the closing gap between misdemeanors and felonies over time relates to the structural changes initiated in the determinate sentencing law and continued with the kinds of mandatory sentences called for by the three strikes law. The laws themselves, as well as the general atmospheric change that brought more public scrutiny to charging decisions, led to an overall trend toward prosecuting felonies over misdemeanors when possible. In her study of the use of discretion in three strikes cases, Jennifer Walsh notes that it became internal policy in many district attorneys' offices to prosecute "wobblers" as felonies; by the beginning of the containment era, state law made most wobbler crimes presumptive felonies, meaning that prisoners would be routinely charged with felonies unless discretion was applied to reduce the felonies to misdemeanors.[45] Where discretion regarding sex offense arrests in the rehabilitative era meant many misdemeanor arrests, in the containment era this discretion is more constrained.

Altogether, this account of the shift toward determinate and mandatory sentences highlights the location of authority in criminal justice decision making. In addition to the rise of the prosecutor and the decline of the judge, the removal of sentence length determination from the parole authority is another important feature of the institutional changes that have shaped prison populations in California since 1980. Prosecutors wield more power than judges in many ways with regard to sentences, and these local actors have replaced the state-level institution of the parole authority in determining the amount of time served. This institutional story is the final source of confirmation that California's sex offender imprisonment shows a tailwind effect of the overall increases in incarceration.

From 1980 until at least 1999, sex offender imprisonment in California appears to be better explained by general trends in imprisonment than by an explanation grounded in our particular aversion to sex offenders. Instead, there are parallels with what Michel Foucault discovered in his account of the birth of the prison as a general tool—in contrast to the self-congratulatory accounts of the reformers, the prison took hold because of its utility for state power.[46] Imprisonment trends before 1980 show the similarity between sex offender arrests and general imprisonment. Legal innovation in sex offender punishment followed the prison population increases and focused largely on strategies for managing sex offenders outside of prison. Finally, the same institutional changes that have impacted the general increases are crucial for determining sex offender punishment—in particular, the shift from charging misdemeanors to charging felonies, which has particular salience for sex crime.

While there is evidence that the tailwind effect explains a significant portion of sex offender imprisonment, the explanation is incomplete. What the large coefficients of determination may mask are the temporal divergences between general and sex offender incarceration, which we begin to see in the late 1990s. Prosecutors over time draw more and more on the arguments made by victim advocates who call for increased punishment for all.

Conclusion

I never had any trouble with guns, I never hurt anyone. Other than death, I don't know what could be any worse. It takes everything away, even if you are not the bogeyman. There's nothing left for me.
—Ryan Johnson, personal correspondence, November 24, 2008

I spoke with Ryan on Thanksgiving Day in 2008. I was taking a few moments to catch up on correspondence before serving my family dinner; he was sitting alone in his temporary housing at the YMCA. Twenty years earlier, almost to the day, Ryan had urinated in the woods because the portable toilets at his jobsite were occupied. A passing police officer spotted him and issued a citation. Ryan was never handcuffed, arrested, or taken to jail. Instead, the State of Florida treated him much like a citizen who is cited for speeding—he was written a ticket, given a date to appear in court, and released. He ultimately pled *nolo contendere* to this single charge and paid $180 in court costs.[1]

During the years after this citation, Ryan married, had twin boys, lived and worked in New York, and then moved to Arkansas to be near his wife's family. On September 10, 2007, Ryan was arrested by officials from the Madison County Sheriff's Office for knowingly failing to register as a "sex offender."

In order to earn release on a $15,000 bond, Ryan was forced to register as a convicted sex offender. So that he could comply with the requirements of the state's Community Notification Act, Ryan vacated the home where he resided with his wife of twenty-five years, Annie, because it was purportedly within 2,000 feet of a private day-care facility. The State of Florida had never required Ryan to register as a sex offender, and Arkansas law does not currently treat his conduct as a criminal sex offense that would trigger notification and registration requirements. Nonetheless, as a result of this wrongful prosecution, Mr. Johnson was ostracized from his community, hounded by the media, and became homeless and unemployed.

Ryan's case is not unique. Rather, it is an example of what happens when laws passed with bogeymen in mind are applied to real people. Other cases like Ryan's include teens like Genarlow Wilson, who was convicted in 2005 of having oral sex when he was seventeen with a consenting fifteen-year-old girl. He spent two years in prison. Genarlow Wilson was an honor student, a football star, and his high school's homecoming king before his conviction, and his case attracted national attention, with the help of former president Jimmy Carter, Reverend Al Sharpton, and other civil rights leaders. Wilson was finally released when the Supreme Court of Georgia overturned his sentence and ruled that he did not have to register as a sex offender. In contrast, although Ryan was able to get legal representation and avoided serving prison time for failing to register, he is still a registered sex offender, facing all the penalties and exclusions that accompany his status. No one will hire him, and even his room at the YMCA is imperiled, since the Y's official policy is that they do not house sex offenders.

Undoubtedly, many people who are subject to these laws are more guilty and more deviant than either Ryan or Genarlow. But the problem is that the laws remove the discretion to differentiate and instead are wildly overinclusive. In addition to the individual injustices, this has broad social and institutional impacts, all of which make it harder, not easier, to prevent and address sexual victimization. Sex offender policies, through the disciplining and governing of individuals and groups, function as symbolic boundary markers that detract from other aspects of the social problem of sexual assault. After explaining the way laws create subjects, I will argue that both the symbolic work done by these policies and their unintended practical effects do more harming than healing.

Sex Offender Laws and Subject Creation

For sociologists since Durkheim, punishment is not aimed at preventing crime. Despite the rhetoric that seeks to justify it, punishment's real intent is not to discipline the offender, but to dramatize the violated norm: "To punish is not to make others suffer in body and soul; it is to affirm, in the face of an offence, the rule that the offence would deny."[2] Punishment maintains social solidarity by dramatizing the superiority of "us" over "them."

In *Discipline and Punish*, Foucault focuses on the body as the unit of analysis, which is often the medium for marking normative boundaries. In each of his studies of abnormality, including *Madness and Civilization*, *The Birth of the Clinic*, and *The History of Sexuality*, transgression comes before the norm. By defining and excluding the abnormal, we establish normality. For example, in *Discipline and Punish*, Foucault describes the way correctional incarceration creates cogs to fit into the disciplinary machine of society. Discipline "compares, differentiates, hierarchizes, homogenizes, excludes. In short, it normalizes."[3] Foucault argues that discipline creates the individual who is the subject of knowledge. This creation of the individual exists reflexively with the rise of expertise and scientific techniques of measurement and classification. The individual is therefore constituted as knowable, subject to examination, correction, and judgment according to normative standards.[4] With sex offender law we see that the legislatures, courts, and law enforcement officials who enact and apply laws like Megan's Law are drawing social boundaries in which the subjects of offender, victim, authority figure, and moral community are regenerated.

Sex Offenders: Governed Subjects

Today when the media and legislators use the term "sex offenders," the public generally interprets this to include men who have perpetrated sexual assault on children or women. This definition is a historically specific delineation of a certain group of people to be targeted by punitive policies; laws are enacted based upon this assumed definition. However, there are many ways in which this assumed group of "sex offenders" requires complication; there are ways in which our collective assumptions may require correcting. Treated uncritically, this assumed notion of "sex offenders" ignores the realities of who is in practice affected by the laws and who avoids legal consequences.

As Wacquant writes, we now treat "sex offenses as the act of a particular species of individual rather than a particular type of legally proscribed conduct. Such legislation and its accompanying trope turns judicial stigma into negative symbolic capital that cannot be shed and will therefore weigh on the bearer for life, like the stain of 'eve' construed as a dishonoring form of denigrated ethnicity."[5] Our preoccupation with monsters ignores the much more common experience of sexual assault within families and among acquaintances. In addition to the harm caused to those victims and to society by overlooking those kinds of assaults, this focus reinforces and replicates itself by the kinds of empirical research about sex offenders that tends to move from scholarly journals into the public arena.

Because most research on "sex offenders" is conducted within correctional populations, that is, those who have been reported, arrested, convicted, and imprisoned, our empirical "picture" of the sex offender is partial.

This partial picture is then entrenched in the law, as through requirements for risk assessments.[6] In addition, this partial view of those who commit sexual assault makes it very easy for "us" to see ourselves as very different from "them"; it verifies a profile made up of the fallacies discussed throughout this book with which real offenders and their victims may not identify. This allows perpetrators to deny their offenses, victims to remain unidentified, and society to remain accepting of highly punitive symbolic policies that do not address root causes of sexual assault.

Authority Figures

In the 1980s and early 1990s, adult victims of child sexual abuse by trusted authority figures came forward with allegations of abuse. Revelations of sexual abuse and subsequent cover-ups by priests, ministers, rabbis, Boy Scout leaders, and preschool teachers have continued since then. Several successful civil suits were brought against religious groups that tried to cover up sexual abuse; damages paid by the Catholic Church to victims of sexual abuse who came forward are estimated in the billions. Similarly, the U.S. military has been rocked by a series of rape and sexual harassment scandals, including Tailhook and the various scandals at West Point and the Naval Academy, as well as more recent reports of sexual abuse of female soldiers stationed in Iraq and Afghanistan.

It is no longer unthinkable to view trusted authority figures as capable of sexual abuse. However, these revelations have resulted in only superficial policy changes and monetary awards for select victims.

Communities and Moral Nonoffenders: Governed Subjects

In *Visions of Social Control*, Stanley Cohen identifies the quest for community as one of our favorite stories of control. He describes the ambiguity of the notion of community, which lacks any negative connotation and instead refers to an idyllic past in which neighbors watched out for one another. Unfortunately, as Cohen and others point out, no such community has ever existed.[7]

In another context, Wacquant defines community as "an elastic term used to designate the various spaces deemed intimate and therefore closed to blacks, from the neighborhood to the club house to the bedroom."[8] He also attributes the popularity of sex offender punishment to neoliberal moralism, functioning similarly to the role of the prison: "Through this triple excommunicating of felons, the prison contributes to the ongoing reconstruction of the 'imagined community' of Americans around the polar opposition between praiseworthy 'working families'—implicitly white, suburban, and deserving—and the despicable 'underclass' of criminals, loafers, and leeches."[9] Sex offender notification laws depend on the community for enforcement. People who enforce and support these laws presume stranger rapists, presume that knowledge equals protection, and—most devastatingly, assume that all potential threats can be identified through past convictions, a logical fallacy. How can such a poorly premised policy have such great appeal? Because it works as a dramatic delineation of who belongs in our community and who does not.

Unintended Consequences

People can access databases of convicted sex offenders and learn the names and addresses of the individuals living in their areas. This is one aspect of the way these databases keep tabs on convicted offenders, by encouraging community members to know the offenders in their neighborhood and presumably to use that knowledge to protect their families. This is social control at the neighborhood level. However, another use of these databases is by law enforcement—frequently, one of the first steps in the investigation of an alleged sex offense involves interrogating the registered offenders in the area. This creates an automatic pool of "suspects" for a current crime based on a past conviction (actuarial justice).

In addition to overt acts of vigilantism, which may actually be "intended consequences" of the policies, there are other side effects that probably were never anticipated. The criminological literature on recent sex offender policy innovations has grown exponentially since 2005, providing ample evidence of the unintended consequences of popular policies. For example, Jill Levenson and Richard Tewksbury conducted an online survey of family members of registered sex offenders, finding that more than half of the respondents reported the effects of teasing, ridicule, fear, anger, or anxiety.[10] More concretely, they also reported employment limitations and financial and housing problems as well as physical and verbal victimization.

Scholars of inequality will be particularly troubled by the impact of sex offender laws on vulnerable communities. A number of recent articles have examined the collateral consequences of these laws on particular communities.[11] In-depth interviews with state officials and residents and local officials in five communities that have dealt with SVP placements suggest that public hostility toward sex offender reentry reflects contestations over government versus citizen responsibility, the best strategies for achieving public safety, and the meaning of citizens' rights.[12] Monica Williams finds that these responses reflect a process by which people express their positions in the ongoing negotiations that constitute the politics of crime control.[13]

Several scholars of rhetoric and philosophy draw our attention to these effects. For example, Pamela Schultz analyzes interviews with convicted sex offenders and finds that framing them as monsters not only dehumanizes them, robbing them of the capacity for choice, but it also undermines treatment (2005). Similarly, John Douard argues that "the media's and lawmakers' framing of sex offenders as monsters, and the incorporation of the monster framework into legal proceedings through the use of psychiatric testimony and diagnoses, results in a nearly invisible, unjust deprivation of liberty."[14] Numerous scholars across the disciplines have emphasized the way sex offender laws like residency restrictions provide a false sense of security, promoting the idea that the bad guys can be easily identified and isolated. Given the reality that the vast majority of sexual crimes are committed by familiars, policies that constitute sex offenders as monstrous others distract us from real dangers.[15]

In another instance like those described at the outset of this chapter, in the early 1980s, a homeless and mentally ill California man, psychotic and unmedicated, urinated in public. He was arrested and convicted of a misdemeanor. Although he never committed another criminal offense, changes in registration laws in the late 1990s forced him to register as a sex offender, making him ineligible for community-based mental health care. After a nonviolent psychotic episode in 2001, he remained in the county psychiatric hospital for ten times as long as the typical stay, not because of his condition but because no programs would accept him. The police officer in charge of sex offender registrations in his area and the social workers involved in his care together tried to convince the court to remove him from the registry, but they failed.[16]

Similar cases have been reported anecdotally about practices in other states. In another case, a severely developmentally disabled man urinated in public, completely unaware that the act was illegal. Nonetheless, he too had to register as a sex offender, and has been denied placement in numerous programs as a result of his status.[17] A recent federal report on the unjust and extended detention of persons in a state psychiatric hospital was explained by doctors within the hospital as largely due to the sex offenders they could not release because they could find no community placements for them because of residency restrictions.[18] Altogether, these offenders are unlike the dangerous "predators" the laws were written to target. There are many people who are swept into the purview of registration and notification laws who were not likely the intended targets, but who suffer as a result and go unnoticed in our punitive fervor. These include mentally ill, noncontact offenders; prostitutes; adolescent experimenters; consensual adults engaged in public or otherwise prohibited sexual activity; and kids in the juvenile system who are disproportionately likely to get "caught" violating sex offense laws.[19]

This consequence could not have been an intention of the laws, though perhaps our sense of "community" *is* meant to exclude the homeless and the mentally ill. There are other numerous examples that are perhaps more palatable to the general public, which does not typically extend much sympathy to the kind of people described above, who often have engaged in other criminal conduct.

Ignored Subjects

The "Unimportant" Affected

Another unintended consequence of these notification laws is the impact on families of offenders and on victims. The crimes for which convicted sex offenders must register sometimes take place within families or neighborhoods. When information about the crime is distributed on the Internet or through flyers, the victim of the crime can be identified, adding to the victim's pain and stigmatization. Family members of the offender can suffer the same kinds of stigmatization and denial of services that the offender endures.[20]

The Benefiting Professionals

Entirely unnoticed by the public, an entire field of professionals benefits from sex offender laws, especially those laws that require extensive evaluation and surveillance during imprisonment and after release. These include sex offender treatment practitioners (who build their profession based on these laws) and police department administrators (who fund their work through federal Byrne and Wetterling grants).

In California, the state coalition of sex offender treatment practitioners has been able to shape the policies they will then be hired to implement. No matter how generously we view the intentions of these aspiring professionals, they are clearly reaping financial and jurisdictional rewards from sex offender policies. In effect, they are a set of "unintended subjects" created by the new laws.[21]

Harmful Distractions

By focusing on sex offenders as being strangers, we don't have to discuss the concerns that feminists have presented about the prevalence of acquaintance rape. Sexual assailants are much more likely to be friends and relatives than strangers. But despite data from victim surveys as well as general surveys of college-age men and women that document this reality,[22] the dominant image of the rapist is the stranger-monster. In a way, the second-wave feminists took less of a scapegoating view: Instead of singling out a subgroup of deviants, their original position against pornography was based on the premise that porn harmed all women by reinforcing the subjection of women; implicit in this is the belief that "all men are potential rapists." This in fact is a more radical view, which would require structural changes in social relations, not just the punishment of individuals.

A more pragmatic concern about notification policies in particular is clearly stated by one of my informants who runs a child-care center. She feels that background checks provide a false sense of security. A wiser emphasis would be a certainty that adults and kids in a particular organization understood the appropriate boundaries and that the administration maintains enough involvement that they are able to intervene when necessary. On the one hand, she fears that background checks do not tell us enough—we need to have a higher standard for the kind of adult we want involved with our kids than just that they have passed a check. She also notes that checks don't cover all offenses (either someone has not gotten caught yet or records have not been exhaustively searched). On the other hand, she also feels that there will be excellent mentors who have overcome criminal pasts, and we need to be able to allow a role for them.

In addition, civilly committing a small proportion of offenders and applying expensive and invasive conditions for release to another relatively small group ignores the reality that there are already many convicted sex offenders in our community and that very few of them receive any treatment or support. "'We can't beam these people to Mars—they're going to be back on the streets eventually,' says Father Stephen J. Rossetti, a psychologist and president of St. Luke Institute, a church-run psychiatric hospital in Silver Spring, Maryland. 'If they get treatment, it reduces the likelihood that they'll re-offend.'"[23] Father Rossetti states a reality that many people simply do not accept: We will eventually have to acknowledge that sex offenders are likely to live next door to us.

In summary, the subjects created by sex offender policies—a limited and biased notion of the offender, an empowered victim identity that also excludes many actual victims, and the moral community constituted and dramatized by expressive punishment—have three main harms: (1) This avoids the search for practices that will actually decrease the offending of the subgroups that are now targeted; (2) this adds to the penalizing, scapegoating, and disabling of the "underclass"; and (3) this avoids more threatening issues, including family violence, the eroticization/objectification of women and children, and the uncertainties of our normative (hetero- and queer-) sexualities.

Beyond Moral Panic

Recently, scholars have paid tribute to the legacy of "moral panic" as a tool for revealing the social constructions of deviance and the unnecessarily punitive responses that often followed.[24] The expressive and constitutive functions of these boundary defenses have been explored by scholars concerned about the exaggerated effects. For example, in 1950, Edwin Sutherland described a policy-making process that began with sensationalized sex crime, relied on power-hungry experts and politicians, and resulted in hasty and shoddy sexual psychopath laws.[25] Since then, critiques of the way sex offender policies are made have often used the analytic of "moral panic." This description of poor process and poor product has unfortunately been taken to reflect skepticism about the existence of a problem in the first place. This is in part a legacy of the larger body of "moral panic" literature, which focused on sensational depictions of crime waves, which had little relationship to actual crime patterns: for example, the European witch-hunt and the "mugging crisis."[26] The concept of moral panic as applied to sexual offending policies thus tended to be taken as indicating disbelief, "that Megan's Law is a hysterical overreaction to a hugely exaggerated problem—that there is no real problem warranting dramatic legal or cultural attention and energy."[27]

But questioning the social construction of a problem need not mean denying the existence of a problem. In addition to its illuminations, however, reliance on moral panic and its related concepts has had unintended consequences, especially when those concepts have served as the *primary* explanations for changes in the penal landscape.[28] Specifically, the paucity of robust theorizing in the area of sex crime and punishment is in part due to the polarizing effects of the moral panic analytic. In particular, the emphasis on exaggeration has chilled critical analysis of current approaches to sex crime and punishment. Further, the most compelling concern underlying moral panic scholarship—that panics will lead to increased punitiveness demonstrable at the level of both policy and practice—may blind us to empirical realities, including the *restraints* on punitiveness, which may have greater impact than the panics and in some cases may even *result from* moral panics. As Jeffrey Victor describes, "In brief, a moral panic is a form of collective behavior characterized by suddenly increased concern and hostility in a significant segment of a society, in reaction to widespread beliefs about a newly perceived threat from moral deviants. Careful, empirical examination at a later time, however, reveals that the perceived threat was greatly exaggerated or nonexistent."[29] This kind of definition has added to the perception that if one criticizes sex offender policy, one is a "left-progressive" who dismisses the needs and experiences of victims.

In the thirtieth anniversary edition of his book *Folk Devils*, Stanley Cohen distinguishes between strong constructionists (who focus exclusively on the discourses and processes) and weak constructionists, who are motivated by the need to issue "reality-checks" by contrasting the discourses with observed realities and who may also wish to be engaged in resolving social problems.[30] It is the latter group that has had special resonance with penologists studying the United States' methods of resolving crime, as well as those scholars who study the reaction to sex crimes in particular. Cohen's book has challenged us to examine moral panics comparatively[31] by scrutinizing historical patterns of sex offender panic and criminal justice responses. My historical comparative research demonstrates that moral panics may actually limit punitiveness as well as expand it.

The most sophisticated historical studies of moral panics surrounding sex crime in twentieth-century America are most successful when they document trends in the discourses and processes surrounding those panics. But they also decry the potential for misuses of state power created by new policies like civil commitment laws for sexual psychopaths. These support this concern with snapshot data from a few localities and draw greater inferences than their data should allow. The longitudinal perspective developed in this book suggests that their concern about penal impact was misplaced and potentially misleading.

While public anxiety may pressure the government to respond, I argue that expertise (located in the social and behavioral sciences and in the form of task executors like police, prosecutors, judges, and parole boards as well as risk assessors and other clinicians) represents a neglected and crucial mediation of punitive policy. Changes in the status of these academic fields and in the insulation of these criminal justice actors have determined both the content of knowledge about sexual offending and how much influence that knowledge has on public policy. Panic, therefore, is not a sufficient explanation for contemporary penality, as other scholars concerned with the structures and politics of criminal justice have also argued.[32]

While many scholars after the cultural turn would not expect to see discourse related directly to changes in practice, many do identify connections between punitive discourse and penal practice. In fact, most contemporary theorists of the present penal situation include some measure of a uniquely punitive public as part of the explanation for the explosion of incarcerated populations since the 1970s. Table 9.1 presents a selection of contemporary theorizing, distilling several of the most influential models into an input, the key explanatory mechanism, and the output.

TABLE 9.1.

	Input	Key Mechanism	Output
Garland	Social structure and politics (late modernity)	Erosion of penal-welfare model	Mass imprisonment, punitive politics
Zimring	Vengeful public, distrust of experts	Policy makers lose insulation	Direct democratic control of punishment
Tonry	Failure of War on Poverty	Cycles of punitiveness	Increasing incarceration of drug offenders
Simon	Policy makers react to fear of crime	Breakdown of social activist–style of governing	Detention and segregation, governing through crime
Wacquant	Neoliberalism	Race acted on through the prison and ghetto	Prison society
Young	Global economic, cultural, and political structures	Othering, deprivation	Vertigo, alienation, punitiveness

This schematic was originally created for Wacquant's graduate seminar "Permutations of Penality" at the University of California, Berkeley, in the fall of 2003. The idea to query these grand theories in terms of explicit causal factors is Wacquant's; my interpretation of each theory reflects his influence as well as our seminar discussants including Victor Rios, Damon Mayrl, Osagie Obasogie, Joshua Page, and Simon Grivet.

Contemporary criminologists offer various and complex explanations for the historical shift from the period extending after World War II though the 1970s to the punitive present.[33] All tend to idealize the previous periods and focus on shifts rather than continuities. Among the cited factors related to the shift are the decline of the New Deal and neoliberalism, economic restructuring into a post-Fordist economy, the rise of conservative politics, political opportunism, and the rising importance of the victim as a site of governance.

Each theory alludes to changes in the social structure related to public intolerance for certain groups, and several use public attitudes of punitiveness as the causal factor. While these theories provide outstanding skeletons on which to hang the meat of empirical research, they sacrifice that sort of empirical grounding in favor of their ability to sketch large trends.

Criminological theorizing at the meta-level, about the connections between political structures and cultural expressions about punishment can be expanded and revised through grounding at the case level. These theories also benefit greatly from historical comparative research, which allows us to test claims about the peculiar present by looking for continuities with the past. The examples of sex offender punishment in California at mid-century and of the current risk assessments of sexual offenders both reveal some of the mediation that insulated experts have been credited with in the hallowed past.[34] Truth in sentencing and other innovations of the late twentieth century have certainly curtailed discretion at the sentencing end. But most of the discretion to bring individuals into the state's systems of control, and much of the discretion to track such offenders, through prosecutorial charging and psychological assessment, remains untouched and largely unreviewed today. There is reason to take this book's grounded approach and examine implementation decisions throughout the criminal justice system. Beneath facially punitive law and beneath therapeutic or retributive rhetoric, what other effects may we find?

No matter our ideological commitments, scholars run the risk of seeing what we want to see, whether we're interpreting a statement or piecing together the meanings of numerical data. Grounding in the social sciences perhaps offers more opportunities to reflect on this than is available to those more squarely located in law and politics. Regardless, all scholars, teachers, and activists should read through our familiar disciplines and perspectives. We must challenge each other's interpretations, and we must acknowledge our subjectivity and its limitations. This does not happen nearly as much as it should when the topics are crime and punishment.

What Happens Next?

The decisions of local actors are very important in determining sex offender punishment, but very little is known about how these decisions are made and how they vary across locations and across time. A general narrowing has taken place in the criminal justice system's working image of the sex offender, now classified as a monster requiring confinement rather than as a nuisance or a potential patient. Both policy and practice now prioritize the public's belief that all sexual offending is harmful, dangerous, and caused by deviant desires that are compulsive beyond control. This is accompanied by a broadened legal arsenal, which compounds the ramifications of being convicted of a sex offense.

This research has also shown that penal practices have not changed in the past because of moral panics surrounding sex offenders. Instead, the public view that sex offenders are all monsters is more or less consistent over the last century—even when the public favored rehabilitation for some, this did not lead to a grand rehabilitative experiment. What appears to have had more impact is the constellation of factors driving criminal justice decision makers, especially prosecutors. The politics of criminal justice and the rise of single-issue advocates seem to have had more impact on sex offender imprisonment than any other factors. This suggests that efforts to create policy that differentiates among sex offenders, selecting those who may be candidates for community supervision without first serving a prison sentence, must be broadly supported by law enforcement and victim advocacy organizations if they will have any chance of turning the punitive tide.

While descriptive quantitative analysis has shown that most sex offender incarceration has been driven by trends in general incarceration, the divergence between the two, which began in 1999, suggests that the monster image of the sex offender may continue to drive those incarceration rates even after general incarceration moderates. As the data in chapter 8 show, prisoners with "other" sex offense convictions are a growing and significant share of prison populations. Although sex offender incarceration has not been the result of unique forces in the past, it may now present unique challenges to modulation.

Reform Strategies

Politicians on the left and right call for more and better punishment, aided by hard-line victim advocates who want to reserve treatment resources for the deserving victims. Criticism of contemporary sex offender punishment policy, though not a major feature of public debate in the containment era,

can be located in a variety of sources. A few academics bemoan the validation of public punitiveness through expensive policies that do not live up to
their promises. A handful of critics on the left emphasize that due process
and liberty interests have been violated by what is cast as the rise of the preventive state. Some feminists and some victim advocates emphasize the need
to focus on assault by familiars and to incorporate policies that differentiate among offenders. Treatment practitioners point out the anti-therapeutic
effects of stigmatization and isolation.

Where can reform go from here? The past does not suggest that experts have
ever driven policy making, though they have certainly had more influence than
they do now. Sutherland and others within law and criminology who criticized
the sexual psychopath laws may have helped to moderate the punitive influence of the policies enacted during that time. In some other states, academic
critics of due process and civil liberty violations created by civil commitment as
social control for sex offenders may have contributed to the downfall of those
statutes in the 1970s. But in California, those concerns were less important than
the concerted efforts of victim advocacy groups like SLAM in overturning the
MDSO law. Experts within law and the social sciences are not likely to drive
policy change in the containment era either. But scholarship and policy analysis that document the way current penal policies impact the criminal justice
and correctional apparatus, as well as the broader goal of public safety, can lend
support to policy changes led by more influential groups.

At best, psych experts may be able to take advantage of another opportunity like the one that occurred in the early 1960s when staff from the
Department of Mental Health (DMH) shaped the civil commitment criteria. Perhaps the 2006 criteria revision, which now authorizes SVP commitment for offenders with only one victim (part of Jessica's Law) will create the
same kinds of institutional pressures on the DMH that led it to push for the
1960s revisions. But even this is uncertain, because the state has invested in
increasing the institutional capacity, providing for hundreds of new beds at
a new facility in Coalinga. Regardless, civil commitment in the containment
era represents only a fraction of the state's social control of sex offenders, so
significant changes must be targeted elsewhere to have widespread impact.

Quiet Politics

One of the practical implications of my findings that public panic is not
determinative is that public education may not be a worthwhile investment
for experts or reformers. While there may be other reasons to try to change

hearts and minds, policy change is not necessarily one of them. If the key mechanism driving containment policies was public panic, then that is what policy reform should address. Instead, public education is less important than structuring government to allow mediation. Those intent on affecting public discourse can aid this by creating a robust debate that includes both practice-based and academic experts, because the public will accept the insulation of such experts if they also trust them.

As the Adam Walsh Act and its broad requirements for inclusion in a sex offender registry have been implemented by the states, its undifferentiated approach has had the effect in some cases of making legislators aware of the rigidity of the act. State legislators who in the past would not consider any revisions to existing sex offender policies that did not extend its punitiveness now acknowledge that there are problems. Advocates have noted that legislators are now willing to discuss reforms in private, whereas in the early 2000s, such doors to dialogue were closed.[35]

Since Iowa's coalition of law enforcement officers spearheaded the retraction of their state's early experimentation with residency restrictions in 2006, a handful of other states have scaled back their registration and residency requirements. Some have chosen the more public route, such as Ohio, where the Public Defender's Office has pursued reforms through the courts and the legislature.[36] In June 2003, the Supreme Court of Ohio overturned the state's AWA, which had re-classified 26,000 offenders by offense conviction alone.[37] Ohio's recent victory in this case and example of legislating more modest juvenile requirements have been modeled by other states.[38] For example, people who fight for more recognition of juvenile justice have used the Ohio example to persuade their own legislators that easing up on registration requirements can be done and that it will not lead to Byrne grant revenue losses.[39] Still others, like advocates in Georgia, strategically use the Ohio example as an extreme to demonstrate that more moderate reforms by legislators are necessary to prevent the courts from intervening.[40]

The registration roll-back in Georgia may provide the most instructive example for other states. Georgia's enthusiastic embrace of the kinds of punitive and inclusive laws that have characterized the containment era resulted in both personal and public shifts in opinion. Cases like Genarlow Wilson's, for example, brought national attention to the harsh sentences juveniles can potentially face. In addition, a former prosecutor who takes credit for writing part of the state's sex offender law has himself begun to campaign for moderation.[41] But perhaps more important, state legislators in Georgia have begun to have personal experience with the laws, as their own children and the children of their friends have been caught in the wide net.[42] These factors, combined with civil liberties groups who sought court reform, allowed a significant shift when legislators undid a 2006 law that prohibited all sex offenders from living and working within 1,000 feet of schools and playgrounds.[43] As the Associated Press reported two months after the law was reversed, "Gov. Sonny Perdue signed the changes into law in May, allowing the 13,000 or so registered sex offenders who committed their offense before June 4, 2003, to live wherever they choose."[44] In addition, Georgia reforms included the institutionalization of a procedure for individuals to petition for removal from the registry, a crucial avenue for individualized decisions as to risk.[45] There were no public pronouncements as these bills were signed, and little attention was paid until after the fact, when a few national news channels featured short stories about the reforms. It is possible that there will be some political consequences for the legislators who voted for these reforms, but the cover provided by the Ohio example and the advocates' general strategy of combining a prosecutor's support with a relatively quiet campaign may ultimately prevail. If it can be done in Georgia, similar reforms may have success elsewhere as well.

Advocates for reform of sex offender laws in New Mexico have led a similar quiet campaign that has already achieved several legislative victories. Like Georgia, their biggest success was achieved by partnering with an original supporter of the registry laws, in this case a victim advocate who not only supported passage of the law, but also actively prompted its enforcement in her community by personally investigating neighbors and insisting on police response. Reform advocates approached her and explained the diluted effect caused by the overbroad registry, and she reportedly joined their efforts to scale it back.[46] Since 2009, the advocates take credit for stalling several bills that would have expanded the punitive approach, largely by overwhelming the legislature with testimony. Their volunteer organization has arranged to have people available at a moment's notice to speak about the effects of registry and residency laws on themselves and their families, and the pages of prepared comments have daunted committee chairs into tabling proposed bills.

Interestingly, even the most punitive of single-issue advocates will occasionally differentiate by severity, as when Mark Lunsford distinguished his eighteen-year-old son's consensual sexual touching of a fourteen-year-old from the conduct of a "pervert."[47] Patty Wetterling, the mother of child victim Jacob Wetterling, is well known for her advocacy of sensible policies that focus on using research and treatment to address problems of sexual violence. Rather than using her son's tragedy for indiscriminate punitiveness, she declares that she's "tired of tough. Everybody wants to out-tough the next legislator. 'I'm tough on crime,' 'No, I'm even more tough.' It's all about ego and boastfulness."[48]

Experts' Role

The most important role psych experts may be able to play is not one tied directly to policy making, or even to public education, because it is the local decision makers who implement policy that seems to drive punishment trends in this area. Instead, psych experts should commit themselves to filling in the knowledge base, beyond the role they currently play in supporting the status quo. Rather than conducting research that builds on assumptions such as uncontrollable compulsion or the connection between sexual fantasy and sexual conduct (or even the assumption that sex offenders are different from other violent offenders), we need methodologically rigorous, controlled experimentation that tests these assumptions and that provides the basis for empirically grounded differentiation among sex offenders.

Canadian experts have modeled this kind of research and have implemented many of their strategies in the correctional system. Recently, clinicians have argued for a move to something more like a self-regulation model of sex offender treatment. This builds on the research of Dr. Karl Hanson, a Canadian correctional clinician and researcher who has both pioneered assessment and treatment approaches and produced the meta-analyses of recidivism studies that yield the most widely supported base rates. The self-regulation model moves from reliance on static risk factors (aspects of an offender's record or identity that cannot change and therefore cannot be affected by treatment) to "dynamic risk factors" for re-offense. Consistent with Hanson's 2007 report on the "Dynamic Supervision Project," which included all of Canada and the states of Alaska and Iowa, research has shown that risk assessments using these kinds of factors can reliably sort offenders into risk categories. If room can be made for community corrections officers in the United States to make supervision decisions based on these tools, perhaps with the additional "cover" of tools like the polygraph, it may be possible to dramatically reduce the unnecessary use of taxpayer money to pay for the incarceration or intensive supervision of the large numbers of offenders who are unlikely to commit new crimes. Future research will examine the effects of this approach to treatment and recidivism.

Few would advocate a return to past practices that dismissed sexual offending as a mere nuisance if it was committed by upstanding citizens or family members. The demise of the discretion to downplay certain kinds of sexual assault based on the status of the offender or the victim should not be mourned. But there are at least two reasons why a new and improved differentiation among sexual offenders should be a policy and research priority. First, it is inevitable that discretion will continue to play a role in criminal justice decision making: Even a very inclusive image of what counts as monstrous sexual offending will not lead to the incapacitation of all sex offenders. Some offenders will still be diverted for failing to match that image; evidentiary and other factors will still mean that not all sex offenders will go to prison. Most important, the reality is that almost all of those sex offenders who do go to prison will eventually be released. Instead of preventing prosecutors and other decision makers from classifying sex offenders who are not monsters, structures and guidelines should channel that discretion.

Second, the need to provide for differentiation is a pragmatic one related to the first. Prisons and civil commitment programs cannot possibly hold all sex offenders indefinitely. The already underfunded and overworked parole system is in no condition to provide intense supervision and accountability for all sex offenders, even with the help of GPS technology (which itself creates new costs to parole agents who must process the data and decide how to respond to them). Even if states continue building prisons and state hospitals, and are somehow able to recruit and retain all the people it would need to staff those facilities and the parole system, the exorbitant costs incurred will eventually require some limits in practice.

The national survey of sex offender treatment providers conducted by the independent Safer Society Institute insists that financial pressures require better use of public money, especially in times of reduced funding, programs and jurisdictions must effectively manage their resources for services to sexual abusers in order to ensure the greatest positive impact. This means, given limited resources, sexual abusers should optimally receive no more than, and no less than, the type and amount of care needed to successfully manage their risk to re-offend and to be productive members of society.[49] Reformers need to heed this advice: Taxpayers should only spend their money on sex offenders when it is empirically justifiable.

Thus, the need to guide discretion and to recognize institutional constraints and budgetary limits means differentiation among sex offenders will happen. It should be the task of policy makers, victim advocates, and criminal justice and correctional actors, as well as experts in the psychological and social sciences, to insist that this differentiation is grounded in what we know about the perpetrators of sexual violence, not what we fear about monsters.

Appendix A

Research Methodology

What does it mean for a discursive turn in the sociology of knowledge? First of all it points to the analytical "business as usual" part in discourse studies. Social sciences' discourse research starts with a theoretically informed research question and a heuristic circumscription of the social phenomenon under examination. In the following step explorative interviews might be conducted to gain further information on the object, appropriate units of analysis (data-format: e.g. documents, flyers, monographs, visual images, newspaper articles) have to be defined and subsequently to be collected. Later on, the leading questions as well as the data sample might be modified, transformed or even replaced by others.

—Keller 2005, 21

Social scientists continue to grapple with how to acknowledge the influence of the researcher on the research. In every study, we choose not only what to "read" as data, but we select among the available interpretations, and this is undoubtedly shaped by who we are. In a mixed methods study of this kind, data could be cherry-picked to tell the tale for which the researcher advocates, rather than allowing the data and the possible interpretations to emerge without forcing them into preferred forms. As with all research, at a certain point we must trust the judgment of the investigator. However, this trust is more deserved after the researcher fully explains her methods and interpretive choices. In this appendix I fully describe the data collection and interpretation that culminated in the stories I tell here.

Data Collection

The historical chapters are based on archival research, for which I combined database-driven research (e.g., looking for all news articles that referred to "sex fiends" in the *Los Angeles Times* and *New York Times* and by reading every eighth California case found using a series of search terms) with a screening "by hand" of all volumes of major journals in the social and behavioral sciences for content relating to sexual offending.[1] Looking through hard-copy volumes containing listings of articles to locate coverage rather than relying on the filtering of keyword searches of databases was possible prior to the 1980s because of the scale. After 1980, I often used databases, such as the Family Studies database. Because two chapters use California for an extended case analysis, I also attempted to locate all published reports from California's Department of Corrections and Department of Mental Health/Hygiene relating to sex offender punishment, as well as reports to the legislative branch.

Bourdieu's concepts of "field" and "doxa" as applied to the legal field are especially useful here. Doxa are "common assumptions and understandings," which Terdiman (Bourdieu's translator) explains as implying "immediate agreement elicited by that which appears self-evident, transparently normal. Indeed, doxa is a normalcy in which realization of the norm is so complete that the norm itself, as coercion, simply ceases to exist as such."[2] I describe the doxa surrounding sex offenders in each era and the contradictory assumptions that were increasingly elided, especially from policy. In the text I use the more widely recognized term "orthodoxy" to refer to this.

These doxa, these prevailing understandings about who sex offenders were and how they should be handled, must be understood in terms of the professional and social structures that support them, what I call the "sex offender discursive field." Bourdieu explains that a field is "a structured, socially patterned activity or 'practice'" and is often "the site of struggle, of competition for control."[3] Struggle for control leads to a hierarchical system within the field. For example, the juridical field "is organized around a body of internal protocols and assumptions, characteristic behaviors, and self-sustaining values—what we might informally term a 'legal culture.'"[4] "The specific codes of the juridical field—the shaping influence of the social, economic, psychological, and linguistic practices which, while never being explicitly recorded or acknowledged, underlie the law's explicit functioning, have a determining power that must be considered if we are to comprehend how the law really functions in society."[5] The field surrounding sex offender social control is analogous to Bourdieu's juridical field, although it encompasses multiple professional groups who accept segments of the sex offender "problem." Data collection and interpretation therefore focused on these groups as well.

The chapters based on the current, containment era, especially chapter 6, also draw heavily from qualitative research with the people who manage sex offenders. I conducted participant observations and formal and informal interviews covering two very different geographical regions, three formal organizations, and about ninety respondents, over a period of about nine years, at more than a thousand hours. I conducted open-ended interviews with correctional officers, therapists, and those who provide risk assessments, as well as lawyers, judges, and offenders (twenty formal interviews, each averaging 2.5 hours), and at least seventy informal conversations during conferences or at field sites and in response to unsolicited phone calls to my office by offenders who found my name, each ranging from ten minutes to sixty minutes in length. The former also included observations of these penal and therapeutic agents in training and at work, including about three hundred observation hours. All research received approval from institutional review boards for the protection of human subjects; sensitive participant information is kept confidential following the preferences of participants, including the alteration of personally identifiable details. Observations occurred at professional meetings, official state proceedings, and clinical practices: I attended the statewide training conference for sex offender treatment professionals in a large state for three nonconsecutive years between 2001 and 2006. I regularly attended the monthly local meetings of one state's Sex Offender Management Board and of two geographically distinct regional associations between 2001 and 2009. I also joined the board of a small national organization devoted to promoting the treatment of sexual abusers, made up of nonexpert volunteers such as clergy members; this group provided an especially useful comparison to the perspectives offered by the quasi professionals, who all had some sort of affiliation with state agencies. Court observation work for a separate project also occasionally informed this work.

My observations with the first two groups consisted of attending meetings, sharing my interests as a researcher, and largely passive note-taking. I also conducted short presentations on policy making and public education at a local, statewide conference and a national conference. My participation in the treatment organization was more active, including serving as a resource for individuals with questions about how to comply with local sex offender laws. This expressed my belief in access to treatment for philosophical, not empirically proven, justifications as I discuss in the text.

In addition to these observations, I recruited interview subjects through these groups, leading to a snowball sample of participants who are likely more experienced and more interested in professionalization, public education, and policy change than typical practitioners in this field—this is an important limitation. However, despite the skew toward more professionally and politically active subjects, I did achieve variation across the types of professionals. My formal interview pool included five probation and parole officers, three lawyers and judges, two psychiatrists, three psychologists, and seven assessors. Interviews were unstructured conversations in which I explained my research interest into how sex offender policies work in practice, and how I sought insight into current laws and their implementations as experienced by the various subjects. Open-ended questions included "What do we need to do to solve the problem of sexual offending?" and "What current law would you like to change and why?" These offered opportunities for reflections on personal as well as professional experiences. Other informants included victim advocates, parents of offenders, and former offenders. I addressed some of the same questions with them, but with less effort at systematic coverage. Finally, I also participated in the evaluation of a commonly used assessment tool, described in chapter 6. I not only observed the tool in action but also personally administered it to twelve individuals. My participation concluded before the results of each offender's assessments were processed, in part due to concerns about the voluntariness of the participating offenders. This constraint, combined with the need to respect the proprietary nature of one of the assessment tools, prevents my direct reporting of data from offenders. These interactions with offenders did shape my interpretation of the tool and what it does. I report here on how the tool was used and what it meant for offenders, but I do not reveal anything offenders said regarding their own deviance or history, following my institutional review board's advice regarding the terminated research.

Interpretation, Bias, and Subject Position

Other scholars who have recently written about sexual offending have either allowed their stories to reveal their subject positions, as in Eric Janus's account of his role on the defense team for a sexually violent predator, told within his book about the failure of the laws, or explicitly describe their personal stake in the storytelling, as Pamela Schultz does by analyzing her own victimization in her account of the stories of imprisoned child molesters.[6] Still others criticize contemporary law with no indication of their active advocacy related to the law. One legal writer in particular has provided critique based on very faulty scholarship, as I have pointed out elsewhere;[7] that writer chose not to reveal her membership on the board of an advocacy organization and chose to present her work as a detached weighing of opposing sides.

I find none of these approaches satisfactory. On the one hand, intellectual honesty, not to mention adequate social scientific technique, requires direct confrontation of the potential biases we may bring to our work. By noting them, and testing our interpretations for their influence, we have the best chance of telling the story as accurately as we can despite our predispositions. This book reflects my evolution from an advocate to a scholar. It took me several years of thinking, writing, and opening my work up to criticism in order to see that the desire to quickly name a problem and suggest a policy fix would blind me to the nuances of a complicated reality. I thank the generosity of the commenters from the Northeastern Law and Society meetings, in particular, for their close engagement with my work and their pointed critiques on this matter.

In terms of the approach that includes the claiming of victim or survivor status as a pathway to authority on this topic, I respect those who have made that choice, but I find it troubling in the context of the larger discourse surrounding victimization, gender, and expertise. However, in the interest of full disclosure I have given expert testimony on what we know about recidivism rates of sex offenders for the defense side, as part of my work as a professor, without additional compensation. I have also consulted with federal prosecutors regarding how to proceed in a case of child abuse that included evidence derived in conflict with professional ethical obligations. I am currently working on a statewide effort to provide services to women in sex work, which includes treatment for their victimization histories and diversion from criminal prosecution. I recently addressed the Reform Sex Offender Laws organization and acted as the faculty advisor to a student charged with failure to register. As a feminist, a woman, and a mother, I probably have more insight into victimization than many who lack these subject positions. In sum, I have had more consistent exposure to the "offender" side than the "victim" side, although most of this book problematizes that divide, as do my interactions with multiple individuals who are both victims and offenders.

Reflection and reflexive research, interpreting data from very different sources, testing interpretations with the "task executors" as well as the proponents and the objects of those laws, brought me to a different place. This book is telling more complicated stories than just making the simple statement "we are doing sexual violence policy wrong." In the conclusion I do point out clear places where policies must change, but these are derived from the stories I was able to hear by listening to as many voices as possible, rather than the story I began the project intending to tell.

Appendix B

Timeline

Contexts of Sex Crime Policy

The Sexual Psychopath Era: 1930–1955

1932: First psychiatrist in California system appointed at San Quentin

1934: American Psychiatric Association forms Section on Forensic Psychiatry

1937: National Committee for Mental Hygiene issues the pamphlet "The Challenge of Sex Offenders"

1937: Michigan passes sexual psychopath law

1938: Illinois passes sexual psychopath law

1939: California passes sexual psychopath law

1947: California passes Sex offender Registration Law

1948: Kinsey's *Sexual Behavior in the Human Male* is published

1950: California passes the Sexual Deviation Research Act

1950: California Penal Code 288a (oral copulation) statute changed to allow judgment as felony or misdemeanor (a wobbler)[1]

1952: In California, the education code prevents licensing and employment for teachers convicted of sex offenses (Stats. 1953, 1st Ex. Sess.1952, ch. 25, p. 389)

1952: The *Diagnostic and Statistical Manual* (*DSM*), first edition, includes homosexuality, fetishism, pedophilia, transvestism, exhibitionism, voyeurism, sadism, masochism, and other unspecified sexual deviations[2]

1952: California Penal Code 286 (sodomy) revised to allow life sentence as punishment

1953: Kinsey's *Sexual Behavior in the Human Female* is published

1954: Atascadero State Hospital opens

1955: Daughters of Bilitis founded in San Francisco, California

1957: California passes the Venereal Disease Law

1962: Illinois becomes the first U.S. state to decriminalize sodomy, after adopting the Model Penal Code

1968: *DSM-II* categorizes sexual deviation as a personality disorder[3]

1969: San Francisco Assemblyman Willie Brown starts an annual tradition of introducing legislation to repeal the state's sodomy law

1970: In California, the MDSO law is revised to remove ninety-day observations

1973: APA membership votes to exclude homosexuality from the *DSM*

1974: California Child Abuse Prevention and Reporting Act is passed

1975: California decriminalizes sodomy

1978: A released mentally disordered sexual offender (MDSO) murders Amy Sue Seitz

1981: The MDSO law is repealed in California

1984: The McMartin preschool accusations become public

1985: The National District Attorneys Association establishes the National Center for Prosecution of Child Abuse

1986: California enacts fifteenth revision to mandated child abuse reporting law

1987: First McMartin trial begins

1990: McMartin trial ends in acquittal; second trial begins and ends in acquittal

1990: California extends and amends statute of limitations in abuse cases

1990: Washington State enacts sexual predator civil commitment

1994: The Jacob Wetterling Act requires states to keep sex offender registries or lose federal funds for criminal justice

1994: California passes One Strike for [some] Rapists law

1996: Polly Klaas case gains nationwide attention

1996: California enacts the Sexually Violent Predator Law

1997: The U.S. Supreme Court upholds civil commitment in *Kansas v. Hendricks*

2001: In *Seling v. Young*, civil commitment is judged not to be second punishment

2006: In California, the Sex Offender Punishment, Control and Containment Act of 2006 is passed; nationwide, the Adam Walsh Act is implemented (followed by state implementations)

2010: The U.S. Supreme Court upholds the indefinite commitment of the Adam Walsh Act in *U.S. v. Comstock*

2012?: *DSM-V* distinguishes paraphilias from paraphiliac disorders and adds "harm" to the definition of these disorders

Notes

INTRODUCTION

1. Throughout the book I use "sex offenders" to refer to people who have committed a range of offenses including hands-off offenses like exhibitionism, as well as violent assaults. Following the FBI's data collection practices as well as public perceptions of what counts as sex crime, I generally exclude crimes related to prostitution and vice. I also focus on male offenders—while female sex offenders have always been acknowledged in a limited way, from the lesbians and prostitutes Cesare Lombroso fixated upon to the Mary Kay Letourneaus of recent years, these offenders are viewed as being in a separate category, one that is characterized by sexuality or promiscuity rather than violence or danger. See Lombroso and Ferrero 2004; Valverde 2005.

2. Zimring et al. 2001.

3. Finkelhor and Jones 2006 (describing child abuse rates in particular); see the Uniform Crime Reports, www.fbi.com/ucr, for trends across other categories.

4. Simon 2007.

5. Furillo 2006.

6. Skelton 2006.

7. Goldenflame, a convicted sex offender, has appeared on Oprah, CNN, and elsewhere to promote his book, *Overcoming Sexual Terrorism*. See http://www.overcomingsexualterrorism.com/jakegoldenflameauthor.html, accessed 12/20/10; CalCASA 2006.

8. See, e.g., Wells and Horney 2002, 2; and generally Bachman and Schutt 2007.

9. Douglas 1966, 39–40.

10. See Logan 2009.

11. Rafter 2007, 416.

12. I conducted a database-driven search in the Historical Newspapers database and included results found from the *New York Times* and the *Los Angeles Times*. The *New York Times* could arguably be called a national newspaper by the early 1920s, while the *Los Angeles Times* remained a regional paper longer, but by the 1960s the *Los Angeles Times* bore many marks of a national paper.

13. Little Hoover Commission 2007.

14. Marques et al. 2005.

15. Garland 2001, x.

16. Ibid., 22.

17. Foucault 1995; Foucault et al. 1991.

18. As Garland notes, "Whether he acknowledged it or not, Foucault's inquiries always carried within them a critical, normative dimension, urging us to identify the dangers and harms implicit in the contemporary scheme of things, and to indicate how our present

social arrangements might have been—and might still be—differently arranged" (2001, 3). This normative dimension is reflected in the writings of Foucault's intellectual descendants as well as his antagonists.

19. Ibid., 13.

20. Rusche et al. 2003.

21. Wacquant 2009.

22. Simon 2007; Garland 2001.

23. Krisberg and Marchionna 2006, 1.

24. Durkheim et al. 1983; Kennedy 2000.

25. Jenkins 1998; Beckett 1996. Building on this rich literature of close readings, which also includes Paula Fass's book about child abduction and Joel Best's identification of the salience of the child-victim, I contrast that framing with other pertinent social constructs and practices (Fass 1997; Best 1990).

26. Ofshe and Watters 1994; Simon 2000; Zimring 2006; Janus 2006; Socia 2010.

27. Cohen 1972, 9.

28. Jenkins 1998.

29. Freedman 1987.

30. Ibid., 88.

31. There are numerous valid ways to periodicize, depending on one's choice of emphasis: Estelle Freedman focuses on 1920–1960 for a similar project and Jenkins reminds us of an earlier cycle during the Progressive era (Freedman 1987; Jenkins 1998; see also Lieb et al. 1998).

32. Jenkins describes the lull as being from 1958 to 1976 (1998, 94–117).

33. Freedman 1987; Jenkins 1998; Chauncey 1993; Miller 2002.

34. Weidlein-Crist 2008, 1.

35. Quinn et al. 2004; Simon and Leon 2007.

36. Greenfeld 1997; Simon and Leon 2007.

37. Clay-Warner and Burt 2005; Bachman and Paternoster 1993; Finkelhor and Jones 2006; Horney and Spohn 1991.

CHAPTER 1

1. Simon 2000, 1111.

2. Herdt 2009.

3. Jenkins 1998, 232–233.

4. Greer 2003, 188.

5. Ibid., 186.

6. Fass 1993, 921.

7. Varela and Black 2002.

8. Slater and Bishop 1964, 158, citing an Atascadero superintendent, possibly Root.

9. Gallo et al. 1966, 792.

10. Douglas 1966, 36–37.

11. Simpson 1996, 550.

12. Ibid., 557.

13. Ibid.

14. Robertson 2001, 12.

15. *Los Angeles Times* [hereafter *LAT*], June 13, 1951.

16. *LAT*, January 6, 1950.

17. Tables for each era that show the characteristics attributed to sex offenders and the strategies promoted, by the various stakeholders, are available from the author.

18. Young 2007.

CHAPTER 2

1. *People v. Northcott* 1930, 643.

2. Healey 1930.

3. See Robertson 2001 on the rise of the mental hygiene movement and the new audience it provided to psychiatric notions of sexual danger.

4. U.S. Public Health Service 1919, No. 17.

5. Ibid., No. 18.

6. Ibid., Nos. 20–22.

7. Ibid., No. 34.

8. Ibid., Nos. 43 and 44.

9. Ibid., No. 32.

10. Lombroso and Ferrero 2004, 2006.

11. Lombroso and Ferrero 2006, 333.

12. Ibid., 332.

13. Ibid.

14. Note that this era overlaps slightly with the therapeutic era, and it could be said to end at either 1950 or 1955. The periodization is not meant to indicate precise starting and ending points but rather to enable characterizations of the dominant influences on each period. The sexual psychopath era might be seen as ending when California's pioneering treatment program at Atascadero opened for business or could extend to include the last of the executions of the "sexual psychopaths," as deemed by the media.

15. Schudson 1978.

16. Ploscowe 1951; Sutherland 1950a, 1950b; Freedman 1987; Jenkins 1998.

17. American Psychiatric Association 1952; Ray 1968.

18. See *LAT* January 16, 1947; *LAT* July 4, 1942; *New York Times* [hereafter *NYT*] April 1, 1948; *NYT* October 9, 1950; Associated Press, September 24, 1950.

19. See the various articles that named people who were being assessed as potential sexual psychopaths, for example, *LAT* June 1, 1940; *LAT* November 18, 1944; *LAT* July 17, 1954. During this period there were also several series that covered "manhunts" for a particular fleeing subject: *LAT* February 24, 1946; *LAT* November 16, 1949; *LAT* June 25, 1956; as well as a few stories about escapees from sexual psychopath wards: *LAT* September 29, 1952; *NYT* October 9, 1950.

20. Fass 1993, 924.

21. *People v. Adams* 1939, 161.

22. Ibid., 163.

23. *LAT* August 27, 1937.

24. *LAT* August 17, 1937.

25. Dyer's nine confessions were the sole basis of his conviction—there were no evidence and no motive other than the sexual appetite that De River ascribed to him. While

De River's testimony formed the basis of Dyer's appeal to the state's Supreme Court, it was not deemed prejudicial enough to have impacted the decision.

26. *LAT* August 7, 1937; *LAT* August 27, 1937.

27. *LAT* August 7, 1937; *LAT* August 27, 1937.

28. For example, a caption related to another story read "Angry throngs of women gathered outside the Hausman house" to protest the family's complicity in allowing another child murderer, Fred Stroble, to live there after they knew he had molested another child.

29. Whitman 1951, 107.

30. *LAT* November 16, 1949.

31. *LAT* March 16, 1957.

32. Nolte 2004.

33. Anhalt 1952; Crowther 1952.

34. Fass 1993, 920.

35. Whitman 1951, 51.

36. His theory regarding the rise of a new category was reviewed uncritically in the *Journal of Criminology*, which praised his sensational tales and his recommendations for more police patrolling as the primary solution to the problem of street crime "Through his deep penetration into the hoodlum trend, the causes and cures of this peculiar vogue of violence, and his analysis of the sex criminal, Howard Whitman has given us an absorbing and significant piece of social commentary."

37. Whitman 1951, 425–427.

38. Associated Press 1949; Hoover 1937; *LAT* January 16, 1947; *LAT* January 17, 1947.

39. Hill 1949.

40. See also Pollack 1950, which warned parents about the risk that children might taunt "neighborhood cranks" to the point of murderous rage and sexual assault.

41. http://www.archive.org/details/boys_beware.

42. Douglas 1966, 163. This may therefore contradict Fass's argument that offenders need to be "democratized" so that the public can learn from their example (Fass 1993, 938).

43. Kirkendall 1952, 18.

44. See, for example, Jenkins 1998 and Meloy 2006.

45. De River 1949, 1958.

46. *NYT* December 23, 1949; Thornton 1950.

47. Helfman 1950.

48. *LAT* May 13, 1924.

49. De River 1958, 21.

50. A significant portion of each book focuses on female sexual psychopaths: primarily lesbians but also infanticides and incendiarists—this parallels Lombroso's chapter and is also noteworthy in its departure from the public discourse. De River includes a set of photos in his book to complement the text; a disproportionate number of these photos portray lesbian sadomasochism and women with masculine gender identities. This fascination presents a sharp contrast with the current notion of the sex offender as largely a male deviant.

51. http://www.policepsychiatrist.com/, accessed December 18, 2008.

52. De River 1958.

53. Hoover 1937, 1947

54. St. Paul Police Department 1941.

55. Satterfield 1951.

56. Ibid., 406.

57. As Stephen Robertson explains, "Part of the turn-of-the-century movement of psychiatry out of the asylum, mental hygiene drew its conceptual basis from dynamic theories of mental illness that focused on functional disorders of the mind and emotional maladjustment rather than on physiological conditions" (2001, 10).

58. Fass 1993, 920.

59. Bowman 1951, 181.

60. *NYT* April 23, 1950.

61. Fass writes that media used psychiatric concepts "without entirely accepting the new authority of psychiatry itself" (1993, 928).

62. Halleck 1965, xi.

63. Ibid.

64. *LAT* December 10, 1948.

65. Ibid.

66. Sutherland 1950a, 1950b.

67. Ploscowe 1951.

68. *LAT* June 22, 1949.

69. Ibid.

70. *LAT* April 11, 1947; December 8, 1949; June 23, 1949.

71. *LAT* February 10, 1948; De River 1958.

72. *LAT* June 17, 1956.

73. *LAT* January 16, 1947.

74. Harris 1949. Both of these statements are corroborated by the yearly admissions reported in the series *California Prisoners*, although typically social scientists would not measure crime by convictions.

75. California Legislature.

76. See Zimring et al. 2001, chapter 10, for an extended analysis of insulation of experts and its erosion.

77. *LAT* 1949.

78. Hill 1949.

79. Upon hearing his death sentence, Dyer asked if this would hurt his chances for getting parole. *LAT* 1937.

80. *LAT* June 20, 1951. For more examples, see the California legislation as described in *LAT* December 4, 1947; December 8, 1949; December 12, 1949; May 5, 1950; June 26, 1951. For the New York legislation see *NYT* December 27, 1943; April 12, 1947; March 14, 1948; April 1, 1948; December 23, 1949.

81. I viewed the Espy data on file with the Inter-University Consortium for Political and Social Research and obtained frequencies coded for the following: rape, rape murder, murder rape robbery, burglary, attempted rape, attempted rape, rape robbery, sodomy, buggery, and bestiality (I chose not to include adultery or criminal assault). If anything, I would view these numbers as underestimates, because the coding may not always have included homicides with sexual components. Espy and Smykla 2004.

82. The Espy coding shows twelve murder/rape executions in California, which did not include the Northcott case. It appears that the Espy offense coding did not account

for male victims of sexual assault, and so those offenses must be discovered through other sources.

83. Randolph 1949.

84. Bonner 1937.

85. *LAT* June 23, 1949.

86. *LAT* May 25, 1951.

87. Hogue 1937.

88. Ibid.

89. Jenkins reads the sterilization laws of the eugenics era as purely aimed at preventing hereditary transmission, though he does note their special application to moral degenerates and perverts (1998, 43).

90. Freedman 1987, 95.

91. *NYT* December 11, 1949.

92. *NYT* March 19, 1947; March 7, 1948.

93. An undated document, released in the 1970s through the Freedom of Information Act, describes such research on sexual psychopaths. Though all names and identifications have been excised, many of the details about the institution point to Sing Sing.

94. See Watts 1968. Neil Miller's account of the Ernest Triplett case in Iowa described the administration of hallucinogenic drugs during his interrogation regarding his involvement in the sexual murder of a young boy (Miller 2002, 28).

95. Bowman 1954.

96. Wagner and Myers 1951.

97. Hoover 1937.

98. Simon 2007, 4.

99. Zimring and Johnson 2006.

CHAPTER 3

1. Cited in Illing 1965, 515.

2. Ibid.

3. Ibid., 514. Illing continued, "Whoever 'Dr. Slater' could be, his claim that he 'founded the group therapy technique for the treatment of sexual offenders' in the California State Prison System is false."

4. Reumann 2005.

5. Bookspan 1991; Cummins 1994; Halleck 1965; Simon 1993.

6. This is the caption for a tabloid story about California's Norwalk State Hospital, pictured as an idyllic retreat complete with palm trees (*Mirror* 1952).

7. Wacquant 2009; Rose 1990; Rothman 1980; Victor 1998; Fass 1993.

8. Hubbart 1959.

9. Ibid.

10. Ibid.

11. Bigart 1963.

12. Hubbart 1959.

13. Reporter 1959.

14. *NYT* November 14, 1961.

15. Weiler 1961.

16. See Jenkins 1998, 108–109.

17. See Valverde 1998.

18. Atascadero Program 1955; Atascadero State Hospital 1959.

19. Atascadero Program 1955.

20. Atascadero State Hospital 1959, 11.

21. Marshall and Marshall 2000.

22. Rose 1990; Lunbeck 1994.

23. Atascadero Program 1955, 1. Prison doesn't work for these "emotionally ill" offenders because it is demoralizing and does not allow for rehabilitation.

24. Nelson 1963.

25. Unpublished "Kinsey notes," dated March 28, 1958, Box SO1, Folder 1D, accessed through the generosity of the Kinsey Institute on Sex, Gender and Reproduction. It was not clear from the archival materials in the Kinsey collection who took the interview notes, although a scholar familiar with Alfred Kinsey's writings believed that the notes were probably written by Kinsey himself.

26. Slater and Bishop 1964, 13–14.

27. Whitman 1951, 109, 111–124.

28. Jenkins 1998.

29. *LAT* November 22, 1949.

30. Dix 1976, 237.

31. Bowman 1951, 254.

32. Jenkins 1998, 98.

33. Brownmiller 1975, 379.

34. See, for example, Robitscher 1966.

35. Marcus and Sidley 1974.

36. Halleck 1966.

37. Miller 2002, 155.

38. Nelson 1963.

39. Ibid.

40. *NYT* May 3, 1960.

41. Beisel 1997.

42. Associated Press [hereafter AP] 1960.

43. Anonymous 1961.

44. Coates 1963.

45. Cal. Pen. 209, enacted in 1947.

46. Hubbart 1959.

47. Gallo et al. 1966, 737.

48. Forst 1978, 71.

49. Gallo et al. 1966, 712.

50. AP 1975; Johnston and Herron 1975.

51. AP 1975.

52. AP 1972.

53. UPI 1976.

54. A judge in 2008 told me essentially the same thing: regardless of personal distaste for castration, if an offender wanted it in order to get out of prison, who was she to say no?

55. See Angela Davis, who argues for the political construction of the black rapist as a justification for lynching black men after slavery. Davis 1983, ch 11; See also Sommerville 2004 which provides a history of rape and race in the nineteenth-century South.

56. Hunter, Ralph, and Marquart 1993; Wolfgang and Riedel 1973.

57. Chalmers 1959.

58. Jenkins 1998, 95.

59. Garland 2005; Zimring 2003.

60. Sittons 1959.

61. The 1949 revision of the sexual psychopath law made proceedings mandatory in all cases involving a victim under 14 if a felony, or if a misdemeanor with a prior sex offenses. Cal. Welf. and Inst. 5501 (b)–(c), enacted 1949.

62. Despite these changes, throughout the era, sex offender civil commitment was available for people who committed sex offenses as well as those who committed nonsexual crimes but were deemed to be sexually deviant and dangerous. No evidence suggests noncriminals were widely targeted; implementation data reviewed in later chapters show the criminal focus.

63. Cal. Welf. and Inst. Code Sec. 6300 et seq (1972). In contrast, contemporary law reserves civil commitment for "a person who has been convicted of a sexually violent offense against two or more victims and who has a diagnosed mental disorder that makes the person a danger to the health and safety of others in that it is likely that he or she will engage in sexually violent criminal behavior. Cal. Welf. and Inst. 6600 (a)(1).

64. After release from civil commitment, defendants who benefited from treatment were usually not sentenced to further confinement, while those deemed dangerous or not amenable usually did serve more time (see Beattie 1972). The contemporary SVP law, in contrast, is triggered by the Department of Corrections review of sex offenders' case files as they approach the completion of their criminal sentence. Thus, the sexual psychopaths and MDSOs entered the Department of Mental Health prior to any criminal sentencing or incarceration, while SVPs are committed after serving their full sentence, without the input of the sentencing judge and sometimes decades after their offense.

65. Hubbart 1959.

66. Merton 1957; Cloward and Ohlin 1960.

67. Davis 1983.

68. Rushton 2000.

69. Hubbart 1959.

70. Unpublished document, Kinsey archives, Box SO1, Folder 1C, "Atascadero State Hospital," May 1, 1955, attributed to Dr. Rood.

71. Unpublished document, Kinsey archives; "Bessant 1952." This echoes the *DSM*'s inclusion of rape only when it included sadism (see the timeline in appendix B).

72. See, e.g., Herek 2000. Early psychiatry did not agree about the etiology of homosexuality—while Kraft-Ebbing coined the term "sexual psychopath" (see Valverde 2005), Freud and Ellis both believed homosexuality to be inborn and not a disease. Later psychoanalysts, influential in psychiatry and popular culture, also disagreed about specifics but tended to view homosexuality as a result of pathological family dynamics. Signaling the entrenchment and influence of this notion of pathology, the first edition of the American Psychiatric Association's *DSM* that was published in the early 1950s included homosexuality among the sexual disorders. The *DSM* continued to include homosexuality

until 1973, when the "weight of empirical data, coupled with changing social norms and the development of a politically active gay community" finally overcame psychiatry's desire to maintain jurisdiction (Herek 2000).

73. American Psychiatric Association 1952, 24.

74. APA 1968, 39.

75. This belief was expressed to me by three different treatment professionals, one of whom holds a national government office; all three claimed to have heard this from a revision task force member.

76. American Psychiatric Association 1980, 266.

77. Ibid., 271.

78. Jenkins 1998, 136.

79. In the 1990s, the religious right protested what they perceived to be a third significant change in the way paraphilia was described. Although the phrasing changed very little, Focus on the Family began a national campaign again the APA's "support" of pedophilia (see Jenkins 1998, 161).

80. Unpublished "Kinsey notes," dated March 28, 1958, Box SO1, Folder 1D.

CHAPTER 4

1. No disaggregated data by offense or diagnosis could be located for commitments prior to 1950.

2. The Department of Mental Hygiene was formed in 1973; civil commitment was under the Department of Health prior to this.

3. Lieberman and Siegel 1957.

4. Beattie and Vanich 1972.

5. Dix 1976, 236.

6. Ibid.

7. Kirk and Kutchins 1992; Kutchins and Kirk 1997; O'Donohue et al. 2000.

8. Lieberman and Siegel 1957, 803.

9. Cal Pen.Code, 242.

10. *People v. Feagley* 1975, 342.

11. Janus 2006, 144.

12. This average masks significant outliers. The misdemeanants demoted from Atascadero to serve out their civil commitment in prison averaged more than forty months—twice that of the Atascadero committees.

13. This may be an effect of civil commitment, because lewd offenders who were civilly committed first might get that time counted toward prison sentences: for example, if they were released from Atascadero as un-amenable to further treatment (Forst is told by attorneys that judges do this kind of calculation, see 133–136).

14. Nelson, *LAT* October 7, 1963.

15. Nelson, *LAT* October 6, 1963.

16. This kind of selective use of civil commitment is seen in other states as well. See Cole 2001 on New Jersey, as well as Robitscher 1966 on Pennsylvania.

17. Lieberman and Siegel 1957.

18 Ibid., 803.

19. Dix 1976, 234.

20. Atascadero State Hospital 196?.

21. Frisbie and Dondis 1965.

22. *People v. Stoddard* 1968; Dix 1976, 237. Dix found particular controversy regarding exhibitionism. Clinicians disagreed over whether exhibitionism was dangerous and, if so, whether the danger came from the likelihood that a flasher would progress to more serious sexual offending or from the nuisance and distress it caused to observers. Dix also refers to the California case law that held that exhibitionism under any circumstances qualified as dangerous, showing the gap between expert and legal assumptions.

23. Lieberman and Siegel 1957, 805.

24. Beattie and Vanich 1972. These figures are statewide, excluding Los Angeles: 50% of the lewd offenders were referred and 18.3% of the rapists were referred.

25. Ibid.

26. Unpublished document, Kinsey archives, Box SO1, Folder 1C, Rood, ASH Fact Sheet, May 1, 1955.

27. Cole 2000, 299.

28. California Division of Criminal Law and Enforcement, California Bureau of Criminal Statistics, and California Youth Authority 1954.

29. Jenkins cites civil commitment patterns in other states including New Jersey and Indiana, which included larger proportions of homosexual offenders, but he also notes that the total number of committees was very small nationwide, with the exception of California (1998, 86–89).

30. Forst 1978, 114–116.

31. Gallo et al. 1966, 783.

32. Robitscher 1966, 158.

33. Forst 1978, 44.

34. Forst writes that probation officers felt free to consider allegations of past criminal conduct, which they included in their recommendations. He writes that when cases deviated from the going rate, it was because the evidence was poor or because of hidden priors (1978, 118).

35. Atascadero Program, 1955.

36. Atascadero State Hospital 1959, 1963?; Lieberman and Siegel 1957.

37. Atascadero State Hospital 1959.

38. Kinsey materials, no date.

39. Ibid.

40. Unpublished "Kinsey notes," dated March 28, 1958, Box SO1, Folder 1D.

41. Ibid.

42. Assembly 1950, as cited in *People v. Feagley* 1975, 393.

43. Atascadero State Hospital 1959, 3.

44. Ibid.

45. 1957, 805.

46. McGrath et al. 2003, 47–48.

47. Atascadero State Hospital 1959, 6.

48. Ibid., 4.

49. Ibid., 8.

50. Atascadero Program 1955; see also Miller 2002.

51. Hubbart 1959.

52. Italics added; Assembly 1950, 172.

53. Assembly 1950, 171, 172.

54. *People v. Feagley* 1975, 394; from statements filed by the Attorney General in the case of In re Abney on Habeas Corpus at 15112.

55. *People v. Feagley* 1975, 398–399.

56. Robitscher 1966, 153–168.

57. Beattie and Vanich 1972.

58. Ibid.

59. *People v. Feagley* 1975, 398–399.

60. Cited in *People v. Feagley* 1975, 373.

61. The graph shows felony sex arrests as being more numerous in the early 1960s, but this is an artifact of poor disaggregation by offense and of poor reporting in general.

62. California Bureau of Criminal Statistics 1958, 1959.

63. The series of reports published as *Delinquency and Probation in California* from 1954 to 1963, includes these numbers, as well as the sample of lower court probation referrals.

64. Frisbie 1969, 139.

65. Gallo et al. 1966.

66. Ibid., 783.

67. Except in rare (and perhaps never-used) cases of voluntary commitment. Commitment to private hospitals may also have occurred, but these data are not available either.

68. Robertson 2001, 5.

69. See Jenkins 1998, 89.

70. UCLA Project 1966, 738.

71. Unfortunately, we don't know the outcome of those not granted probation; therefore, we cannot determine whether the disparity led to more or less punitiveness.

72. *Delinquency and Probation in California 1957,* 118.

73. Odem 1995.

74. Amir 1971.

75. See Wheeler and George 2005, 39, in Barrett and George 2005.

76. Beattie and Vanich 1972, 11.

77. Ibid.

78. Kirk 1975, 299.

79. Ibid., 300.

80. Ibid., 301.

81. Gallo et al. 1966, fn. 63.

82. Halleck 1965.

83. Director of a California Sex Offender Program, as quoted in Slater and Bishop 1964, 158–159.

84. Not all were trained in psychiatry but nevertheless can be viewed as part of correctional or forensic psychiatry because of their work in diagnosis and treatment: thus I call them "psych experts."

85. Note that the offense breakdown is not as precise as we'd like—"other" includes all nonrape sex offenses, but other data indicate that it is dominated by child molesting offenses.

86. Forst 1978, 44; *People v. Feagley* 1975.

87. Forst 1978, 199.

88. Simon 2007.

CHAPTER 5

1. English et al. 1996; Lynch 2002.

2. In 2007, a Philadelphia judge would not allow the prosecution of men who raped a prostitute but insisted it be charged as robbery: "I thought rape was a terrible trauma." A case like this, she [Judge Deni] said—to my astonishment—"minimizes true rape cases and demeans women who are really raped" (Porter 2007).

3. Shaw 1990, as cited in Earl 1995.

4. For more detail, there are numerous articles and books available, some of which include the recollections of the defendants in the case (Buckey et al. 1990; Butler 2001; Earl 1995). For a perspective on the satanic abuse accusations that spread beyond McMartin, see Lawrence Wright's *Remembering Satan* (1994), as well as other excellent journalistic and sociological accounts (Nathan and Snedeker 1995; Richardson et al. 1991; Showalter 1997).

5. Wakefield 1995.

6. See Jenkins 1998, 216.

7. Earl 1995.

8. Buckey et al. 1990.

9. See Jenkins 1998, 232, describing the globalization of child abuse panics.

10. Stewart and Scott 1984.

11. Hernandez 1984; Ingram 1984.

12. Jenkins 1998, 118, 121.

13. Ibid., 128.

14. Loftus and Doyle 1987; Loftus and Ketcham 1994; Ofshe and Watters 1994.

15. Jenkins 1998, 188.

16. Jenkins provides a history of "predator" with its contemporary connotations, noting its first use in this way around 1990 (1998, 193–195).

17. Fechter had not seen *The Mark* prior to creating *The Woodsman*, personal correspondence.

18. This echoes a comment made to me by a sex offender on probation, who described carrying coins in his pocket at all times in case he was violated and needed to make a call.

19. See also the hit cable series *Dexter*—the pilot episode featured the triumphant execution of a homicidal child molester.

20. Lynch 2002.

21. Ibid., 557.

22. California legislators passed the Sex Offender Containment Act in 1999, which Governor Wilson vetoed, but many aspects of the model have been implemented at the agency level. It also reflects the orientation of CCOSO and ATSA to sex offender management—and their members are the ones who put policy into practice.

23. English et al. 1996.

24. Abbott 1988.

25. As noted early in this era, "One of the crucial factors in combating the sexual molestation of children is the identification and treatment of the offender. Yet most clinicians are not being trained to work with such clients in the course of their graduate schooling. As a result, offenders continue to be recycled back into the community without the support services necessary to reduce the risk of recidivism" (Gary et al. 1982, 143).

26. McGrath et al. 2003, 25–26.

27. Robinson 2003, 5.

28. Kiersh 1990, 179.

29. Ibid., 185.

30. Ibid.

31. Gathright 2001; Goodnough and Davey 2007; Marosi 2001.

32. *Coker v. Georgia*, 1977.

33. *State v. Wilson* 1996, 1067.

34. According to Louisiana's Justice Project, the exception exists in twenty states and in the federal code 404B, but the Louisiana statute only names it a lustful disposition: all others create exceptions for bringing in other crimes' evidence, but most are for showing a modus operandi or "signature"—not propensity but generally geared toward an independent, relevant aspect (personal correspondence, December 17, 2008).

35. Hanson and Bussiere 1998; Hanson and Morton–Bourgon 2004; Langan 2002.

36. The Louisiana Justice Project brought me in as an unpaid expert to present recidivism data in the case of *State v. Vessell* in support of a motion calling Louisiana code 412.2 unconstitutional on January 16, 2009. The motion failed and the prior evidence was allowed, but the defendant was later found not guilty.

37. See, for example, California Penal Code §§311, 314.

38. See the DOJ overview of SORNA's complicated requirements at http://www.ojp. usdoj.gov/smart/pdfs/faq_sorna_guidelines.pdf, accessed January 6, 2009.

39. As of this writing, the DOJ had deferred state compliance until July 2010 and is expected to issue an additional year's deferral, which would postpone compliance until July 2011. However, states that are determined to be noncompliant with the act face severe consequences, such as a 10% reduction in criminal justice funding from the federal government's Byrne grant system. As a result, many states have amended their laws to meet the requirements in whole or in part.

40. In general, a person convicted of a registerable felony sex offense who fails to register is guilty of a felony. A person convicted of a registerable misdemeanor sex offense who fails to register is guilty of a misdemeanor on the first violation, but subsequent failures are felonies. Cal. Pen. §290(g).

41. The bill failed to pass in 2009 but was introduced again in 2010 as HR 5138.

42. In addition to removal from the doctoral program, following his PO's inaccurate advice led to a new felony failure to register charges, still pending in Delaware.

43. See also Leon et al. 2011.

44. Pub. L. 104-236, 110 Stat. 3093.

45. Logan 2009.

46. Terry et al. 2008.

47. Pub. L. 104-145, 110 Stat. 1345.

48. See, for example, http://www.meganslaw.ca.gov/, which also allows citizens to report information on sex offenders in violation of the law: "Once you have read and acknowledged the disclaimer on the next page, you may search the database by a sex offender's specific name, obtain ZIP Code and city/county listings, obtain detailed personal profile information on each registrant, and use our map application to search your neighborhood or anywhere throughout the State to determine the specific location of any of those registrants on whom the law allows us to display a home address. . . . This website

indicates that many of these registrants are currently in violation of their registration requirements. Any information you may have on these individuals should be reported to your local law enforcement" (accessed March 6, 2007).

49. Pub. L. 104-236, 110 Stat. 3093nd 2000.

50. For information on the efficacy of other types of sex offender policies at reducing sex crimes, see the review by Socia and Stamatel (2010), and the studies in the May 2010 issue of Criminal Justice and Behavior, as introduced by Harris and Lurigio (2010).

51. Harris et al. 2010.

52. Ibid.

53. Hanson and Morton-Bourgon 2009.

54. See the essays in the November 2010 issue of *Criminology and Public Policy* for more detail on residency restrictions and their political and empirical contexts, including Leon 2010.

55. Koch 2007.

56. Rothfeld 2009.

57. "Residents list the camp as their official address on their driver's licenses—'Under the Julia Tuttle Causeway'—and some say their probation officers ordered them to live there" (Loney 2009).

58. Casady 2009; Levenson 2008; Minnesota Department of Corrections 2003.

59. Hughes and Burchfield 2008.

60. Minnesota Department of Corrections 2007, 25.

61. Duwe and Donnay 2010.

62. Levenson 2009.

63. New York approved a new law in early 2007 that differs in several ways.

64. In some cases, civil commitment before 1980 led to confinement for low-level offenders like exhibitionists who otherwise would probably have received probation and/or a fine (see the next chapter). But these were numerically far fewer. In addition, offenders released from civil commitment as "unamenable" to treatment could end up serving time in prison if the sentencing judge decided—a reversal of the sexual predator laws, but also resulting in a total amount of months in confinement far smaller than the truly indeterminate confinement of today.

65. Davey and Goodnough 2007.

66. See Szasz 1963.

67. See American Friends Service Committee 1971; Mitford 1973; Szasz 1963; Freedman 1987; Jenkins 1998.

68. All figures in this paragraph are from Davey and Goodnough 2007.

69. Lohn 2010.

70. Participant Observation 2005–2006; Davey and Goodnough 2007; Gathright 2001.

71. Commitment admissions for the period 1998–2009 derived from the data provided by the California Department of Mental Health.

CHAPTER 6

Material in this chapter surveying the status of empirical knowledge regarding sex offender treatment will appear in the *Sage Handbook on Corrections, Sex Offender Treatment*.

1. Halleck 1965.

2. Ibid., v.

3. Wakefield 2006.

4. Carey 2004.

5. Note that research on behavior modification and later on chemical castration did appear in other journals, including the *British Journal of Psychiatry, Acta Psychiatrica Scandinavia* (reporting on Stèurup's work with the "untreatable" and various clinical publications like the *Treatment of Sexual Aggressiveness News.*

6. Quoted in *People v. Feagley* 1975, 369.

7. CSOM 1996.

8. Breiling 2003; Prentky 2003.

9. Breiling 2003.

10. Prentky 2003.

11. Hanson and Bussiere 1998.

12. I conducted both broader and deeper searches than Prentky did, which are the basis for my claim that offenders were the focus until the 1980s, when a reversal took place. For searches that extended Prentky's analysis through 2008, I found similar concentrations of topics. See appendix A.

13. Unpublished document in Kinsey archives, Box SO1, Folder 1A: "the Emotional Security Program."

14. Guttmacher 1951.

15. General Accounting Office 1996.

16. Marques et al. 2005.

17. Hanson 2002.

18. Lösel and Schmucker 2005.

19. McGrath et al. 2003, 2.

20. Zimring 2006.

21. Robinson 2003.

22. Robinson also recounts the U.S. Department of Justice's realization in 1993 that sex crimes had become a crucial problem for governance and its invitation for a briefing by experts in the field (2003, 2). This briefing revealed a "knowledge gap" within expertise as well and led to the founding of the Center for Sex Offender Management to promote research, training, and public education (3).

23. First and Pincus 2002.

24. American Psychiatric Association 2000, 522–532.

25. Spitzer and Wakefield 1999.

26. Ibid.

27. http://www.dsm5.org/ProposedRevisions/Pages/proposedrevision.aspx?rid=416#, accessed July 23, 2010.

28. Ibid.

29. Rind et al. 1998.

30. Cole 2000, 13.

31. Garrison and Kobor, 2002.

32. Material in this section has also been published in "Over, under and Back Again? Unintended Consequences of Sex Offender Policies" (forthcoming in a special issue of the *International Journal of Law and Psychology*); De River 1949.

33. Marcus and Sidley 1974. See discussion of Dr. Henry Davidson who "warned psychiatrists from becoming Dr Fixits even if asked to assume that role by courts" (Robitscher 1966, 156).

34. Gee et al. 2003; Abel et al. 1977.

35. Blanchard and Freund 1981.

36. A 1998 article debunking the arousal-action connection put it this way: "The allied concept that deviant sexual arousal will be associated with sexual offending has appeared to many clinicians (and the criminal justice system) to be axiomatic, although a review of the relevant literature reveals that such a relationship is, at best, an uncertain one" (Howes 1998, 184).

37. Ibid., 185.

38. McGrath et al. 2003.

39. For a full discussion of bias, interpretation, and methodology, see appendix A.

40. See Zimring et al. 2001, chapter 10, for an extended analysis of insulation of experts and its erosion.

41. Bradberry and Tester 2005, 13.

42. This discussion is based on a study authorized, but not commissioned, by the proprietors of the tool (PRV-3 is not the real name). My research assistant and I received no compensation of any kind for our work, although an associated clinician did receive a computer for use in future assessments and receives ongoing compensation as one of the only paid assessors for the region. My participation in that study ended before any data were analyzed; the data may be published elsewhere. Before being trained, I signed a nondisclosure statement agreeing not to reveal specific trade secrets; the sanctions would include monetary relief as well as injunctions from publication. However, after I raised objections to the original nondisclosure document, adequate revisions and verbal assurances made me confident that I could engage in the research without sacrificing academic freedom or my obligation to be truthful.

43. In practice, it is given in prisons in less controlled environments.

44. As I have only been trained by one individual and have spoken with but not actually observed others in practice, I have no way of knowing if the other assessors speak in similar terms. However, this assessor had reviewed his "script" with the proprietors and they generally approved.

45. After the test taker concludes the two part of the test, the test computer sends information to the PRV-3's proprietors, who return a report to the assessor that includes scores for several commonly used psychometric assessments as well as the comparison with the denier group.

46. Scholars who have critiqued the tool and its proprietors have focused on the tool's inability to statistically support the claims made by the proprietors. The proprietor's publications have rarely been vetted through peer review. When they do, the statistical findings are reported in vague terms that prevent replication. In response to this critique, the proprietor responded that those critics had themselves failed to meet standards of scientific inquiry. He failed to address the request for a transparent statistical evaluation of the assessment tools. This academic debate reveals the heart of this case study: the lack of outside and open review of the assessment tools, which are the key features of sex offender knowledge work. Many researchers, including the critics mentioned above as well as this author, agree that the tool is a promising one but should be further refined.

Indeed, with an open academic debate on the empirical merits of the tool, the necessary refinement could be achieved.

47. The assessor's account of this negative feedback was confirmed by the supervisor in question, who volunteered the same information to me.

48. While this seems like a hefty fee, recall that the assessment takes several hours to complete and requires a secluded quiet environment. As a result, it takes a significant investment of time for the assessor, time that could be spent running treatment groups for Medicaid reimbursal; Jacob and Eisenstein 1977, x.

49. It is worth emphasizing here that my findings are limited by the sampling to assessors with more professional and public policy interests but is not limited to "defense-side experts." Rather, there is such limited availability of these sex offender assessors that it is not possible for them to specialize; all receive state contracts, and many may do private assessments for attorneys as well.

50. In the sense of lessened state control.

51. Helpful unless they wanted those treatment spots, as some did, in part because those spots would be much more affordable than private treatment, and their treatment participation would offer further "proof" of attempts at internal control.

52. Simon and Leon 2007.

53. Ward 2006.

54. Hanson 1999.

55. Huot 1999, 6–4.

56. Ibid.

57. Witt and Barone 2004, 172.

58. But see Lave 2009. See, for example, Hanson and Bussiere 1998; for criticism of MnSOST, see Gunderson 2007.

59. Langan 2003.

CHAPTER 7

1. Wilson 1994. A bill enacted in 1994 had also been called a "one strike" law for sex offenders, but it actually addressed repeat offenders, mandating a twenty-five-year sentence for crimes including rape, forcible spousal rape, and lewd and lascivious conduct with a child under the age of fourteen if the offender had two prior felony convictions.

2. Wilson's one-strike proposal faded away, which Zimring and colleagues explain as a timing problem: The coalition that had supported the three strikes law was still focused on the upcoming November election and did not welcome more distractions (Zimring et al. 2001, 140).

3. Simon 2007, 7.

4. Sandalow 1994.

5. Greer 2003.

6. *LAT* February 27, 1946.

7. *LAT* December 10, 1948.

8. Ibid.

9. Garland 2001; Scheingold 1997; Simon 2007; Zimring et al. 2001.

10. Luther 1984.

11. Lindgren and Luther 1984.

12. Ibid.

13. *LAT* December 12, 1949.

14. Anderson 1976.

15. http://www.alcoda.org/about_us/history, accessed December 20, 2010. This prominence is especially striking given the recent coverage of the case, casting doubt on Abbott's guilt and on police practices; see Nolte 2004.

16. Anderson 1976. " 'These crimes are most heinous.' [Judge] Di Giuseppe said, adding that the mental hospital treatment was recommended in both psychiatric and probation reports. He said Atascadero could mean lifetime confinement whereas De Caro would 'technically be eligible for parole before he even got to state prison. If I were to send him to prison he probably would spend four years there.' After the hearing he said no one is released from Atascadero in less than two years and that he has issued an order that De Caro not be paroled or released without court approval." (Anderson 1976).

17. Lindgren 1984.

18. This distaste for feminists persists—in a 2004 police training book, the author's eminently reasonable tone in relating research and data-supported conclusions about sexual offending shifts into a hostile diatribe against university feminists who stir things up (Carney 2004, 112–113).

19. Mathews 1982.

20. Ibid.

21. The United States Department of Justice honored Linebaugh in 1985 as part of its celebration of Crime Victims' Rights Week. http://www.ojp.usdoj.gov/ovc/ncvrw/1985/honorees.htm, accessed March 1, 2007.

22. Mathews 1982.

23. "Most state courts operate on the principle that molesters can be cured or at least are not enough of a threat to society to merit long prison terms" (Mathews 1982).

24. Zimring et al. 2001. A 1996 police research report explains that "the many groups or organizations dedicated to the protection of children . . . are passionate about their cause and dedicated to making a positive difference. They are well organized, well funded and powerful. Smart public policy makers and law enforcement leaders will recognize the benefits of associating with these groups in an effort to accomplish missions which benefit the primary cause" (Finch 1996, 12–13). The MDSO law was replaced with a voluntary program for imprisoned sex offenders who sought treatment, but this was extremely restricted in availability.

25. Brennan 1984.

26. Vachss 2005.

27. http://www.protect.org/about/mission, accessed December 20, 2010.

28. Gloria Allred, http://www.protect.org/california/caSB33Supporters.shtml, accessed April 4, 2007. (The Web site is not currently active; hard copy is on file with the author.)

29. Zimring et al. 2001.

30. Kim 2003.

31. Morgenthau 2005.

32. http://www.protect.org/agenda.html, accessed April 1, 2007. (The Web site is not currently active; hard copy is on file with the author.)

33. De Quervain et al., 2004.

34. *Philadelphia Inquirer* June 11, 2009.

35. In fact, reform opponents often use examples of sex offenders to challenge drug sentencing reforms. When California voters had the opportunity to amend the three strikes law to restrict it to violent offenses (Prop 66), campaign phone calls to voters said that a yes vote on Proposition 66 would "release 26,000 murderers, rapists and child molesters into their communities." I received such a call in October 2004.

36. Merton 1972.

37. Maeve and Vaughn 2001, 48.

38. Simon 2007; Zimring and Johnson 2006; Garland 2001. Garland writes, "Any untoward attention to the rights or welfare of the offender is taken to detract from the appropriate measure of respect for victims. . . . Paradoxically, this vision of the victim as Everyman has undermined the older notion of the public, which has now been redefined and dis-aggregated" (2001, 11).

39. As quoted in *Counterpunch*, March 4–5, 2006, available at http://www.counter-punch.org/pariah03042006.html.

40. Zimring 1997. Note that the measure of recidivism includes failure to register as well as other nonviolent offenses, making the real sex offense repeat rate even lower.

41. Zimring 2006. See Zimring and Leon 2008 for an extensive examination of recidivism rates and their misrepresentation by scholars and advocates.

42. Wakefield 2006.

43. Robinson 2003, 4, 5–6.

44. Packer 1968; see also Feeley and Levine 2001.

45. Brownmiller 1975, 178–180.

46. Ibid., 179.

47. Karpman 1965; Gebhard et al. 1965; Guttmacher 1951; *LAT* January 6, 1950 (quoting Abrahamsen).

48. Schultz 2005.

49. Ibid.

50. Little and Lyon 2001, 44, as cited in Robinson 2003, 5.

51. Hudson 2002.

52. See, e.g., Koss et al. 2004.

53. Koss et al. 2004, 1448.

54. Cormier 2002.

CHAPTER 8

1. Lave 2009.

2. Data on file with the author, from the Crime in California series.

3. Drake and Barnoski 2006, 3.

4. Finkelhor and Jones 2006.

5. But the inconclusiveness of these patterns are revealed by the UCR's compilation of an "other" sex offense category for California (the dotted line beginning in 1990)—this is a higher rate than the one I calculated using all the nonrape sex offenses reported in Crime in California (California Bureau of Criminal Statistics and Special Services et al.).

6. See Klein 2004, which includes Alabama, Tennessee, Minnesota, Michigan, Georgia, Ohio, Florida, Louisiana, Texas, New York, New Jersey, Washington and California.

7. Ibid.

8. Jenkins 1998.

9. The Bureau of Justice Statistics calls its "other" category "other sexual assaults," but the close correlation between the rate of increase it shows nationally with California's "other" sex offense rate suggests that the agencies are counting similar offenses.

10. Few states make long-term correctional trends available online or in other formats. To compile the California data, I spent many long hours in the University of California archives copying numbers. Similar archival research across several other states would be very helpful for assessing the variation in state sex offender incarceration since the 1970s. Nonetheless, the California and national data are themselves very useful as harbingers of other state correctional systems, which may lag in following their example.

11. See Illinois data available at http://www.idoc.state.il.us/subsections/reports/statistical_presentation_2004/part1.shtml#8. Data calculated from numbers in the annual reports available at http://www.dcor.state.ga.us/Reports/Annual/AnnualReport.html.

12. Drake and Barnoski 2006, 7.

13. Bradberry and Tester 2005, 7.

14. California Prisoners series, 1960–2007.

15. This is the offense that makes up the bulk of the "other" sex offense category referred to in the arrest and imprisonment data.

16. Drake and Barnoski 2006, 10.

17. See, for example, Bardach 1977; Berk et al. 1977; Feeley 1992; Galanter 1974; McCoy 1993; Scheingold 1974.

18. Zimring et al. 2001, 125–147.

19. Jenkins 1998, 72; Edelman 1985.

20. See, e.g., Cole 2000, 299; Freedman 1987; see also Chauncey 1993.

21. See also Jenkins 1998, 61–64.

22. See Jenkins 1998; Lynch 2002; Simon and Leon 2007.

23. Zimring et al. 2001, 161.

24. Zimring and Hawkins 1992, 11–14.

25. Hill et al 2007, 683, 740.

26. Zimring and Hawkins 1992.

27. Zimring et al. 2001.

28. Ibid., 112–113, 144–145.

29. Goodyear and Hallissy 2003; Lindgren and Luther 1984; Timnick 1984; UPI 1963; Wagner and Myers 1951.

30. Barker 2007, 624–625.

31. Terry Glenn Lilley has suggested this, and it is certainly confirmed by the highly visible political activism that family member victim advocates played in the series of cases in California described in this book. However, this reveals a limitation of the data used here—the "behind-the-scenes" and arguably more influential advocacy that took place but did not make it into the media or other historical documents available to me cannot be used to falsify my interpretation. Future research is needed that utilizes deep case studies and interviews with victim groups in order to make comparisons across types.

32. In chapter 6 I described the victim advocates who succeeded in eliminating the California MDSO law.

33. See the Fox Newscast that aired on July 26, 2010, available at http://www.youtube.com/watch?v=fCc4yZoSbrU.

34. Anderson 2007.

35. Zimring et al. 2001, 26.

36. Simon 2007, 33.

37. Albonetti 1986; Frohmann 1997; Beichner and Spohn 2005.

38. See, e.g., Stover 1981; Thomas and Fitch 1976; Walsh 2004.

39. Gallo et al. 1966, 736–738.

40. The increase around 1995 in the "other" felony sex offense rate may be related to the 1994 three strikes initiative and other factors that would have weighed in favor of prosecuting lewd wobblers as felonies.

41. Zimring and Hawkins 1991, 1992.

42. Beattie and Vanich 1972, Tables 4A–4C.

43. Ibid.

44. California Prisoners 1973, 1983, Table 18A.

45. Walsh 2004.

46. Foucault 1995; Garland 2001.

CHAPTER 9

1. This account is based on personal correspondence with Ryan (not his real name), as well as the documents filed in his case. It is possible that Ryan's account is deceitful and that his conduct was more menacing than he claims. Even if this is true, and he was purposely exhibiting his genitals, little if any of what happened to him subsequently would be justified.

2. Durkheim 1983, 176.

3. Foucault 1995, 183.

4. Thanks to Damon Mayrl for this phrasing.

5. Wacquant 2009, 78.

6. Lave 2011.

7. Cohen 1985.

8. Wacquant 2009, 39.

9. Ibid., 116.

10. Levenson 2009.

11. Hughes and Burchfield 2008; Hughes and Kadleck 2008.

12. Williams 2009.

13. Ibid.; see also Barker 2007.

14. Douard 2008–9, 33.

15. Finkelhor et al. 2004.

16. Conversation with a psychiatric social worker in Alameda County, California, November 23, 2001.

17. Conversation with a social worker who works in a private, community-based mental health facility in Maryland, November 2001. Delaware social service providers report numerous similar stories, despite a new administration at the state level that is willing to release mentally ill and disabled clients with sex convictions from the state hospital, in contrast to previous unwritten policy which kept all such individuals indefinitely, see Leon et al. 2011.

18. Confidential interview, November 12, 2010.

19. Ibid.

20. See Laura Rapp, "Women in Relationships with Men Convicted of Sex Offenses." Unpublished dissertation on file with the author.

21. For example, the California group CCOSO has been able to influence policy because of a severe shortage of practitioners. There are about ninety thousand registered sex offenders living in California and only one hundred treatment providers (as counted by CCOSO). As a result, the CDC is sensitive to the concerns of CCOSO members because it needs those members to apply for its grants. The CDC has acknowledged that by discussing revisions of a recent Request for Funding Proposal (RFP) with CCOSO members, it permitted conflict of interest. But because there were so few treatment practitioners interested in the RFP, if they excluded those from the revision meetings there would be no one left to apply for the grants (Tobin 2002).

22. See, e.g., Finkelhor 1980; Russell 1986; National Victim Center 1992.

23. Marsa 2002.

24. See, e.g., Feeley and Simon 2007; Welch and Schuster 2005; Cohen 2002.

25. Sutherland 1950a, 1950b.

26. Ben-Yehuda 1981; Hall et al. 1978.

27. Corrigan 2006, 274.

28. For example, Jenkins 1998.

29. Victor 1998, 543.

30. Welch and Schuster 2005, 399; Cohen 2002.

31. Cohen 2002, xxi.

32. Zimring and Johnson 2006.

33. For example, Feeley and Simon describe the shift from the old penology to the new; Garland describes the erosion of penal welfarism and the rise of the culture of control; Jock Young describes a transformation into an exclusive society; Simon explains the efficacy of governing through crime; Michael Tonry documents the return to unthinkable punishments; and Zimring shows the effects of mistrust and of removing the insulation of decision makers from the public.

34. For example, Zimring et al. 2001.

35. Personal correspondence regarding ACLU efforts in an eastern state, 2010.

36. See http://www.opd.ohio.gov/AWA_Information/Adam_Walsh.htm, accessed July 30, 2010.

37. Grieco and Gokavi 2010.

38. The advocacy revised proposed versions of SB 10 so that just nine kids were included on the registry, down from 2000 in early versions. Statement of Amy Borror at the Reform Sex Offender Laws meeting, June 27, 2010.

39. Nicole Pittman, Defender Association of Philadelphia, testimony to the Delaware House Judiciary Committee, March 31, 2010.

40. AP July 19, 2010; see also a Georgia advocates blog, http://justdamn-vdog.blogspot.com/, posted Thursday, July 29, 2010, which explicitly compares the Georgia reforms to Ohio's as the lesser of two evils.

41. AP October 29, 2007, quoting Tom Morgan.

42. Personal communication with the mother of one such offender, June 27, 2010.

43. Georgia *HB 571*, enacted May 21, 2010.

44. AP July 19, 2010.

45. Official Code of Georgia Annotated *Section 42-1-19.*, available online at: http://www.lexisnexis.com/hottopics/gacode/Default.asp

46. Unconfirmed statement by Lloyd Swartz describing state lobbying efforts at the RSOL national meeting, June 27, 2010. Full transcript on file with the author.

47. AP May 31, 2007.

48. Gunderson 2007.

49. McGrath 2003, 4.

APPENDIX A

1. Specifically, these stories are the product of a search for articles that discussed sexual psychopaths, sex fiends, etc., prior to 1960 in the Historical Newspapers (Proquest) database (containing full texts of the *Los Angeles Times*, *New York Times*, and *Wall Street Journal*). Once I identified a particular case, I expanded the search to include the relevant names. All of the articles that resulted were published between 1937 and 1958. Other sources including court documents revealed three other publicized cases that, though not discussed explicitly as sexual psychopaths, also informed policy. I prefer the approach of screening by hand, but the quantity of material made it impossible to screen newspaper accounts and relevant case law without using a database search. The journals I searched were *American Psychologist*, *American Journal of Psychiatry/Insanity*, *Criminology*, *Journal of Crime and Criminology/Police Science*, and *Journal of Research in Crime & Delinquency*. I coded them Clinical/descriptive, Theory of Causation/Etiology, Classification of kinds of disorders, Treatment, Recidivism, Impact on Victims, Punishment, Prostitution, and Pornography.

2. Terdiman 1987, 809.

3. Ibid.

4. Ibid., 806.

5. Ibid., 807.

6. Janus 2006; Schultz 2005.

7. Zimring and Leon 2008.

APPENDIX B

1. *Cal.* Stats. 1950, 1st Ex. Sess. ch. 56, §1, at 512, added "or by imprisonment in the county jail not to exceed one year." See also Gallo et al. 1966, 678. This change may have been part of the "catch and treat them early" strategy recommended by the psychiatrists at Warren's special session, but this is only a guess. Intriguingly, this change, accompanied by the 1952 sodomy revision, meant that throughout the 1950s and 1960s, California had one of the most liberal oral copulation laws but one of the most stringent sodomy laws. See Gallo et al 1966, 677–679.

2. Sexual Deviations are included in the section on Personality Disorders and Certain Other Non-Psychotic Mental Disorders. *DSM-I* does not contain diagnostic guidelines, but the list is preceded by this explanation: "This category is for individuals whose sexual interests are directed primarily toward objects other than people of the opposite sex, toward sexual acts not usually associated with coitus, or toward coitus performed under bizarre circumstances as in necrophilia, pedophilia, sexual sadism, and fetishism. Even

though many find their practices distasteful, they remain unable to substitute normal sexual behavior for them. This diagnosis is not appropriate for individuals who perform deviant sexual acts because normal sexual objects are not available to them" (American Psychological Association 1952, 44).

3. "This diagnosis is reserved for deviant sexuality which is not symptomatic of more extensive syndromes such as schizophrenic and obsessional reactions." The term includes most of the cases formerly classed as "psychopathic personality with pathologic sexuality. The diagnosis will specify the type of the pathologic behavior, such as homosexuality, transvestism, pedophilia fetishism and sexual sadism (including rape, sexual assault, mutilation)" (American Psychiatric Association 1968, 38–39).

Bibliography

Abbott, Andrew Delano. (1988). *The System of Professions: An Essay on the Division of Expert Labor.* Chicago: University of Chicago Press.

Abel, G. G., D. H. Barlow, E. G. Blanchard, and D. Guild. (1977). The components of rapists' sexual arousal. *Archives of General Psychiatry, 34,* 895-903.

Albonetti, Celesta A. (1986). Criminality, prosecutorial screening and uncertainty: Toward a theory of discretionary decision-making in felony case processings." *Criminology, 24*(4), 623-644.

American Friends Service Committee. (1971). *Struggle for justice. A report on crime and punishment in America, prepared for the American Friends Service Committee.* 1st ed. New York: Hill & Wang.

American Psychiatric Association. (1952). *Diagnostic and statistical manual of mental disorders* Washington, DC: American Psychiatric Association.

———. (1968). *Diagnostic and statistical manual of mental disorders: DSM-II* (2nd ed.). Washington, DC: American Psychiatric Association.

———. (2000). *Diagnostic and statistical manual of mental disorders: DSM-IV-TR* (4th ed.). Washington, DC: American Psychiatric Association.

American Psychiatric Association and Task Force on *DSM-IV.* (1994). *Diagnostic and statistical manual of mental disorders: DSM-IV* (4th ed.). Washington, DC: American Psychiatric Association.

American Psychiatric Association and Task Force on *DSM-IV.* (1995). *Diagnostic and statistical manual of mental disorders: DSM-IV: International version with ICD-10 codes* (4th ed.). Washington, DC: American Psychiatric Association.

American Psychiatric Association and Work Group to Revise *DSM-III.* (1980). *Diagnostic and statistical manual of mental disorders: DSM-III.* Washington, DC: American Psychiatric Association.

American Psychiatric Association Committee on Nomenclature and Statistics. (1952). *Mental disorders; diagnostic and statistical manual.* Washington, DC: American Psychiatric Association.

Amir, M. (1971). *Patterns in forcible rape.* Chicago: University of Chicago Press.

Anderson, C. (2007, March 8). Sex offender guilty in Florida girl's death. Associated Press.

Anderson, P. (1976, August 15). Rapist sent to asylum; women upset. *Los Angeles Times.*

Anhalt, E., and Anhalt, E. (1952). *The Sniper*—from research to shooting. *New York Times.*

Anonymous. (1961). Study urged on crime and pornography. *Los Angeles Times.*

Assembly. (1950). *Preliminary findings.* Sacramento: Subcommittee on Sex Crimes of the Assembly Interim Committee on Judicial System and Judicial Process.

Associated Press (AP). (1948, November 26). Woman slain in brutal attack by sex fiend. *Los Angeles Times*.

————. (1950, September 24). Missing boy slain, buried. *Los Angeles Times*.

————. (1972, April 8). Sex offender's castration case given to doctors to investigate. *New York Times*.

————. (1973, January 25). Sex offenders being "castrated." *Washington Post*.

————. (1975, October 2). Two sex offenders sent to prison after plea for castration fails. *New York Times*.

————. (2007, October 27). Critics decry states' teen sex laws. MSNBC.com.

————. (2007, May 31). Mark Lunsford's son, 18, accused of sexual conduct with a minor.

————. (2010, July 19). Georgia forced to soften famously strict laws against sex offenders.

Atascadero State Hospital. (1959). *Therapeutic community program*. Atascadero, CA: Atascadero State Hospital.

————. (196?). *Youth maturity program: From boys to men*. Sacramento: Atascadero State Hospital.

Atascadero State Hospital: Emotional Security Program [cited as Atascadero Program]. (1955). *The new approach: Sex offender to good citizen*. Sacramento: Atascadero State Hospital.

Bachman, R., and Paternoster, R. (1993). A contemporary look at the effects of rape law reform: How far have we really come? *Journal of Criminal Law and Criminology, 84*, 554–574.

Bachman, R., and Schutt, R. K. (2007). *The practice of research in criminology and criminal justice*. 3rd ed. Los Angeles: Sage.

Barker, V. (2007). The politics of pain: A political institutionalist analysis of crime victims' moral protests. *Law and Society Review, 41*(3), 619–663.

Barrett, K., and George, W. (2005). *Race, culture, psychology, and law*. Thousand Oaks, CA: Sage.

Beattie, R., and Vanich, V. (1972). *The mentally disordered sex offender in California*. Sacramento: Bureau of Criminal Statistics.

Beckett, K. (1996). Culture and the politics of signification: The case of child sexual abuse. *Social Problems, 43*(1), 57–76.

Beisel, N. K. (1997). *Imperiled innocents: Anthony Comstock and family reproduction in Victorian America*. Princeton: Princeton University Press.

Best, J. (1990). *Threatened children: Rhetoric and concern about child-victims*. Chicago: University of Chicago Press.

Bigart, H. (1963, September 27). Killing of 2 girls yields no clue; police question 500 in a month. *New York Times*.

Blanchard, R., and Freund, K. (1981). "Assessment of sexual dysfunction and deviance." In M. Hersen and A. Bellack (Eds.), *Behavioral assessment: A practical handbook*. 2nd ed. New York: Pergamon.

Bonner, A. B. (1937, October 3). Letters to the times: The sex fiend. *Los Angeles Times*.

Bookspan, S. (1991). *A germ of goodness: The California state prison system, 1851–1944*. Lincoln: University of Nebraska Press.

Bourdieu, P. (1987). "The force of law: Toward a sociology of the juridical field." *Hastings Law Journal, 38*(5), 814–853.

Bourdieu, P., and Wacquant, L. J. D. (1992). *An invitation to reflexive sociology*. Chicago: University of Chicago Press.

Bowman, K. (1951, October). The problem of the sex offender. *American Journal of Psychiatry*, 250–258.

———. (1954). *Final report: California's sexual deviation* research. Department of Mental Hygiene, Langley Porter Clinic.

Bradberry, C., and Tester, D. (2005). *Sex offenders in South Carolina: An overview of the population and the nexus of community supervision and mental health services.*

Breiling, J. (2003). Etiology research as the route to science-based prevention. *Annals of the New York Academy of Sciences, 989*, 150–153.

Brennan, P. (1984, October 18). Law professor's answer for molesters: Jail former prosecutor says psychiatric treatment doesn't protect children." *Los Angeles Times.*

Brownmiller, S. (1975). *Against our will: Men, women, and rape.* New York: Simon and Schuster.

Buckey, P., Buckey, R., and Buckey, P. A. (1990). "After the McMartin trials: Some reflections from the Buckeys." *Issues in Child Abuse Accusations, 2.*

Butler, E. W. (2001). *Anatomy of the McMartin child molestation case.* Lanham, Md.: United Press of America.

CalCASA. (2006). *Press release: Sexual assault coalition announces opposition to Jessica's law.* Sacramento: California Coalition Against Sexual Assault.

California Bureau of Criminal Statistics and Special Services. (1978, 1989). "Criminal justice profile; statewide."

California Bureau of Criminal Statistics and Special Services. Division of Law Enforcement., California. Bureau of Criminal Statistics., California. Division of Criminal Law and Enforcement., California. Bureau of Criminal Information and Analysis, California. Law Enforcement Information Center, and Criminal Justice Statistics Center (Calif.). (1965, 2001). *Crime and Delinquency in California.* Sacramento: Department of Justice, Division of Criminal Justice Information Services.

California Division of Criminal Law and Enforcement, California Bureau of Criminal Statistics, and California Youth Authority. (1954). *Delinquency and Probation in California.* Sacramento: Bureau of Criminal Statistics.

California Legislature. Senate, Economic Development Agency of the State of California, California. Dept. of Finance, and California. Legislature. Senate. Fact-Finding Committee on Commerce and Economic Development. (1958; 2004). California statistical abstract.

California Offender Information Services Branch. Data Analysis Unit. (1988). *California Prisoners and Parolees.* Sacramento: Youth and Adult Correctional Agency, Dept. of Corrections, Administrative Services Division, Offender Information Services Branch, Data Analysis Unit.

Carey, B. (2004, November 9). Long after Kinsey, only the brave study sex. *New York Times.*

Carney, T. P. 2003. *Practical investigation of sex crimes: A strategic and operational approach.* CRC Series in Practical Aspects of Criminal and Forensic Investigations. Boca Raton, Fla.: CRC Press.

Center for Effective Public Policy. (1996). *Strategies to promote public safety through the effective management of sex offenders in the community.* Report produced with the Center for Sex Offender Management.

Chalmers, A. K. (1959, June 26). Florida verdict praised: Stride toward equal justice seen in white youths' conviction. *New York Times.*

Chauncey, G. (1993). The postwar sex crime panic. In W. Graebner (Ed.), *True stories from the American past* (pp. 160–178). New York: McGraw-Hill.

Chivers, M. L., Seto, M., and Blanchard, R. (2007). "Gender and sexual orientation differences in sexual response to the sexual activities versus the gender of actors in sexual films." *Journal of Personality and Social Psychology, 93*(1108), 1121.

Clay-Warner, J., and Burt, C. (2005). Reporting rape: Have things really changed. *Violence Against Women, 11*, 150–176.

Cloward, R. A., and Ohlin, L. E. (1960). *Delinquency and opportunity; a theory of delinquent gangs*. Glencoe, Ill.: Free Press.

Coates, P. (1963, May 21). "Book burners: Latest flare-up gets writer hot under collar." *Los Angeles Times*.

Cohen, S. (1972). *Folk devils and moral panics: The creation of mods and rockers*. New York: St. Martin's.

———. (1985). *Visions of social control*. Cambridge: Polity Press.

———. (2002). *Folk devils and moral panics: The creation of mods and rockers* (3rd ed.). London: Routledge.

Coker v. Georgia. 433 US 584 (1977).

Cole, S. (2000). From the sexual psychopath statute to "Megan's law": Psychiatric knowledge in the diagnosis, treatment and adjudication of sex criminals in New Jersey, 1949–1999. *Journal of the History of Medicine, 55* (3). 292–314.

Commission on California State Government Organization and Economy. (2007). *Solving California's corrections crisis: Time is running out*. Sacramento, Calif.: Little Hoover Commission.

Cormier, R. B. (2002). *Restorative justice: Directions and principles—Developments in Canada*. Department of the Solicitor General.

Corrigan, R. (2006). "Making meaning of Megan's Law." *Law and Social Inquiry, 31*(2), 267–312.

Crowther, B. (1952, May 10). Five newcomers begin runs. *New York Times*.

Cummins, E. (1994). *The rise and fall of California's radical prison movement*. Palo Alto: Stanford University Press.

Dabney, D. A., and Vaughn, M. S. (2000). Incompetent jail and prison doctors. *The Prison Journal, 80*, 151–183.

Davey, M., and Goodnough, A. (2007, March 4). Doubts rise as states detain sex offenders after prison. *New York Times*.

Davis, A. Y. (1983). *Women, race and class*. New York: Vintage.

de Quervain, D. J. F., Fischbacher, U., Treyer, V., Schellhammer, M., Schnyder, U., Buck, A., and Fehr, E. (2004). The neural basis of altruistic punishment. *Science, 305*(5668), 1254.

De River, J. P. (1949). *The sexual criminal: A psychoanalytical study*. Oxford: Blackwell.

———. (1958). *Crime and sexual psychopath*. Springfield, Ill.: C. C. Thomas.

Delaware, Office of Management and Budget. Statistical Analysis Center. (2007). Recidivism of Delaware juvenile sex offenders released in 2001.

Department of Corrections. (1945–1953). Adult authority and board of trustees of the California Institution for Women, 1945/49–, and Bureau of Criminal Statistics 1952–. *California Bureau of Criminal Statistics. California Prisoners; Summary statistics of prisoners and parolees*. Sacramento.

Dix, G. E. (1976). Differential processing of abnormal sex offenders: Utilization of California's mentally disordered sex offender program. *Journal of Criminal Law and Criminology, 67*(2), 233–243.

Douard, J. (2008–9). Sex offender as scapegoat: The monstrous offender within. *New York Law School Law Review, 53*, 31–53.

Douglas, M. (1966). *Purity and danger: An analysis of concept of pollution and taboo.* London: Routledge.

Dowd, M. (1983, September 5). "Rape: The sexual weapon." *Time.*

Drake, E., and Barnoski, R. (2006). *Sex offenders in Washington state: Key findings and trends* (No. 06-03-1201). Olympia, Wash.: Washington Institute for Public Policy.

Durkheim, E. (1997 [1933]). *The division of labor in society.* New York: Free Press.

Durkheim, E., Lukes, S., and Scull, A. T. (1983). *Durkheim and the law.* New York: St. Martin's.

Earl, J. (1995). The dark truth about the "dark tunnels of McMartin." *Issues in Child Abuse Accusations, 7.*

Edelman, M. J. (1985). *The symbolic uses of politics.* Illini books ed. Urbana: University of Illinois Press.

Eisenstein, J., and Jacob, H. (1977). *Felony justice: An organizational analysis of criminal courts.* Boston: Little, Brown.

English, K., Pullen, S., and Jones, L. (Eds.). (1996). *Managing adult sex offenders on probation and parole: A containment approach.* American Parole and Probation Association.

Espy, M. W., and Smykla, J. O. (2004). *Executions in the United States: 1608-2002* (4th ed.). Inter-University Consortium for Political and Social Research. doi:ICPSR Study 8541

Fass, P. S. (1993). Making and remaking an event: The Leopold and Loeb case in American culture. *The Journal of American History, 80*(3), 919–951.

———. (1997). *Kidnapped: Child abduction in America.* New York: Oxford University Press.

Federal Bureau of Investigation. Uniform Crime Reports. http://www.fbi.gov/about-us/cjis/ucr/ucr.

Feeley, M., and Simon, J. (2007). Folk devils and moral panics: An appreciation from North America. In D. Downes, P. Rock, C. Chinkin, & C. Gearty (Eds.), Crime, social control and human rights: From moral panics to states of denial, essays in honour of Stanley Cohen (pp. 39–53). Portland, OR: Willan.

Finch, J., Downey Police Department. (1996). *Meeting the challenge of repeat child molesters.* Sacramento: California Commission on Peace Officers Standards and Training.

Finkelhor, D. (1980). "Sex among Siblings: A Survey on Prevalence, Variety and Effects." *Archives of Sexual Behavior, 9*(3): 171–194.

Finkelhor, D., and Jones, L. (2006). Why have child maltreatment and child victimization declined? *Journal of Social Issues, 62*(4), 685–716.

First, M. B., and Pincus, H. A. (2002). The DSM-IV text revision: Rationale and potential impact on clinical practice. *Psychiatric Services, 53*(3), 291.

Forst, M. L. (1978). *Civil commitment and social control.* Lexington, MA: Lexington Books.

Foucault, M. (1990). *The history of sexuality.* New York: Vintage.

———. (1995). *Discipline and punish: The birth of the prison* (2nd ed.). New York: Vintage.

Foucault, M., Burchell, G., Gordon, C., and Miller, P. (1991). *The Foucault effect: Studies in governmentality: With two lectures by and an interview with Michel Foucault.* Chicago: University of Chicago Press.

Freedman, E. B. (1987). "Uncontrolled desires": The response to the sexual psychopath, 1920–1960. *The Journal of American History, 74*(1), 83–106.

Frisbie, L. V. (1969). *Another look at sex offenders in California.* Sacramento: State of California, Dept. of Mental Hygiene.

Frisbie, L. V., and Dondis, E. H. (1965). *Recidivism among treated sex offenders.* Sacramento: State of California, Dept. of Mental Hygiene.

Frohmann, L. (1997). Convictability and discordant locales: Reproducing race, class, and gender ideologies in prosecutorial decisionmaking. *Law and Society Review, 31*, 531.

Furillo, A. (2006, October 24). Crackdown urged on sex offenders; critics see flaws. *Sacramento Bee.*

Gallo, J. J., Mason, S. M., Meisinger, L. M., Robin, K. D., Stabile, G. D., and Wynne, R. J. (1966). The consenting adult homosexual and the law: An empirical study of enforcement and administration in Los Angeles county. *UCLA Law Review, 13*, 647–832.

Garland, D. (1991). Punishment and culture: The symbolic dimension of criminal justice. *Studies in Law, Politics and Justice, 11*, 191–222.

———. (2001). *The culture of control: Crime and social order in contemporary society.* Chicago: University of Chicago Press.

Garrison, E. G., and Kobor, P. C. (2002). Weathering a political storm: A contextual perspective on a psychological research controversy. *American Psychologist, 57*(3), 165.

Gary, T. S., Groth, A. N., and Hobson, W. F. (1982). The child molester: Clinical observations. *Journal of Social Work and Human Sexuality, 1*(1), 125–144.

Gathright, A. (2001, August 23). Sex offender pays for his own castration. *San Francisco Chronicle.*

Gebhard, P. H., Gagnon, J., and Pomeroy, W. (1965). *Sex offenders.* New York: Harper and Row.

Gebhard, P. H., Johnson, A. B., Kinsey, A. C., and Institute for Sex Research. (1979, 1998). *The Kinsey data: Marginal tabulations of the 1938–1963 interviews conducted by the Institute for Sex Research.* Bloomington: Indiana University Press.

Gee, D., Ward, T., and Eccleston, L. (2003). The function of sexual fantasies for sex offenders: A preliminary model. *Behaviour Change, 20*(1), 44–60.

General Accounting Office, and United States Congress. House Committee on the Judiciary. Subcommittee on Crime. (1996). *Sex offender treatment: Research results inconclusive about what works to reduce recidivism: Report to the chairman, subcommittee on crime, committee on the judiciary, House of Representatives.* Washington, DC.

Glaser, B. (2003). Therapeutic jurisprudence: An ethical paradigm for therapists in sex offender treatment programs. *Western Criminology Review, 42*(2), 143–154.

Goldstein, M. J., Kant, H. S., and Legal and Behavioral Institute. (1973). *Pornography and sexual deviance: A report of the legal and behavioral institute, Beverly Hills, California.* Berkeley: University of California Press.

Goode, E., and Nachman, B.-Y. (1994). Moral panics: Culture, politics and social construction. *Annual Review of Sociology, 20*, 149–171.

Goodnough, A., and Davey, M. (2007, March 5). A record of failure at center for sex offenders. *New York Times.*

———. (2007, March 6). Therapy's benefits for sex offenders is disputed. *New York Times.*

Goodyear, C., and Hallissy, E. (2003, August 21). Data on sex offenders riddled with mistakes many addresses out of date, state audit finds. *San Francisco Chronicle.*

Greenfeld, L. A. (1997). *Sex offenses and offenders* (No. NCJ 163392). Bureau of Justice Statistics, Office of Justice Programs, U.S. Department of Justice.

Greer, C. (2003). *Sex crime and the media: Sex offending and the press in a divided society.* Portland, OR: Willan.

Grieco, L., and Gokavi, M. (2010, July 21). Reclassifying sex offenders sends courts into chaos. *Dayton Daily News.*

Gunderson, D. (2007, June 18). Sex offender laws create unintended consequences. Minnesota Public Radio.

Guttmacher, M. S. (1951). *Sex offenses; the problem, causes and prevention.* New York: Norton.

Hall, S. (1978). *Policing the crisis: Mugging, the state, and law and order.* New York: Holmes & Meier.

Halleck, S. L. (1965). American psychiatry and the criminal: A historical review. *American Journal of Psychiatry, Supplement* (March), i–xii.

Hanson, R. K., and Buissiere, M. T. (1998). Predicting relapse: A meta-analysis of sexual offender recidivism studies." *Journal of Consulting and Clinical Psychology, 66*(2), 348–362.

Hanson, R. K., and Morton-Borgoun, K. E. (2009). The accuracy of recidivism risk assessments for sexual offenders: A meta-analysis of 118 prediction studies. *Psychological Assessment, 21,* 1–21.

Harris, A., Lobanov-Rostovsky, C., and Levenson, J. (2010). Widening the net: Effects of transitioning to the federally-mandated Adam Walsh Act classification system. *Criminal Justice and Behavior, 37*(5), 503–519.

Harris, A., and Lurigio, A. (2010). Sex offenses and offenders: Toward evidence-based public policy. *Criminal Justice and Behavior, 37*(5), 477–481.

Harris, R. E. G. (1949, December 13). State hunts solution of sex maniac riddle. *Los Angeles Times.*

Healey, F. (1930, October 3). Northcott executed. *Los Angeles Times.*

Helfman, H. M. (1950). Police science book review: 12 against crime. *Journal of Criminal Law and Criminology, 41*(4), 547.

———. (1951). Review: Terror in the streets. *The Journal of Criminal Law, Criminology, and Police Science, 42*(4), 510.

Herdt, G. H. (2009). *Moral panics, sex panics: Fear and the fight over sexual rights.* New York: New York University Press.

Herek, G. (2000). Homosexuality. In A. E. Kazdin (Ed.), *Encyclopedia of psychology.* Washington, DC: American Psychological Association and Oxford University Press.

Hernandez, M. (1984, April 6). Public support for tougher law on molesters sought. *Los Angeles Times.*

Hill, G. (1949, December 8). California moves to curb sex crime. *New York Times.*

Hogue, F. (1937, December 19). Social eugenics. *Los Angeles Times.*

Hoover, J. E. (1937). War on the sex criminal! *Los Angeles Times.*

———. (1947, April 20). How good a parent are you? *Los Angeles Times.*

———. (1960). *FBI chief urges drive to bar smut.* Washington, D.C.

Horney, J., and Spohn, C. (1991). Rape law reform and instrumental change in six urban jurisdictions. *Law and Society Review, 25*(117).

Howes, R. J. (1998). Plethysmographic assessment of incarcerated nonsexual offenders: A comparison with rapists. *Sexual Abuse: A Journal of Research and Treatment, 10*(3).

Hubbart, J. (1959, August 9–15). California's penal system designed to cure criminals: 6-part series. *Los Angeles Times*.

Hudson, B. (2002). Restorative justice and gendered violence: Diversion or effective justice? *British Journal of Criminology, 42*, 616–634.

Hughes, L. A., and Burchfield, K. B. (2008). Ex offender residence restrictions in Chicago: An environmental injustice? *Justice Quarterly, 25*, 647–673.

Huot, S. (1999). The referral process. In A. M. Schlank and F. Cohen (Eds.), *The sexual predator: Law, policy, evaluation and treatment* (Vol. 1, pp. 6-1–6-10). Kingston, N.J.: Civic Research Institute.

Illing, Hans A. (1957). Group psychotherapy and group work in authoritarian settings. *Journal of Criminal Law, Criminology and Police Science, 48*(4), 387.

————. (1965). Review: Sex offenders in group therapy. *The Journal of Criminal Law, Criminology, and Police Science, 56*(4), 515–516.

Ingram, C. (1984, April 11). Senate panel advances two child abuse bills. *Los Angeles Times*.

Israel, C. E. (1958). *The mark, a novel*. New York: Simon and Schuster.

Janus, E. S. (2006). *Failure to protect: America's sexual predator laws and the rise of the preventive state*. Ithaca: Cornell University Press.

Jenkins, P. (1998). *Moral panic: Changing concepts of the child molester in modern America*. New Haven: Yale University Press.

Karpman, B. (1954). *The sexual offender and his offenses; etiology, pathology, psychodynamics, and treatment*. New York: Julian Press.

Keller, R. (2005). Analysing discourse: An approach from the sociology of knowledge. *Forum: Qualitative Social Research, 6*(3).

Kennedy, J. E. (2000). Monstrous offenders and the search for solidarity through modern punishment. *Hastings Law Journal, 51*, 829.

Kiersh, T. A. (1990). *Bulleting of the American Academy of Psychiatry and the Law, 18*(2), 180.

Kim, S. (2003). *Analysis of Assembly Bill 1101*. Sacramento: Judiciary Committee.

Kirk, S. A. (1975). The sex offenses of blacks and whites. *Archives of Sexual Behavior, 4*(3), 295.

Kirk, S. A., and Kutchins, H. (1992). *The selling of DSM: The rhetoric of science in psychiatry*. New York: A. de Gruyter.

Kirkendall, L. A. (1952). Review: The dangerous stranger. *The Coordinator, 1*(2).

Klein, L. (2004). *There oughta be a law: Oh yeah, we have sex offender legislation*. Ann Arbor, MI: ICPSR Summer Institute.

Knopp, F. H., Rosenberg, J., Stevenson, W., and Prison Research/Education/Action Project (New York State Council of Churches). (1986). *Report on nationwide survey of juvenile and adult sex-offender treatment programs and providers, 1986*. Syracuse, NY: Safer Society Press.

Koch, W. (2007, February 25). Sex-offender residency laws get second look. *USA Today*.

Koss, M. P., Bachar, K. J., Quince Hopkins, C., and Carlson, C. (2004). Expanding a community's justice response to *sex crimes* through advocacy, prosecutorial, and public health collaboration: Introducing the RESTORE program. *Journal of Interpersonal Violence, 19*(12), 1435–1463.

Krisberg, B., and Marchionna, S. (2006). *Attitudes of U.S. voters toward prisoner rehabilitation and reentry policies*. National Council on Crime and Delinquency.

Kutchins, H., and Kirk, S. A. (1997). *Making us crazy: DSM: The psychiatric bible and the creation of mental disorders*. New York: Free Press.

Langan, P., and Levin, D. (2002). *Recidivism in prisoners released in 1994*. Washington, D.C.: Department of Justice, Office of Justice Programs, Bureau of Justice Statistics.

Lave, T. (2009). Only yesterday: The rise and fall of twentieth century sexual psychopath laws. *Louisiana Law Review, 69*.

———. (2011). Controlling sexually violent predators: Continued incarceration at what cost? *New Criminal Law Review, 14*(2).

Leon, C. S. (2010). As well as expected: Women's performance in problem solving courts. Meeting of the Law and Society Association, Chicago.

Leon, C. S., Burton, D. L., and Alvare, D. (2011). The overuse of registration and residential treatment for youth who commit sex offenses. *Widener Law Review, 17*(1).

Levenson, J. S. (2009). Collateral consequences of sex offender residence restrictions. *Criminal Justice Studies, 21*, 153–166.

Lieb, R., Quinsey, V., and Berliner, L. (1998). Sexual predators and social policy. *Crime and Justice, 23*, 43.

Lieberman, D., and Siegel, B. (1957). A program for sexual psychopaths in a state mental hospital. *American Journal of Psychiatry* (March), 801–807.

Lindgren, K., and Luther, C. (1984, April 17). Higher priority urged to fight child abusers. *Los Angeles Times*.

Loftus, E. F., and Doyle, J. M. (1987). *Eyewitness testimony: Civil and criminal*. Kluwer Evidence Library. New York: Kluwer Law.

Loftus, E. F., and Ketcham, K. (1994). *The myth of repressed memory: False memories and allegations of sexual abuse*. 1st ed. New York: St. Martin's Press.

Logan, W. A. (2009). *Knowledge as power: Criminal registration and community notification laws in America*. Critical Perspectives on Crime and Law. Stanford, Calif.: Stanford Law Books.

Lohn, M. (2010, June 21). $175,000 per offender? get-tough sex predator 'treatment' busts state budgets. *Cleveland Daily News*.

Lombroso, C., and Ferrero, G. (2004). *Criminal woman, the prostitute, and the normal woman* (M. Gibson, Trans.). Durham: Duke University Press.

———. (2006). *Criminal man, fifth edition, 1896–1897* (M. Gibson, Trans.). Durham: Duke University Press.

Loney, J. (2009, July 9). Sex offenders under bridge sue Florida county. Reuters.

Lösel, F., and Schmucker, M. (2005). The effectiveness of treatment for sexual offenders: A comprehensive meta-analysis. *Journal of Experimental Criminology, 1*.

Lucas, G. (1994, February 8). Wilson talks tough at crime summit: Blend of politics, pathos at Hollywood event. *San Francisco Chronicle*.

Lunbeck, E. (1994). *The psychiatric persuasion: Knowledge, gender, and power in modern America*. Princeton: Princeton University Press.

Luther, C. (1984, April 23). Pinpointing "right" issues election key. *Los Angeles Times*.

Lynch, M. (2002). Pedophiles and cyber-predators as contaminating forces: The language of disgust, pollution, and boundary invasions in federal debates on sex offender legislation. *Law and Social Inquiry, 27*(3), 529.

Maeve, M. K., and Vaughn, M. S. (2001). Nursing with prisoners: The practice of caring, forensic nursing or penal harm nursing? *ANS Advances in Nursing Science, 24*(2), 47–64.

Marcus, E. H., and Sidley, N. T. (1974). Letter to the editor: "Dangerousness" of sex offenders; Dr. Sidley replies. *American Journal of Psychiatry, 131*(1), 105.

Marosi, R. (2001, March 2). Some sex offenders seeking castration in bid for freedom. *Los Angeles Times.*

Marques, J. K., Wiederanders, M., Day, D. M., Nelson, C., and Van Ommeren, A. (2005). Effects of a relapse prevention program on sexual recidivism: Final results from California's sex offender treatment and evaluation project (SOTEP). *Sexual Abuse: A Journal of Research and Treatment, 17*(1).

Marshall, W. L., and Marshall, L. E. (2000). The origins of sexual offending. *Trauma, Violence, and Abuse, 1*(1), 250.

Mathews, J. (1982, May 18). An angry grandmother leads drive against child molesters. *Washington Post.*

McCoy, C. (1993). *Politics and plea bargaining: Victims' rights in California.* Law in Social Context Series. Philadelphia: University of Pennsylvania Press.

McGrath, R. J., Cumming, G. F., and Burchard, B. L. (2003). *Current practices and trends in sexual abuser management.* Safer Society Foundation.

Meloy, M. L. (2006). *Sex offenses and the men who commit them: An assessment of sex offenders on probation.* Hanover: University Press of New England for Northeastern University Press, Boston.

Merton, R. K. (1957). *Social theory and social structure.* Rev. and enl. ed. Glencoe, Ill.: Free Press.

Miller, N. (2002). *Sex-crime panic: A journey to the paranoid heart of the 1950s* (1st ed.). Los Angeles: Alyson.

Minnesota Department of Corrections. (2003). *Level Three sex offenders residential placement issues.* St. Paul, Minn.

————. (2007). *Residential proximity and sex offender recidivism in Minnesota.* St. Paul, Minn.

Mirror, The. (1952). California copes with a menace. *Los Angeles Times (1886-Current File).*

Mitford, J. (1973). *Kind and usual punishment; the prison business.* 1st ed. New York: Knopf.

Nathan, D., and Snedeker, M. R. (1995). *Satan's silence: Ritual abuse and the making of a modern American witch hunt.* New York: Basic Books.

National Victim Center. (1992). Rape in America: Report to the Nation. Arlington, VA: National Victim Center.

Nelson, H. (1963, October 6). Better cure rate for sex offenders sought. *Los Angeles Times.*

————. (1963, October 7). 26% of sex offender patients recommitted. *Los Angeles Times.*

Nolte, Carl. (2004). "Elsie Abbott: Mother in sensational murder case dies at 100; she never gave up on son's innocence." San Francisco Chronicle.

Odem, M. E. (1995). *Delinquent daughters: Protecting and policing adolescent female sexuality in the United States, 1885–1920.* Chapel Hill: University of North Carolina Press.

O'Donohue, W., Regev, L. G., and Hagstrom, A. (2000). Problems with the DSM-IV diagnosis of pedophilia. *Sexual Abuse: A Journal of Research and Treatment, 12*(2), 95–105.

Ofshe, R., and Watters, E. (1994). *Making monsters: False memories, psychotherapy, and sexual hysteria.* New York: Charles Scribner's.

Other books of the week. (1949, December 4). *New York Times.*

Packer, H. L. (1968). *The limits of the criminal sanction.* Stanford, Calif.: Stanford University Press.

Pariah (pseudonym). (2006, March 3). Sexual fascism in progressive America. Message posted to http://www.counterpunch.org/pariah03042006.html.

People v. Adams. (1939). 93 P.2d 146. Supreme Court of California.

People v. Feagley. (1975). 14 Cal.3d 338. Supreme Court of California.

People v. Northcott. (1930). 289 636. Supreme Court of California.

People v. Stoddard. (1968). 227 Cal. App. 2d 40. Supreme Court of California.

Ploscowe, M. (1951). *Sex and the law.* 1st ed. New York: Prentice-Hall.

Pollack, J. H. (1950, May 28). What you should know about neighborhood cranks. *Los Angeles Times.*

Porter, J. (2007, October 12). Hooker raped and robbed—by justice system. *Philadelphia Daily News.*

Prentky, R. A. (2003). A 15-year retrospective on sexual coercion: Advances and projections. *Annals of the New York Academy of Sciences, 989,* 13–32.

Quinn, J. F., Forsyth, C. J., and Mullen-Quinn, C. (2004). Societal reaction to sex offenders: A review of the myths surrounding their crimes and treatment amenability. *Deviant Behavior, 25*(3), 215.

Rafter, N. H. (2007). Crime, film and criminology: Recent sex-crime movies. *Theoretical Criminology, 11*(3), 403.

Randolph, N. K. (1949, November 23). Letters to the *Times*—sex crime curb. *Los Angeles Times.*

Ray, I. (1968). *Mental hygiene.* The History of Medicine Series, no. 35. New York: Hafner.

Reinhold, R. (1990, January 24). The longest trial—a post-mortem. Collapse of child-abuse case: So much agony for so little. *New York Times.*

Reporter. (1959, October 16). Get license number: Police ask help in nabbing molesters. *Los Angeles Times.*

Reumann, M. G. (2005). *American sexual character: Sex, gender, and national identity in the Kinsey reports.* Berkeley: University of California Press.

Richardson, J. T., Best, J., and Bromley, D. G. (1991). *The Satanism scare.* Social Institutions and Social Change. New York: A. de Gruyter.

Rind, B., Tromovitch, P., and Bauserman, R. (1998). A meta-analysis examination of assumed properties of child sexual abuse using college samples. *Psychological Bulletin, 124*(1), 22–53.

Robertson, S. (2001). Separating the men from the boys: Masculinity, psychosexual development, and sex crime in the United States, 1930s–1960s. *Journal of the History of Medicine, 56,* 3–35.

Robinson, L. O. (2003). Sex offender management: The public policy challenges. *Annals of the New York Academy of Sciences, 989,* 1–7.

Robitscher, J. B. (1966). *Pursuit of agreement: Psychiatry and the law.* Philadelphia: Lippincott.

Rose, N. S. (1990). *Governing the soul: The shaping of the private self.* London: Routledge.

Rothfeld, M. (2009, January 16). There's no evidence Jessica's law works, California officials say. *Los Angeles Times.*

Rothman, D. J. (1980). *Conscience and convenience: The asylum and its alternatives in progressive America.* Boston: Little Brown.

Rusche, G., Kirchheimer, O., and Melossi, D. (2003). *Punishment and social structure.* New Brunswick, NJ: Transaction.

Russell, D. E. H. (1986). *The secret trauma: Incest in the lives of girls and women.* New York: Basic Books.

St. Paul (MN) Police Department (Producer). (1941). *Saint Paul police detectives and their work: A color cartoon.* [Video/DVD] Accessed through Prelinger Archives.

Satterfield, V. B. (1951). The education of a metropolitan police department respecting sex molestation. *The Journal of Criminal Law, Criminology, and Police Science, 42*(3), 403–408.

Scheingold, S. A. (1997). *Politics, crime control and culture.* International Library of Criminology, Criminal Justice and Penology. Aldershot, U.K.: Ashgate.

Scholefield, H. K. (1949, November 29). Sex crime surgery. *Los Angeles Times.*

Schudson, M. (1978). *Discovering the news: A social history of American newspapers.* New York: Basic.

Schultz, P. D. (2005). *Not monsters: Analyzing the stories of child molesters.* Lanham, Md.: Rowman & Littlefield.

Scully, J. (2006, October 4). Make California's communities safer. *Sacramento Bee.*

Sedlack, A. J., Finkelhor, D., and Hammer, H. (2004). *National estimates of children missing involuntarily or for benign reasons.* Washington, D.C.

Shepard, P. (1937, April 25). When strikes! *Los Angeles Times.*

Showalter, E. (1997). *Hystories: Hysterical epidemics and modern media.* New York: Columbia University Press.

Sidley, N. T., and Stolarz, F. J. (1973). A proposed "dangerous sex offender" law. *American Journal of Psychiatry, 130*(7), 765–768.

Simon, J. (1993). *Poor discipline: Parole and the social control of the underclass, 1890–1990.* Studies in Crime and Justice. Chicago: University of Chicago Press.

———. (1998). Managing the monstrous: Sex offenders and the new penology. *Psychology, Public Policy and Law, 4*(1), 452–467.

———. (2000). Megan's law: Crime and democracy in late modern America. *Law and Social Inquiry, 25*(4), 1111.

———. (2003). Managing the monstrous: Sex offenders and the new penology. In B. J. Winick and J. Q. La Fond (Eds.), *Protecting society from sexually dangerous offenders: Law, justice, and therapy.* Washington, D.C.: American Psychological Association.

———. (2007). *Governing through crime: How the war on crime transformed American democracy and created a culture of fear.* New York: Oxford University Press.

Simon, J., and Leon, C. (2007). The third wave: American sex offender policies since the 1990s. In S. G. Shoham (Ed.), *International handbook of penology and criminal justice.* Tel Aviv: CRC Press, Taylor and Francis Group.

Simpson, R. (1996). Neither clear nor present: The social construction of safety and danger. *Sociological Forum, 11*(3), 549–562.

Sittons, C. (1959, May 3). Lynching points up continuing tension: "Classic" violence diminishes but racial friction remains strong. *New York Times.*

Skelton, G. (2006). Republicans' anti-molester measure puts democrats in a tough spot. *Los Angeles Times.*

Slater, M. R., and Bishop, G. V. (1964). *Sex offenders in group therapy; the personal experiences of a clinical psychologist in criminal group therapy.* Los Angeles: Sherbourne Press.

Socia, K. M., and Stamatel, J. P. (2010). Assumptions and evidence behind sex offender laws: Registration, community notification, and residence restrictions." *Sociology Compass, 4*(1), 1–20.

Sommerville, D. M. (2004). *Rape and race in the nineteenth-century south.* Chapel Hill: University of North Carolina Press.

Spitzer, R. L., and Wakefield, J. C. (1999). DSM-IV diagnostic criterion for clinical significance: Does it help solve the false positives problem? *American Journal of Psychiatry, 156*(12), 1861.

State v. Wilson, 685 So.2d 1063 (La. 1996).

Steele, A., and Moran, R. (2009, June 3). "Person of interest" held in child-rape case. *Philadelphia Inquirer.*

Sterngold, J., and Martin, M. (2005, July 3). Hard time California's prisons in crisis—high price of broken prisons tough sentencing creates overcrowding that endangers inmates, haunts taxpayers. *San Francisco Chronicle.*

Stewart, R. W., and Scott, A. (1984, March 22). Five on school staff held in molestations. *Los Angeles Times.*

Stover, C. (1981) "Prosecution in Middle County: An application of organization theory to criminal justice." *Criminal Justice Review, 6*(1), 26–35.

Sutherland, E. (1950a). The diffusion of sexual psychopath laws. *American Journal of Sociology, 56*(2), 142–148.

———. (1950b). The sexual psychopath laws. *Journal of Criminal Law and Criminology, 40*(5), 534–544.

Szasz, T. S. (1963). *Law, liberty, and psychiatry; an inquiry into the social uses of mental health practices.* New York: Macmillan.

Terdiman, R., and Bourdieu, P. (1987). Translator's introduction: The force of law: Toward a sociology of the juridical field. *Hastings Law Journal, 38*(5), 805–813.

Terry, K. J., Furlong, J. S., Dropkin, J., and Rahmberg Walsh, E. (2008). *Sex offender registration and community notification: A "Megan's Law" sourcebook.* 2nd ed. Kingston, N.J.: Civic Research Institute.

Thornton, N. (1950). Police science book review: The sexual criminal. *Journal of Criminal Law and Criminology, 41*(3), 389–390.

Times, Los Angeles [LAT]. (1924, May 13). Art of changing noses.

———. (1937, August 27). Dyer found guilty.

———. (1937, August 7). Women storm hall of justice as dyer trial opens in triple child murder.

———. (1937, August 17). Dyer's horror story placed before jury.

———. (1937, August 21). Dyer trial climax set for Monday.

———. (1937, August 27). Jury decrees dyer must die for murders.

———. (1940, June 1). Mental test set in morals case.

———. (1942, July 4). Shallow, weed-covered grave yields body of lost boy, 7.

———. (1944, November 18). Slayer adds to details in killings of women.

———. (1946, February 24). Great posse searches for kidnaping victim.

———. (1946, February 27). Parents to pay "any price" for kidnapped child.

———. (1947, January 16). Girl victim of sex fiend found slain.

———. (1947, January 17). Sex fiend slaying victim identified by fingerprint records of F.B.I.

———. (1947, August 11). Mutilated body of bride found; husband among four held.

———. (1948, December 10). Sex perverts pour in here, inquiry told.

———. (1949, December 4). Assemblymen speed up hearing on sex crimes.

———. (1949, November 16). Mexico-U.S. hunt on for girl's slayer.

———. (1949, December 8). Psychiatrists' view.

———. (1949, November 22). Special session to deal with sex cases urged.

———. (1949, December 10). State plans more aid to psychopaths.

———. (1949, December 12). Warren bills ready for legislature.

———. (1950, January 6). Jurist opens fire on penal system.

———. (1950, January 7). Five sex crime bills get Warren signature.

———. (1950, May 5). Warren signs sex offender register law.

———. (1951, May 25). Law change to give death penalty in sex case kidnaping urged by roll.

———. (1951, June 20). Easy dealing with sex offenders.

———. (1951, June 13). Freedom over (photo caption).

———. (1951, July 26). Life or knife fallacy.

———. (1951, July 26). Warren signs student body card measure.

———. (1952, September 29). Three fugitives hunted after hospital escape.

———. (1954, July 17). Jury finds woman who beat daughter was sane.

———. (1956, June 25). Kidnapper of Palmdale girl hunted.

———. (1957, March 16). Gov. Knight call late to halt Abbott death.

Times, New York [NYT]. (1943, December 27). New curbs are urged for sex offenders.

———. (1947, March 19). Summary of proposals approved and rejected by the legislature.

———. (1947, April 12). Bill for confining sex insane vetoed.

———. (1948, March 14). Major bills voted by legislature.

———. (1948, April 1). State staffs get 20 million pay raise.

———. (1949, December 23). Psychiatric help asked in sex cases.

———. (1950, January 31). Sex-crime laws held ineffective—"fallacies" are cited.

———. (1950, April 23). View is modified on sex offenders.

———. (1950, October 9). Yale professor slain, wife shot in home by an "insane" intruder.

———. (1960, May 3). Treatment urge for sex criminals.

———. (1961, November 14). 7 Men arrested by policewoman.

Timnick, L. (1984). "Abuse in the nursery school—a license is no safety guarantee." *Los Angeles Times.*

Tobin, T. (2002). *RFP history.* CCOSO.

Trust, Albany. (Ed.). (1963). *Homosexual law reform; sexual deviation from the psychiatric standpoint; parliament and the Wolfenden report; sociological aspects of homosexuality; sex and the family; towards a sexually sane society.* London: Albany Trust.

UPI. (1963, June 11). Mahoney says high court makes law-enforcing hard. *New York Times.*

UPI. (1976, April 28). Sex slayer dies during "last chance" castration. *Los Angeles Times.*

U.S. Department of Justice, Bureau of Justice Statistics. "Survey of inmates in state and federal correctional facilities, 2004." ICPSR04572-v1. Ann Arbor, MI: Inter-university Consortium for Political and Social Research. doi:10.3886/ICPSR04572. Complete series is available at http://www.icpsr.umich.edu/cocoon/NACJD/SERIES/00070.xml.

U.S. Public Health Service. (1919). *Keeping fit* (48 poster series ed.).

Vachss, A. (2005). The incest loophole. *New York Times.*

Valverde, M. (1998). *Diseases of the will: Alcohol and the dilemmas of freedom.* Cambridge: Cambridge University Press.

———. (2005). Lombroso's criminal woman and the uneven development of the modern lesbian identity. *American Society of Criminology,* Toronto, CANAFA.

Varela, D., and Black, D. W. (2002). Letters to the editor: Pedophilia treated with carbamazepine and clonazepam. *American Journal of Psychiatry, 159*(7), 1245–1246.

Victor, J. (1998). Moral panics and the social construction of deviant behavior: A theory and application to the case of ritual child abuse. *Sociological Perspectives, 41*(3), 541–565.

Wacquant, L. J. D. (2009). *Punishing the poor: The neoliberal government of social insecurity* [Punir les pauvres]. Politics, History, and Culture. Durham: Duke University Press.

Wagner, L. E., and Myers, J. (1951, May 25). Letters to the *Times*—where do we fail? *Los Angeles Times.*

Wakefield, H. (1995). Editor's note. *Issues in Child Abuse Accusations, 7*(2).

———. (2006). The effects of child sexual abuse: Truth versus political correctness. *Journal of the Institute for Psychological Therapies, 16.*

Watts, A. (1968). Psychedelics and religious experience. *California Law Review, 56*(1).

Weidlein-Crist, P., and O'Connell, Jr., J. P. State of Delaware, Office of Management and Budget. Statistical Analysis Center. (2008). *Delaware sex offenders: Profiles and criminal justice system outcomes.*

Weiler, A. H. (1961, October 8). Provocative duo: *The Hustler* and *The Mark* again show films can hit social ills. *Los Angeles Times.*

Welch, M., and Schuster, L. (2005). Detention of asylum seekers in the UK and USA: Deciphering noisy and quiet constructions. *Punishment and Society, 7*, 397.

Wells, W., and Horney, J. (2002). Weapon effects and individual intent to do harm: Influences on the escalation of violence. *Criminology, 40*, 265–296.

Whitman, H. (1951). *Terror in the streets.* New York: Dial Press.

Williams, M. (2009). Community response to sex offenders: The case of residency restrictions. Philadelphia, Pa.

Wilson, P. (1994, March 2). 3 strikes too many when rapists are involved. *San Francisco Chronicle.*

Wilson, R. J., Picheca, J. E., and Prinzo, M. (2005). *Circles of support and accountability: An evaluation of the pilot project in south-central Ontario* (No. 021192). Correctional Service of Canada.

Witt, P. H., and Barone, N. (2004). Assess sex offender risk: New Jersey's methods. *Federal Sentencing Reporter, 16*(3), 170–175.

Wright, L. (1994). *Remembering Satan.* New York: Knopf.

Yantzi, M. (1996). You're doing what? Working with society's "untouchables"—male sex offenders. *Everyman,* (19).

Young, J. (2007). *The vertigo of late modernity.* London: Sage.

Zimring, F. E. (1997, May 5). The truth about repeat sex offenders. *Los Angeles Times.*

———. (2004). *An American travesty: Legal responses to adolescent sexual offending.* Chicago: University of Chicago Press.

———. (2006). *Legislating in the dark: The nightmare of American sex crime policy.* Presented at the Annual Meeting of the Association for the Treatment of Sexual Abusers.

Zimring, F. E., and Hawkins, G. (1991). *The scale of imprisonment.* Chicago: University of Chicago Press.

———. (1992). *Prison population and criminal justice policy in California.* Berkeley: Institute of Governmental Studies Press University of California.

Zimring, F. E., Hawkins, G., and Kamin, S. (2001). *Punishment and democracy: Three strikes and you're out in California*. Studies in Crime and Public Policy. New York: Oxford University Press.

Zimring, F. E., and Johnson, D. (2006). Public opinion and the governance of punishment in democratic political systems. *The Annals of the American Academy of Political and Social Science, 605*(1), 265.

Zimring, F. E., and Leon, C. S. (2008). A cite-checker's guide to sexual dangerousness: Reply to Ruby Andrew. *Berkeley Journal of Criminal Law, 13*(1), 65–76.

Index

control (*cont'd*): as personal volition, 17, 23, 27, 114; "situational lapse," sexual criminality as, 59, 76; will/willpower, 26–27, 91. *See also* containment model; social control, formal
crackdown. *See* "moral panic"

danger, 20–21, 32, 40, 108, 147; as criteria for civil commitment, 72, 85–90, 100, 102; escalation, 18, 21, 24, 51, 85, 89, 105; parent-blaming for, 57; "stranger danger," 34, 76, 186. *See also* Douglas, Mary; images/portrayal of the sex offender; punishment, sex offender, public attitudes towards, race; risk assessment/ prediction; social construction
Dangerous Stranger, The, 33, 34, 37
death penalty, 44–49, 148; execution, 7, 70–71, 115–16, 148
degenerate, 25, 47; "feeble-minded," 29, 33, 49; sexual degeneracy, 33
Delaware, 11, 14
De River, Dr. J. Paul, 28, 33, 35, 44, 133; and the LAPD Sex Crimes Bureau, 38–41
deviance, 23, 112, 130, 133; measurement of, 39, 135–43. *See also* danger; homosexuality; fantasy, deviant; images/portrayal of the sex offender; patient/reformable deviant; risk assessment/prediction
diagnosis. *See* DSM; mental illness
difference/uniqueness of sex offenders, 19, 23 36; differentiation, 27, 59, 74, 76, 78, 86–91, 102, 120, 124, 140, 151, 161, 195–96. *See also* experts; images/portrayal of offenders, race
discourse, 3, 7, 17, 21, 52–3, 76, 135, 161, 188, 197–99; discursive field, 4, 9, 27–37; discursive shifts, 13, 29–30, 108, 111–13, 125, 150–51. *See also* Bourdieu, Pierre; Foucault, Michel; govermentality/governance
discretion, 103–6; diverting offenders at the individual level, 45–46, 53, 65, 85, 88–90, 99–102, 104, 124, 160; effecting de-criminalization at the offense level, 20, 147, 151; judicial, 89, 90, 99, 107; local, 174–77, 191; not to register sex offenders, 68–69, 184; and preventive detention,

81, 88, 94–96, 121; prosecutorial, 94, 105, 124, 167, 172–78; public pressure not to enforce against pillars of the community, 36; and "wobbler," 98, 175, 177. *See also* difference/uniqueness of sex offenders; experts; misdemeanor; race; sentencing
district attorney. *See* prosecutor
diversion, 103–6, 121, 160, 196. *See also* discretion
Doe v. Lafayette, 120
Douard, John, 184
Douglas, Mary, 3, 20, 37
Dowd, Maureen, 107
DSM (Diagnostic and Statistical Manual), 74–75, 79, 130–32, 158, 203, 204
Durkheim, Emile, 7; theory, 24, 32, 113, 153, 180. *See also* symbolic law
Dyer, Albert, 32, 33, 35, 45, 47, 50

emotion, 41, 68; emotional disease/ disorder, 66, 77, 93; Emotional Security Program, 60, 91–93. *See also* Atascadero State Hospital
empirical evidence: cognitive dissonance of 35–7, 155–156; disregard for, 91, 115, 120, 134, 157; implementation data (of sex offender law) 77–106, 119, 121, 161–178, 187–190, 202; lack of, 92, 115, 126, 187–188; LSD interrogation research, 51, 115; research sites, California, 38, 50–51; research sites, New York 50–51; Sexual Deviation Research Act/Study 44, 46, 51, 91; against sexual psychopathy, 41; study of sexuality, 9, 55. *See also* recidivism
excuse: pathology as, 19, 75, 130, 133; sex offender apologists, 63, 158; sexual offending and, 18–19, 158. *See also* fallacies surrounding sex crimes, victim-or-offender
exhibitionism. *See* indecent exposure
experts: as critics, 2, 42, 50, 67, 122, 159, 192; challenges to, 130–34; court testimony, 33, 65; criminology, 4, 44; disagreement, differences between, 29–30, 41, 55, 65, 91; disregard of, 2, 6, 17, 37, 68, 172; insulation/mediation, 52, 124, 167, 188–89, 193;

and policy-making, 10, 129, 192–93; in public debate, 2, 40, 42, 48, 56, 76, 110, 153–54; paraprofessionals and sex offender evaluators, 2, 65, 114, 131, 133–136; professional status and jurisdiction, 56, 104, 106, 110, 114–15; 131–36; and reform, 151, 153–54; 189, 195; victim as, 154–60, 201. *See also* discretion; governmentality/governance; "psych experts"; risk assessment/prediction; treatment, sex offender

fallacies surrounding sex crimes, 22, 58, 125, 133–34, 182–86; bogeyman, 7, 23, 145; continuum to homicide, 18, 24, 44, 62, 103; increasing incidence and/or prevalence, 23, 40, 43, 44, 56, 148, 167; knowledge-is-power, 24, 54, 58, 118–19; new law, 24, 44, 103, 110, 148; past as predictor, 155; recidivism, high, 1, 155; singular/unique sex offender, 23, 117; victim-or-offender, 13, 16, 24, 64, 126, 148, 150, 154, 157–58, 173, 201. *See also* danger; harm, beliefs regarding
false sense of security, 48, 186
family violence/offending by familiars, 20–21, 33, 35, 147, 152–53; lack of recognition of, 107–8, 111, 147, 186, 192. *See also* incest loophole
fantasy, deviant, 17–18, 130; arousal-action nexus, 131; PRV–3, 136–41; sexual preference hypothesis, 134; and violence against women, 67. *See also* risk assessment/prevention
Fass, Paula, 16, 31, 35, 41
Feagley, Chester, 80–81, 94–96, 102, 127
fear, sex offenders and, 1, 45; public anxiety, 30, 147. *See also* danger; "moral panic"; politics of sex offender law
feminists/feminism, 62–64, 67, 104, 110, 146, 149, 152, 157, 163, 186, 201
Finkelhor, David, 163
Florida, 120
Forst, Martin, 89–90, 97
Foucault, Michel, 180–81. *See also* discourse, governmentality/governance; "normal"
Frank, Theodore, 149–50

Freedman, Estelle, 8–10, 38, 103
Freud, Sigmund/Freudian theory, 58, 68, 76; importation of, 9, 39

Garland, David, 5–6, 189
gender: attitudes/statements regarding women, 14, 15, 33, 40, 73, 149; general attitudes about, 8, 27, 48, 53, 187; and power, 73, 113, 201; and social control, 71; trans-gender, 51, 210n95
Glucoft, Linda Joyce, 33–35, 43, 144–45. *See also* Stroble, Fred
going rate, 88, 90, 98, 103
govermentality/governance, 9, 52–53, 147–49, 189; "Crime is a genre...," 14; governing through sex crime, 108–10, 119, 145, 153; governmental authority, 14, 172–78; inaction on sex crime as failure of, 21, 44, 51, 145, 148, 150, 172–73; ways of knowing and acting/measurement, 22, 26, 106, 115, 126–29, 158
Greer, Christopher, 16
Guttmacher, Manfred 62, 128, 158

Halleck, Seymour, 42, 126
Hanson, Karl, 128
harm: beliefs regarding, 18, 27, 62–64, 131, 152–53, 156, 172, 203; of child molestation, 63, 86, 90, 112, 132–33, 146, 151, 153; considerations of, in California rehabilitative era, 78, 85–88; dismissal of, 90, 107, 156; "harmless perverts," 52; as injury, 22, 63, 107, 146; and morality, 156; of rape, 86, 107, 145–46; as trauma, 63, 90, 132–33, 145, 153
homosexuality, 26, 51, 89; arrests, 89, 98, 99; as criminal/"crime against nature," 20, 26, 86; civil commitment for, 76, 89; conviction, 89, 99; as deviant 8, 25; "lesbianism," 27; as mental illness 36, 74, 204; as motive for murder, 25; and pedophiles, 16, 132; as research subject, 51, 142; treatment through hetero-normative recreation, 93. *See also* harm; nuisance; gender, trans-gender
Hoover, J. Edgar, 36, 40, 51–52, 67

molester/molestation. *See* child abuse

monster, 7, 13, 17–18, 36, 37, 46, 111, 129, 143, 150, 156, 191; predators, sexual, 1, 9, 81, 111, 141; sex fiend, 13, 17, 29, 33, 67–68, 148, 165, 185

"moral panic," 8, 29, 30, 52, 161, 169, 187–88; evidence disputing panic/crackdowns, 10–11, 13, 35, 89, 100, 104, 155, 164–78; and pornography, 67; satanic abuse panic/hysteria, 7, 107–10, 155; and sex offender crackdowns, 6, 16, 78, 103

Nathan, Debbie, 155

neighborhood watch, 147

net widening, 91, 103–6, 193–94

"normal," 29, 54, 55, 111, 130, 181, 198; narrative strategies of similarity/"normalizing discourse," 16, 24, 27, 35, 39–40, 57–59, 61–62, 66, 73–74, 76, 111–13. *See also* Foucault, Michel; treatment, sex offender

Northcott, Gordon, 25, 31, 32, 45, 48. *See also* perversion/pervert

nuisance, 19–22, 80–81, 89, 146, 149–51, 153, 195; indefinite confinement of, 80, 94–96. *See also* Feagley, Chester; homosexuality; misdemeanor; sex crimes; stories

Ofshe, Richard, 7

other sex offenses, 161–78, 191; arrest rates of, 99; incarceration rates of, 29–30, 83–84; tracking of, 163–65

Packer, Herbert, 157

paraphilia, pedophilia. *See* biological defect or paradigm; DSM

parole, 84, 89, 111, 114, 120

patient/reformable deviant, 18–19, 57–59, 99, 103, 129, 149–51, 153; as good citizen, 59–62, 91–93. *See also* discretion; treatment, sex offender

patriarchy, 73; patriarchal society, 75

Paulette, Henry, 146

penile plethysmograph, 137, 142

perversion/pervert, 31, 39, 112; masher, 40; "moral pervert," 25. *See also* homosexuality

police, 34, 36, 50, 55, 81, 111, 153; Los Angeles Police Department Sex Crimes Bureau, 38; and sex offenders as promotional tools, 40–42. *See also* discretion

policy reform, 13; evidence-based, 132, 157, 194; Georgians for Reform, 193–94; New Mexico, 193, 194; New York, 152; Ohio, 193, 194; successful efforts, 150–52, 174, 192–95. *See also* experts; governmentality/governance; punishment; rape; sex offender; SORNA; symbolic law

politics of sex offender law, 1–3, 51–53, 147, 152–58, 172–78, 184, 193

polygraph, 114–15, 136, 195

pornography, 55, 67, 108, 113, 139, 143

Prentky, Robert, 127

prison. *See* incarceration

probation/probation officer, 65, 76, 88, 97, 98, 114, 118, 138–40, 146

prosecutor, 13, 14, 34, 44, 81, 117, 126, 149, 150, 172–78, 193; Attorney General, 147, 148; reprimand for prejudice, 32; role of, 174–75; Scully, Jan, 1, 17; and sentencing, 76, 124, 148

prostitutes/prostitution, 14, 185

"psych experts," 19, 50, 55, 74, 124, 127, 129–36; 153, 192, 194

psychiatrists/psychiatry, 4, 8, 13, 41–44, 115, 125–26; constrained/influenced by institutional factors, 42–33, 88, 196; forensic, 9, 126; psychiatric criminology, 126; in rehabilitative era 64–66; in sexual psychopath era, 43–45. *See also* experts; Freud, Sigmund/Freudian theory; "psych experts"

psychology 4, 115, 156. *See also* experts; "psych experts"

punishment: causal models, 6, 53; general trends, 6; goals of, 12, 16, 19; politics of criminal justice and, 9; punitiveness, 10, 16, 29, 35, 105. 152, 159, 172–73, 188, 193, 194–95; satisfaction of punishing evil, 112–13, 153 punishment, sex offender: effect on families of offenders and victims, 185; need for more, 12, 46, 64, 156, 191–92; public attitudes towards, 9–11, 17–18, 29, 107. *See also* governmentality/governance; incarceration; stories, sex crime sex offender; symbolic law

race: "black rapist," 70, 72–73, 101, 102; and class differentiation, 39–40, 73, 78, 89, 99–102, 182–83; disparity in criminal justice processing, 70, 73, 100–101, 106; of offenders, 71–74, 100–102; racial boundaries, 25–26, 182–83; racism, 70–71; and rehabilitative ideal, 61, 66, 74; of victims, 25–26, 31; "whitewashing," 102. *See also* bogeyman view/approach; lynching; rape

Rafter, Nicole Hahn, 4

rape, 145; arrests, 163; compared to "other" sex offenses, 98–99, 104; and the DSM, 74–75, 131–32, 158; forcible, 29–30, 75, 86–87, 139, 169; national trends, 12, 163–64; "normal," 73, 104, 158; reform, 104, 152; reporting, 161; Uniform Crime Reports, 163–67. *See also* gender; victims

recidivism, 1, 4, 119, 121, 126, 127–28, 142, 155–56, 195, 201

reform. *See* policy reform

registration, sex offender, 68–69, 117–19; California law, 51, 68; community notification, 118–119, 172, 183; "failure to register," 118, 121, 201; and law enforcement, 51, 68, 118; Megan's Law, 118, 119; tier placement, 119–20; unintended consequences, 68–69, 118, 178–79, 184; web-based, 119. *See also* discretion; fallacies surrounding sex crimes, continuum to homicide; fallacies surrounding sex crimes, knowledge-is-power

rehabilitation: in California, "how it worked," 77–106; as instrumental, 96–102; public support for, 7, 43, 105, 148, 150, 173; rehabilitative debate era, 4, 54–76; of the sexual psychopath, 29, 43, 150, 203; techniques, 13; treatment to

rehabilitate 18, 43, 66–67, 81, 150. *See also* treatment, sex offender

residency restrictions, 2, 119–20, 167, 173; Georgia, 120; local ordinances, 120; Minnesota, 117; unintended consequences, 120–21

RESTORE program, 160

risk assessment/prediction, 79, 91, 115, 182, 190, 195; Canada, 195; conviction/offense-based, 87, 120; evaluation for confinement, 88–90, 124, 141, 195; measurement/objectivity, 65, 79, 134–42, 200; Minnesota, 141; New Jersey, 141–42; South Carolina, 136. *See also* Adam Walsh Child Protection and Safety Act; danger; deviance; treatment, sex offender

Robertson, Stephen, 21

Robinson, Laurie, 129, 157

Safer Society Foundation, 129, 196

Schultz, Pamela, 159, 184, 201

sentencing: indeterminate/determinate, 2, 17, 56, 105; effect on prison populations, 167; reform, 1, 106, 152, 167. *See also* diversion; going rate; incarceration; policy reform

sex crimes: causes of, 24, 72–76; narratives, importance of, 41; panic, eras of, 8–9; under-reporting, 100. *See also* addiction; biological defect or paradigm; child abuse, child molester/molestation; control; indecent exposure; lewd and lascivious conduct; other sex offenses; rape; victims

Sexually Violent Predators (SVP), 21 79, 96, 121, 167, 172. *See also* civil commitment

Sexual psychopath, 4, 25–53, 150, 158. *See also* civil commitment; monster

Simon, Jonathan, 7, 41, 52, 106, 174, 189; *Governing Through Crime*, 14

social construction, 7, 12, 16, 22, 100, 180–90. *See also* difference/uniqueness of sex offenders; media; punishment, sex offender, public attitudes towards; race social control, 24; through confinement, 81–84, 93–96; explanations for trends in, 83–84, 91, 103–6, 167–78, 187–88; field of, 198; formal, 5, 9, 78, 103, 192; gendered and racialized, 71; medicalization of crime and social control, 29, 55–63, 122, 129; neighborhood, 183. *See also* civil commitment; incarceration

social movements, 26–27, 62, 67, 104, 110, 149, 192

solutions/strategies to address sexual violence: individual level victim, 36–37; individual level offender, 38, 43, 44–51; institutional/legal change, 43, 47, 56, 97, 191–92; public education, 40, 51–52, 192–93, 195, 199; social change, 12, 24, 187, 191. *See also* fallacies surrounding sex crimes

SORNA (Sex Offender Registration and Notification Act), 117–19

sterilization laws, 4; incapacitation through, 46–49

stigma and shame: about sexuality/sexual health, 26–27, 45; of sex offenders, 17, 54, 58–59, 61–62, 179–82; victim-blaming, 8, 27, 56, 63

stories, sex crime/sex offender, 12, 111–13, 200–201; "Crime is a genre...." 14; narrative strategies comparing to non-sex offenders, 18. *See also* Foucault, Michel; discourse; images/portrayal of the sex offender; "normal"

Stringfellow, Bernard, 21, 147

Stroble, Fred, 34, 36, 37, 45, 47, 62. *See also* Glucoft, Linda Joyce

symbolic law, 11, 15, 19, 21, 32, 64, 109, 113, 115, 152, 156, 167, 174, 180, 187, 191–92

Sutherland, Edwin, 44, 184, 187

surveillance and supervision, 50–51, 114, 160, 195; GPS monitoring, 2, 136; sexual psychopath era, 51; surveillance-as-deterrent, 112. *See also* fallacies surrounding sex crimes, knowledge-is-power; polygraph; probation/probation officer

tailwind theory of sex offender punishment, 169–78

Tewksbury, Richard, 183

three strikes laws, 1

Tonry, Michael, 189

treatment professionals, 38, 92, 185

treatment, sex offender, 5, 200; accreditation for, 115; amenability/not amenable, 60–62, 78, 80, 87, 93, 94–96, 106, 141; civil commitment and, 49–50, 76, 124, 127; and cure, 19, 24, 43, 48, 54, 75, 91, 93, 106; evaluation for, 94; group therapy, 76, 92; Langley-Porter Clinic, 51; limitations and limits of, 91–93; California MDSO Program, 5; California rehabilitation era, 91–94; popular books about, 39, 54–55, 57, 61–62; in prison, 81, 93, 148; and recidivism rates, 91, 127–29, 157; Sex Offender Treatment and Evaluation Project, 5, 124; under sexual psychopath laws, 49; therapeutic community, 91–92. *See also* Bowman, Dr. Karl; experts; fallacies surrounding sex crimes

victims: adult, ix, 14, 116; advocates, 13, 115, 147–51, 157, 172, 192, 194; Black Dahlia, 38, 40; child, 25, 34, 49, 90, 116, 132–33; dismissal/undervaluing of, 14, 71, 90, 100, 146; dominance of stories about children, 15, 33, 146, 147, 158; media coverage/valorization of, 31, 33, 56, 113, 172; National Victims' Rights Week, 147; sympathy/empathy for, 85, 112, 141; symptoms of, 127, 132–33; testimony of, 14, treatment, 126. *See also* fallacies surrounding sex crimes, victim-or-offender; gender; punishment; stigma and shame

Victor, Jeffrey, 188

vigilantism, 153, 183

violence. *See* danger; family violence/offending by familiars; rape

Wacquant, Loïc, 6, 181, 182, 189

Warren, Earl, 38, 43, 45, 48

Wetterling, Jacob, 118, 194, 204; Wetterling, Patty, 194